# Better with Jesus

## A Mission 119 Guide Through Hebrews

# Hutson Smelley

Better with Jesus

Copyright © 2015 Hutson Smelley

Unless otherwise indicated, Bible quotations are taken from The King James Bible.

Cover art by Dwayne Smith

ISBN: 978-0-9861336-0-2

www.proclaimtheword.me

# Other Works by the Author

Love, Romance and Intimacy, A Mission 119 Guide to
the Song of Solomon (2016)

Chasing Jonah: A Mission 119 Guide to Jonah (2018)

Living Hope: A Mission 119 Guide to First Peter (2019)

Deconstructing Calvinism - Third Edition (2019)

# Dedication

This volume of the Mission 119 Series is dedicated to Lester Hutson, my friend, mentor and pastor whose now 50 plus years of ministry continues to bring the Word of God to people with depth, conviction, and grace, and whose life reflects the faithful endurance the author of Hebrews taught should characterize all Christians.

# Table of Contents

# Preface

## Preface to the Mission 119 Series

The psalmist declares, "Thy word is a lamp unto my feet, and a light unto my path." (Psalm 119:105) The Bible is unlike all other books, not only in its grandeur and scope, but because its words are God's Words. The Bible presents to us God's special revelation of Himself, His biased view of history past and future, the reality of who we are, and a picture of all that we can be. Woven within its pages and spilling over is God's redemptive plan for humanity, with Jesus Christ as centerpiece. We do not study the Bible merely to accumulate head knowledge, but with the earnest expectation of knowing God more and drawing near to Him. Each page has something for us, sometimes encouraging us, sometimes reproving us, always revealing God, and every jot and tittle a precious morsel for our souls. Against the backdrop of a world encased in darkness, it is the light of truth that pierces through all the deceptions and puts reality in clear focus.

Every generation faces challenges, and the present generation is challenged about truth and whether any absolute truths are knowable. Like all the ones before it, this generation needs to hear God's Word taught boldly, with clarity, without apology, in grace and love. And this generation needs to be reminded by those who teach that the Bible was written for everyone. God has spoken with clarity so that all believers who come to the Bible yielded to what God has for them can know its truths as they grow and mature. The aim here is to strike the proper balance between too little detail to elucidate the message and superfluous detail that obscures, so that this volume is accessible and profitable to laypersons and teachers alike who seek to understand the author's original intended meaning and the continuing relevance of that message today. With this in mind, the Mission 119 Series is designed to provide guidance for the exposition of books of the Bible with depth and a commitment to a plain sense interpretation tethered first and foremost to the context and flow of argument of the book under consideration before comparison is made to other books and the perceived systematic theology of the Bible. Of a certainty, the Bible has one author and contains neither error nor contradiction, but each of the 66 books and letters in the Bible must be allowed first to speak for itself as the teacher helps learners see the message of the book in context and its application principles.

A common sentiment today is that people need only "relevant" teaching from the Bible, which suggests portions of the Bible are irrelevant, and too often means they want three steps to raising teens in place of the perfections of God, five steps to a better marriage in place of how a believer matures and walks in the Spirit, how to find blessing and wealth in place of God's demand for holy living, and so forth. May I say that every word God ever spoke was relevant and remains so today. Those who would step forward as teachers of the Word of God only do people a disservice by trying to conform God's Holy Word to the world's bankrupt self-help counterfeits when what is most needful today is the plain teaching of the whole Bible as it is. Believers engaged in the Word and yielding to the Holy Spirit will find the most practical of wisdom and grace enablement for all areas of their lives as they draw near to God in the transformative experience of knowing Him more and more. May I also suggest that while some people will flee teaching that has depth and conviction, far more people in churches today are thirsty for more depth in the teaching. They want to see that the Bible is not clichés and recycled sugar sticks but truly a light from God unto their paths. In this vein, it is my prayer that this volume of the Mission 119 Series will be a useful guide for teachers of the Bible and a special blessing for students of the Word who aspire to know God more.

## Preface to Hebrews

Hebrews is a doctrinally rich book laced with Old Testament quotations and allusions written to a first century Jewish Christian audience. Unfortunately, the book is not often expositionally preached, and yet it is as needful today as when it was written in the first century. As with the original audience of Hebrews, Christians today are being constantly challenged to conform to the world and compromise Bible teaching in order to get along, to be "politically correct," to avoid ridicule (like being accused of hating), and even to avoid physical persecution. The first century recipients of Hebrews faced persecution from non-believing Jews (see Hebrews 10:26-36, 12:3-4, 13:10-14; also note indications of persecutions and trials back in Judea from verses like Acts 11:27-30; Romans 15:25-26; 1 Corinthians 16:3; 1 Thessalonians 2:14). It is apparent from the substantial material devoted to showing that the new order in Jesus Christ is superior to the Law of Moses, as well as passages like Hebrews 6:4-6 and 10:26-31, that in the face of their trials, they were tempted to turn from Jesus back to the Jewish religious system that rejected him. Accordingly, the fundamental message that Jesus is better than everything the old religious system had to offer, and that being a partaker with him in blessings *and* sufferings is better than compromise, is vital today.

In broad terms, the first ten chapters set forth detailed theological arguments that Jesus is better than the religion associated with the Mosaic Covenant, which was rendered obsolete when Jesus died on the cross as a once for all time sacrifice for sins, and for that reason, they would be insane for returning to the Mosaic Covenant and its animal sacrifices that cannot take away sins. Within these technical theological arguments are four "warning passages" about the severity of the consequences if they should give up on their faith in Jesus and return to Judaism. (Hebrews 2:1-4, 3:7-4:13, 6:4-8, and 10:26-31) A fifth warning passage appears within the exhortations of chapter 12. (Hebrews 12:25) These "warning passages" have led to extensive debate about exactly what consequences the recipients of Hebrews are being warned about. It has been rightly said that there are three sides to every issue. The two dominant positions are as follows: (1) continued disobedience leads to loss of salvation (justification); and (2) continued disobedience reflects that a professing believer was never saved (justified) to begin with. These warning passages are addressed in the notes and it will be shown that neither the context nor the language of the warning passages lend to these interpretations. Instead, the author is warning believers that if they turn from the Word of Christ back to the Jewish religious system of

4

their day, they may suffer negative temporal (immediate) consequences and a loss of privileges and blessings in the future kingdom. In view of this, the primary exhortation is that they need to live obediently to Jesus and steadfastly endure in the face of life's trials.

Related to the warning passages, the book of Hebrews has a pervasively eschatological or kingdom orientation to it. (e.g., Hebrews 1:2, 6, 8, 12, 14; 2:3, 5, 8; 6:5, 12; 9:28; 10:13, 35-37; 11:10, 13-16, 39; 12:22, 28; 13:14) The author will quote verses about Messiah's kingdom, tell us in 2:5 that the subject matter at hand is the "world to come" that will be placed in subjection to Jesus, speak of Christians in 6:5 as having "tasted...the powers of the world to come," admonish us to be "followers of them who through faith and patience inherit [this is future] the promises [i.e., the fulfillment]," focus on the future salvation (e.g., 9:28) into the kingdom when Jesus "shall...appear the second time," teach in 10:13 that Jesus is presently waiting until "his enemies be made his footstool," say in 10:36-37 that we should exercise endurance to do "the will of God" now so that "ye might [future] receive the promise" because in "a little while...he that shall come will come, and will not tarry," explain in 11:10 and 11:13-16 that Old Testament saints lived in view of a promised future heavenly city, explain in 11:39 that the Old Testament heroes of the faith lived in light of promises that they would not see fulfilled in their lifetimes, say in 12:22 that New Testament believers are coming to the heavenly city, in 12:28 that we are "receiving a kingdom which cannot be moved," and in 13:14 that we should "seek one [heavenly city] to come." The reason the author is so focused on the future fulfillment of the great kingdom promises is that the

Christian is not ensured a life of ease and comfort. Those facing trials, in order to endure and mature, cannot live on the basis of present circumstances, but by faith in God's promises about the future. The author's fundamental message throughout will be an exhortation to his audience to steadfastly endure in obedience to God's Word, living faithfully today with the firm conviction of God's promised future blessings to be enjoyed in the Messianic Kingdom. While the entire downside of failing to endure is not delineated in the Hebrews warning passages, it is plain that the believer stands to lose some aspect of those future blessings that will be available in the Messianic Kingdom just as the generation that Moses led out of Egypt died in the wilderness having forfeited the experience of entering the Promised Land because of their failure of faith. (Numbers 13-14)

The heavy reliance on Old Testament quotations coupled with the apparent concern that his audience may return to Judaism leaves little doubt the audience is comprised of Jewish believers. There are numerous indicators in the text that the intended audience is believers—3:1 ("holy brethren, partakers of the heavenly calling"), 3:12 ("brethren...[don't depart] from the living God"), 4:14 ("we have a great high priest...let us hold fast our profession"), 6:9 ("beloved"), 10:22 ("Let us hold fast the profession of our faith"), 10:25 ("Not forsaking the assembling of ourselves together"), 10:32 ("after ye were illuminated"), 10:34 ("knowing in yourselves that ye have in heaven a better and an enduring substance"), 10:39 ("we are not of them who draw back unto perdition; but of them that believe to the saving of the soul"), 12:1 ("let us run with patience the race that is set before us"), 12:2

("Looking unto Jesus the author and finish of our faith"), and 13:20-21 ("Now the God of peace...Make you perfect in every good work to do his will"). Not only are they believers, but they are believers who know the Old Testament scriptures. (Hebrews 5:12) Further, the audience is likely outside of Jerusalem. We know that the Jerusalem church endured poverty (e.g., Acts 11:20, 1 Corinthians 16:1-8) and martyrdom among its members (e.g., Acts 7:59-60, 12:2), but the audience of Hebrews is referred to as having the resources to be charitable (10:34) and having not yet been persecuted to the point of death (12:4). While there is considerable debate about whether they are within Jerusalem or somewhere else, with many scholars advocating that they are in Rome, the better position is that they were in and around Judea since the book emphasizes the coming judgment on the Jewish nation and the possibility of their suffering under that temporal judgment.

The author of Hebrews does not identify himself (the Greek of 11:32 suggests a male author) and while the apostle Paul has been long favored among many Christians as the author, numerous others have been proposed from at least the second century forward, including Apollos, Barnabas, Silas, Phillip, John Mark, and Luke. Given the author's intimate knowledge of the Old Testament and Judaism, it appears likely the author is a Jewish Christian, and certainly Paul was capable of writing Hebrews. The author also speaks of the "great salvation... which at the first began to be spoken by the Lord, and was confirmed unto us by them that heard him." (Hebrews 2:3) The author includes himself in "us," suggesting that he is a second generation Christian, having heard the good news from the apostles rather than directly from Jesus. This possibly excludes Paul (see Galatians 1:15-2:9), but at the end of the day, we simply cannot be dogmatic about who authored Hebrews since the true author, God the Holy Spirit, did not name the human author within the inspired text.

Hebrews was referenced by the church father Clement of Rome in A.D. 96, and so we know the book was written before then. The book also references Timothy (13:23), who was likely evangelized by the apostle Paul (Acts 16:1-3) around A.D. 50, and thus we have a possible time interval of A.D. 50 to 96. Further, the author speaks of the presently existing Levitical sacrifices (see 10:11), which means the Temple was still standing. This shortens the possible time interval to A.D. 50 to 70 since the Temple was destroyed in A.D. 70 by the Romans. We know the recipients are second-generation believers who have not suffered to the point of death yet, which tends to separate them from the early Jerusalem church persecutions (e.g., the martyrdom of Stephen) by several years. The preferable date is therefore in the 60's.

A basic outline of the book is as follows:

I. PROLOGUE: Jesus is better (1:1-4)

II. BETTER THAN ANGELS (1:5 – 2:18)

   a. Because he is a Son not a servant (1:5-14)

   b. First warning passage (2:1-4)

   c. Because the world to come will be subjected to Jesus (2:5-9)

   d. Because of his victory over death and the devil (2:10-18)

In our generation, Christians are under overwhelming pressure to conform to the world to fit in, to be accepted, to avoid ridicule and persecution. Particularly strong influences come from entertainment (including sports), various media (including the internet), and a culture that generally does what is right in its own eyes. (Judges 21:25) The message of Hebrews to be obedient and endure in the midst of our challenging culture is as needed in our generation as it was in the first century.

# Chapter 1

# God's Ultimate Revelation

According to *The New Century Dictionary Volume Two* (copyright 1948), the term "ultimate" can be defined as "last, as in a series," "final and decisive," and "forming the final aim or object." A lot of things happen in a succession and lead to an ultimate conclusion, whether it is a sporting event, a construction project, or human life itself. The unfolding "story" of the Bible is a woven tapestry of many threads, each leading to a conclusion – a conclusion to death, a conclusion to the evil one (Satan), a conclusion to the power of sin, a conclusion to the present heavens and earth, and so on. All of these are ultimate conclusions, but the overarching thread is God revealing Himself and His redemptive plan to us. Theologians speak of God's natural revelation, which is simply the revealing of God in creation, a creation that (at a minimum) affirms God's existence and power but does not yield the fine details of His person and plan. But it is God's special revelation in the Bible that gives us the details that God chooses to make known about Himself. God's self-revelation was not presented to the world in a moment in time but progressively, and like the other threads in God's self-revelation, the progressive revelation itself was leading to the ultimate. While we might expect that the "ultimate" would be a greater message through a greater prophet, the author of Hebrews wants his readers to know that the self-revelation of God to man reached its "ultimate" in a person, Jesus Christ, the Son of God, "Emmanuel, which being interpreted is, God with us." (Matthew 1:22) And with that knowledge comes a decision and consequences.

## Scripture and Comments

As discussed in the preface, the audience is composed of believing Jews who have begun to endure persecution, but have not yet faced death. (Hebrews 10:26-36, 12:3-4; see also Romans 15:25-26; 1 Corinthians 16:3; 1 Thessalonians 2:14-15) In the face of this persecution, some stopped assembling for church and others were contemplating a return to Judaism to end the persecution. They had walked with the Lord and endured, but for some of them, the trials were becoming too much. The opening four verses of the book form a prologue that cuts straight to why it would be foolish to turn aside from Jesus in favor of a return to the empty Judaism of the first century. In short, Jesus is the creator, sustainer and owner of the universe and the ultimate revelation of God to humanity. Anything else is less.

> Hebrews 1:1 God, who at sundry times and in divers manners spake in time past unto the fathers by the prophets, 2 Hath in

> these last days spoken unto us by *his* Son,
> whom he hath appointed heir of all things,
> by whom also he made the worlds; 3 Who
> being the brightness of *his* glory, and the
> express image of his person, and upholding
> all things by the word of his power, when
> he had by himself purged our sins, sat
> down on the right hand of the Majesty on
> high; 4 Being made so much better than
> the angels, as he hath by inheritance
> obtained a more excellent name than they.

The prologue to Hebrews sets up contrasts that are particularly relevant to the Jewish Christian audience. The first is God's prior special revelation contrasted with the revelation in *his* Son. The revelation of God to Israel (contextually the author has primarily the Old Testament in view) was made at **sundry times**. The term **sundry** means various, and thus we are told that God's revelation to Israel in the past was progressive (made at various times) as opposed to all of the revelation being made at once. That practice continued with the New Testament, which was also written at sundry times, probably with the book of James being written first in or around A.D. 44 or 45 and the Revelation penned in the last decade of the first century.

The revelation to Israel was also **in diverse manners...by the prophets.** Remember that the prophet's task was to speak God's Words, and sometimes this involved forthtelling (commenting on current events) and sometimes it involved foretelling (speaking of the future). As we read through the Old Testament, we find that God spoke through prophets by various means. God spoke to Moses (and thus to Israel through the written Word) in Exodus 3 in a burning bush. Sometimes God spoke directly to people, as with Noah, and sometimes through angels, as he did through the angel Gabriel to Daniel. (Daniel 8-9) Sometimes prophets were directed to go to the people and say, "Thus saith the Lord...." Other times, as was often the case with Ezekiel, for example, prophets acted out a divine object lesson. (e.g., Ezekiel 4) Sometimes God spoke in parables (e.g., 2 Samuel 12) and sometimes in apocalyptic terms (e.g., much of Daniel and Zechariah), sometimes He gave visions to the prophets and sometimes a dream. This progressive and diverse revelation was provided **unto the fathers**. He does not mean that the revelation was provided only to the patriarchs (Abraham, Isaac, Jacob), but rather, the generations before the current one to whom God spoke through the prophets.

The phrase **these last days** and similar expressions (e.g., latter days, that day) were a common part of God's Old Testament revelation through the prophets that looked forward to the time of Messiah. The New Testament refers to the present time as the "last days" (e.g., Acts 2:17; 2 Timothy 3:1; 2 Peter 3:3) because we are after the cross and the next event in God's program will be Christ's return. The contrast established by the author is between the Old Testament progressive revelation and God's different type of revelation in **these last days**. In particular, in **these last days** God's revelation came **unto us** (i.e., to Israel) **by *his* Son**. (see Jesus' parable on this in Luke 20:9-19) This, of course, is "Jesus revelation," although the name "Jesus" is not mentioned until Hebrews 2:9. The emphasis here is on Jesus' position as Son, and so more appropriately we should speak of "Son revelation." The *his* is in italics in most KJV printings to indicate that it does not appear in the original text, but reads "by Son," thus placing the emphasis on **Son**, a title pregnant with significance. We may be reminded of the comment in Matthew 7:29 that Jesus "taught them as one having authority, and not as the scribes" or the comment in John 7:46 that "never man spake like this man," but the author of Hebrews has much more in mind. Indeed, seven reasons are provided to impress upon his readers the contrast of prior revelation through the prophets compared to **Son** revelation in **these last days:**

- **whom he hath appointed heir of all things:** The author will build on this issue as the book unfolds, but the point here, simply, is that Son revelation is superior because the Son will inherit the universe.

- **by whom also he made the worlds:** The Greek term translated **worlds** is not the familiar *kosmos* (e.g., John 3:16, "For God so loved the *kosmos*..."). Instead, it is the term *aiones*, which Strong's defines as "properly, an age; by extension, perpetuity (also past); by implication, the world." The term carries the sense of both time and space, and speaks to the Son's role in creating the time-space universe. The overall thought here parallels Paul's words in Colossians 1:16-17, "For by him were all things created, that are in heaven, and that are in earth, visible and invisible, whether they be thrones, or dominions, or principalities, or powers: all things were created by him, and for him: And he is before all things, and by him all things consist." This parallel and others are the reason many hold to Pauline authorship, or at least that the author was heavily influenced by Paul.

The revelation of God through **Son** / Creator is superior to that through the prophets. Note that the reference to making the worlds parallels Hebrews 11:3, which expressly teaches creation *ex nihilo*: "Through faith we understand that the worlds were framed by the word of God, so that things which are seen were not made of things which do appear."

- **who being the brightness of his glory**: When Philip said to Jesus, "Lord, shew us the Father, and it sufficeth us," Jesus responded, "Have I been so long time with you, and yet hast thou not known me, Philip? He that hath seen me hath seen the Father; and how sayest thou then, Shew us the Father?" (John 14:8-9) The point is that to look upon Jesus is to see the very glory of God. If you want to see God, look at the **Son**, who is God incarnate. (see John 1:1-3,14) If you want to know how God would talk if He were a man, listen to Jesus. If you want to know how God would treat other people if He were a man, look how Jesus treated those around him. If you want to know how God would love others if He were a man, stand in the crowd and observe the **Son**. We tend sometimes to think of God's revelation only in terms of a message, but the revelation in God's **Son** was more than words. It was a message lived out before people, revealing God exactly, not just in words and deed, but in His very essence and person.

- **the express image of his person**: The Greek term translated **express image** is *charakter*. The term, according to Strong's, refers to a graver (i.e., engraver) and can refer to the tool or the person. The idea here is that if you could engrave an exact cast of God, that cast / *charakter* would be the **Son**. He is an exact representation of God, not merely almost like God or very much like God but exactly a representation of God's essential nature and person. We can understand why John commented, "No man hath seen God at any time; the only begotten Son, which is in the bosom of the Father, he hath declared him." (John 1:18) As the exact representation of God, the revelation in **Son** is superior to all other revelation of God. Prior revelation was words about God, but the **Son** reveals God directly in his very person.

- **upholding all things by the word of his power**: The **Son** is not only creator, but sustainer, and he sustains by his Word. The word **upholding** means to bear or carry. This strongly argues the point that what the **Son** has to say, which sustains the universe itself (and thus your next breath), is superior to prior revelation through the prophets.

- **he had by himself purged our sins**: Characteristically, Israel has yet to appropriate Christ by faith, but he humbled himself on a cross and thereby purged the sins of those that have placed their faith in him (the **our** refers to the author and his believing audience). Here, the **Son** did what no prior priest or prophet of Israel could accomplish.

- **sat down on the right hand of the Majesty on high**: This does not picture the **Son** enthroned, but the **Son** finished with his high priestly work of providing a sacrifice for the purging of our sins, a point the author will revisit later in the book. As John captures Jesus' Words in his "high priestly" prayer, "I have glorified thee on the earth: I have finished the work which thou gavest me to do." (John 17:4) Thus, the final word recorded of Jesus on the cross in John's Gospel is, in Greek, *tetelesti* (being translated, "it is finished").

In verse 4, the author provides a summary statement of the point he will make in his first fully developed "Jesus is better" argument. Of course, within the first three verses, the author argued that "**Son** revelation" is superior to all prior revelation, so in that sense he has already made one argument that Jesus is better. But what follows, namely that Jesus is better than angels, is fully developed and provides support to the prologue statement that "**Son** revelation" in superior. The Old Testament does not plainly state that the Law was delivered to Moses through angels, but that is revealed in the New Testament: "Wherefore then serveth the law? It was added because of transgressions, till the seed should come to whom the promise was made; ***and it was ordained by angels in the hand of a mediator.***" (Galatians 3:19) The point, then, is that if Jesus is superior to angels, then the revelation of God in Jesus the Son is superior to the revelation of God through angels (i.e., the Law).

Note that the author uses the term **better**. This term is used 13 times in Hebrews to contrast the new order in Christ with the old order in the Law of Moses. The point is not that the Law was bad, for of course it was God's Word, and as Paul said, "Wherefore the law is holy, and the commandment holy, and just, and good." (Romans 7:12) The issue here is which revelation is better, and the answer is that "**Son** revelation" is better because Jesus was **made so much better than** or exalted in rank and status above **the angels.** The author will provide a defense of this claim in the balance of chapter 1 through verse 2:18. The central points are that Jesus is deity and **hath by inheritance obtained a more excellent name than they.** The author will demonstrate from the Old Testament that it is the Son who was vindicated through the resurrection, and became heir of all things, in contrast to angels, who are merely servants. The concept of a **name** often speaks of the person and reputation (e.g., John 17:6, Romans 2:24), and here **a more excellent name** refers to Jesus' exalted status. The one who humbled himself and allowed people to crucify him for the sins of the world (e.g., Philippians 2:5-8) has been highly exalted by the Father, i.e., given **a more excellent name** / status than angels (see also Philippians 2:9).

Now we must consider that if the person of Jesus is the ultimate revelation of God to humanity, what do we do with that knowledge? The first century audience of Hebrews was faced with the prospect of "going along to get along" by returning to Judaism. (e.g., Hebrews 10) This did not necessarily mean they would deny Christ. One can imagine how they might defend their defection. What is the big deal if we start back at the synagogue? Maybe Bob will get his job back at the mill and the neighbors' kids will play with our kids again and the people at the market will sell to us again, etc. Sin always tries to sell itself as deceptively harmless. When a salesman presents us with "the greatest deal ever," we demand to know the price, but sin lies about the price. Hebrews will show us the high price of defection from Jesus. And in our modern context, the defection occurs when we turn aside from the teaching of Jesus and his call to holy living to compromise with and conform to the world. Compromise starts with what we perceive as the little things until the spiritual senses are numbed so that the other things also seem little. But in reality there is no small compromise, and the consequences of turning aside from the Son are substantial, as we shall see.


## Closing

We read in Genesis that God said, "Behold, I have given you every herb bearing seed, which is upon the face of all the earth, and every tree, in which is the fruit of a tree yielding seed; to you it shall be for meat." (Genesis 1:29) We also read, "But of the tree of the knowledge of good and evil, thou shalt not eat of it; for in the day that thou eatest thereof thou shalt surely die." (Genesis 2:17) The story of creation is almost always reviewed through the lens of the forbidden tree, and that is the *modus operandi* of the world that beckons us to fixate on what God withholds from us instead of the great liberty and bounty God makes available. To humanity in the Garden, God forbade only the one tree (for our own good), but all the others were available. Instead of enjoying to the fullest the blessing God provided, Eve was deceived into picking the one tree God withheld from her. And within the deception Satan lied about the benefits and the price. At the end of the day, Eve began by questioning whether God was holding back His best and then chose immediate flesh gratification over long-term blessings. Henceforward, that same decision would play out over and again as people reject God's best in favor of the world's pittance. Believers face this sort of decision when they choose between following the commands of Jesus and compromising, especially where that means looking profoundly different than the world, listening to different music, dressing differently, talking different, etc. And every time the decision is just as foolish as the fateful choice Eve made. Hebrews presents Jesus as God's ultimate revelation and assures us that being a companion of the Son in both his blessings and sufferings is better than anything the world offers.

## Application Points

- **MAIN PRINCIPLE:** Jesus is the ultimate revelation of God to humanity, the creator / sustainer of the universe, the one who inherits everything, the Son who finished his priestly work purging our sins and is seated at the right hand of God.

- As we develop a true picture of Jesus Christ in our confessional theology (what we say we believe), that confession should transfer into what we do, what we say and how we think, as we strive to follow him.

## Discussion Questions

1. What did Jesus create? What did Jesus not create?

2. How did God reveal Himself to humanity in time past?

3. How did Satan reveal himself to humanity in time past?

4. When did "the last days" start? When does it end?

5. What are the implications of Jesus being the sustainer of the universe? What would happen if he stopped sustaining it?

6. If Jesus is seated at the right hand of the Majesty on high, does that mean he is seated on a throne? If so, over what is Jesus presently ruling?

7. If Jesus is the ultimate revelation of God, what implications does that have on whether as believers today we should be looking for further revelation from God through modern apostles, prophets, popes, etc.?

# Chapter 2

# Better than Angels - Part 1

In the book of Acts there is a church established in a town called Berea, about which Luke records this compliment: "These were more noble than those in Thessalonica, in that they received the word with all readiness of mind, and searched the scriptures daily, whether those things were so." (Acts 17:11) Then, as now, there were all kinds of ideas in the world about religion, the God of the Bible, and especially about Jesus. Even when Paul said it, the Bereans looked to the "scriptures" (the Old Testament) for confirmation. That is a quality the author of Hebrews expects of his audience (see Hebrews 5:12), and so he sets out to "prove it" from the one authority they would all accept, the Old Testament. And therefore, in this second lesson, we find an inspired illustration for us of how to "rightly divide the word of truth." But much more than that, we find an argument that Jesus is better than angels because he is God. The world sometimes argues Jesus never existed, and sometimes allows for his existence but argues he was just a good man or good teacher or simply a martyr for social justice, but the reality is that Jesus was crucified because he claimed to be the Son, making himself equal with God. (e.g., John 5:18, 8:55-59, 10:27-31) The divisiveness of Jesus, then and now, is his claim to deity. It is not uncommon today to hear someone suggest that the Bible never claimed Jesus is God, when in fact Jesus' deity drips from the pages, and especially does so here in Hebrews 1. This leads to the simple but probing question Jesus asked his disciples and the question we must all answer, "But whom say ye that I am?" (Matthew 16:15)

## Scripture and Comments

The Prologue culminated in the statement that Jesus was "made so much better than the angels, as he hath by inheritance obtained a more excellent name than they." The author now sets out to prove what he claimed from the Old Testament by quoting "chapter and verse."

> 1:5 For unto which of the angels said he at any time, THOU ART MY SON, THIS DAY HAVE I BEGOTTEN THEE? And again, I WILL BE TO HIM A FATHER, AND HE SHALL BE TO ME A SON?

Here, the author asks the rhetorical question, **For unto which of the angels said he at any time....?** The context demands the answer "none," that is, God never said to the angels, **Thou art my Son, this day have I begotten thee.** He quotes from Psalm 2:7. The second Psalm pictures the rebellion of the Gentile "kings of the earth" as they seek to break free from God's authority. God responds by indicating that "I have set my king upon my holy hill of Zion" and then God issues the decree quoted here in Hebrews 1:5 and applied to Jesus. The reader would naturally think not only of what is quoted, but of the context and of what follows:

> Psalm 2:7 I will declare the decree: the LORD hath said unto me, Thou *art* my Son; this day have I begotten thee. 8 Ask of me, and I shall give *thee* the heathen *for* thine inheritance, and the uttermost parts of the earth *for* thy possession. 9 Thou shalt break them with a rod of iron; thou shalt dash them in pieces like a potter's vessel.

The author of Hebrews focuses on Psalm 2:7 because God calls the king he will install "my Son." And in what follows—a point the author of Hebrews will return to—God tells the Son that when the Son asks, He will give him the nations (i.e., those under the rule of the "kings of the earth" in rebellion) and, indeed, the entire earth so that the Son can defeat the enemies of God. These promises were made by God the Father to the Son, not to any angel, as the plain words say, **Thou art my Son.**

Moreover, the Psalmist records God's Words, **this day I have begotten thee.** Some have taken this to suggest that Jesus was created, which flies in the face of the rest of Hebrews 1 and other New Testament revelation. There need be no debate here because Paul explicitly interprets this phrase in his sermon in Acts 13:

> Acts 13:30 But God raised him from the dead: 31 And he was seen many days of them which came up with him from

Galilee to Jerusalem, who are his witnesses
unto the people. 32 And we declare unto
you glad tidings, how that the promise
which was made unto the fathers, 33 God
hath fulfilled the same unto us their
children, in that he hath raised up Jesus
again; as it is also written in the second
psalm, **Thou art my Son, this day have I
begotten thee**.

As Paul explains, when God vindicated Jesus by raising
him from the dead, He fulfilled the promise given to the
fathers, and in particular, the promise of Psalm 2:7.
Thus, the phrase, **this day have I begotten thee**, does not
indicate the creation of Jesus, but God the Father raising
Jesus from the dead. God never decreed that an angel
would inherit the world, nor did He raise an angel from
the dead (there is no indication in scripture that angels
can die). Rather, the point of Psalm 2:7 is that there
would be a man whom God would raise from the dead
and call "Son" and make him heir of the world. This
point comes to bear in other places in the New
Testament. In Luke 1:32, Gabriel tells Mary, "He shall be
great, and shall be called the Son of the Highest: and the
Lord God shall give unto him the throne of his father
David." (Luke 1:32) And at the baptism of Jesus, God
said, "Thou art my beloved Son, in whom I am well
pleased." (Mark 1:11) As the revelation in Hebrews 1
unfolds, we will see that this is not just any man, but the
unique God-man, who is called Son.

He continues with the connective **and again** to introduce
the next Old Testament proof, this time from 2 Samuel
7:14, **I will be to him a Father, and he shall be to me a**

**Son.** Again, the point being made is that this was not spoken to an angel, but to a Son. It helps here to see the fuller context from 2 Samuel 7, wherein we find the text theologians often refer to as the Davidic Covenant. This quote in Hebrews, to his Jewish audience, would certainly conjure in their minds the whole of this significant prophetic passage about the Messiah. David wanted to build the Temple for God and inquired about building God a "house." God tells David through the prophet Nathan that He selected and protected David, that He would provide Israel a future in the land and security from her enemies (this is an elaboration of the promises made to Abraham, e.g., Genesis 15:3-6). As part of that future there would be a "house" God would make for David:

> 2 Samuel 7:8 Now therefore so shalt thou say unto my servant David, Thus saith the LORD of hosts, I took thee from the sheepcote, from following the sheep, to be ruler over my people, over Israel: 9 And I was with thee whithersoever thou wentest, and have cut off all thine enemies out of thy sight, and have made thee a great name, like unto the name of the great *men* that *are* in the earth. 10 Moreover I will appoint a place for my people Israel, and will plant them, that they may dwell in a place of their own, and move no more; neither shall the children of wickedness afflict them any more, as beforetime, 11 And as since the time that I commanded judges *to be* over my people Israel, and have caused thee to rest from all thine

enemies. Also the LORD telleth thee that
he will make thee an house.

David would die but through his lineage after him, God
would establish a king and a kingdom. While in the near
term, Solomon would build the Temple and God would
establish Solomon as a king whose kingdom extended
beyond David's in terms of its boundaries, that kingdom
ended in the next generation as the kingdom split, and
ultimately, the Northern Kingdom was defeated by the
Assyrians in 722 B.C. and the Southern Kingdom (Judah)
was defeated by the Babylonians in 586 B.C. This passage
looks to a future "son" over a future kingdom that "shall
be established for ever":

> 2 Samuel 7:12 And when thy days be
> fulfilled, and thou shalt sleep with thy
> fathers, I will set up thy seed after thee,
> which shall proceed out of thy bowels, and
> I will establish his kingdom. 13 He shall
> build an house for my name, and I will
> stablish the throne of his kingdom for ever.
> 14 I will be his father, and he shall be my
> son. If he commit iniquity, I will chasten
> him with the rod of men, and with the
> stripes of the children of men: 15 But my
> mercy shall not depart away from him, as I
> took *it* from Saul, whom I put away before
> thee. 16 And thine house and thy kingdom
> shall be established for ever before thee:
> thy throne shall be established for ever.
> 17 According to all these words, and
> according to all this vision, so did Nathan
> speak unto David.

The promise of a permanent throne of David in a Son was not fulfilled in Solomon or any mortal Davidic king thereafter. Indeed, many messianic prophecies looked forward to this: "Behold, the days come, saith the LORD, that I will raise unto David a righteous Branch, and a King shall reign and prosper, and shall execute judgment and justice in the earth. <u>6</u> In his days Judah shall be saved, and Israel shall dwell safely: and this *is* his name whereby he shall be called, THE LORD OUR RIGHTEOUSNESS." (Jeremiah 23:5-6; see also Daniel 7:13-14) As indicated above, the message from Gabriel to Mary was that Jesus would be "called the Son of the Highest" and shall have "the throne of his father David," in direct fulfillment of 2 Samuel 7.

What the author selects to emphasize from 2 Samuel 7 is God's promise about the future king: **I will be his father, and he shall be my son.** The prophecy was spoken to David, not angels, and was to be fulfilled in a son, not an angel. From these two Old Testament quotes, we see that the term Son is a Messianic title that uniquely sets apart the coming Messiah. To be sure, these promises were not given to angels, but the Son / king over a "forever" kingdom, thus establishing his superiority over angels.

> <u>6</u> And again, when he bringeth in the firstbegotten into the world, he saith, AND LET ALL THE ANGELS OF GOD WORSHIP HIM.

The author continues his "chapter and verse" argument that Jesus is superior to angels with the connective **and again** and provides a time-marker, **when he bringeth in the firstbegotten into the world, he saith.** As we shall see, the reference to his being brought **into the world** is not to the first advent, but the second and still future advent of the Son. And the term **first begotten** is the Greek *prototokos*, meaning firstborn not first created, a different term altogether. This is a legal term, as used in Psalm 89:27 of Messiah, when God equates "I will make him my firstborn" with "higher than the kings of the earth." In other words, this has nothing to do with the concept of creating the Messiah or his being born, but of establishing his legal position exalted above all other kings.

Note that the author quotes from Deuteronomy 32:43 taken from the Septuagint (the Greek translation of the Old Testament often denoted the "LXX"). In the KJV, Deuteronomy 32:43 reads:

> Rejoice, O ye nations, *with* his people: for he will avenge the blood of his servants, and will render vengeance to his adversaries, and will be merciful unto his land, *and* to his people.

Notably missing are the words, **and let all the angels of God worship him**. The KJV translates the Old Testament from the Masoretic Text, and the oldest such manuscript copies we have date from the 9th century A.D. The older LXX and a copy of Deuteronomy from the Dead Sea Scrolls (which date before the first century A.D.) include the phrase in Deuteronomy 32:43, "And let all the angels of God worship him," placed as indicated below (noting also the additional words in italics):

> Rejoice, O ye nations, *with* his people, **and let all the angels of God worship him,**

*Rejoice with his people, you Gentiles, and let all the angels be strengthened in him*: for he will avenge the blood of his servants, and will render vengeance to his adversaries, and will be merciful unto his land, *and* to his people.

The KJV and many newer translations follow the Masoretic Text and leave out these additional words. It is beyond the scope of this book to address these issues in any further detail, but what is important is that within the Song of Moses found in Deuteronomy 32, the Song itself culminates with a reference to the Messiah to come in the future who will avenge Israel against her enemies, and the author of Hebrews tells us that the Messiah that Moses preached was the Son, whom the angels were ordered to worship. A few points must be made. First, a Jewish reader would immediately think of the first of the Ten Commandments: "Thou shalt have no other gods before me." (Exodus 20:3) Here, we have God Himself instructing the angels to worship the Son, which demands the conclusion that the Son must also be God. And second, if the angels worship the Son, since of necessity the lesser must worship the greater, the Son is superior to angels. Third, the event referred to when the angels worship the Son was future from Moses' time and did not get fulfilled in the first advent. At that time, Jesus did not avenge Israel (e.g., he fulfilled Zechariah 9:9 but not 9:10). We see in the Gospels that there was an expectation that Messiah would avenge Israel at that time, but he did not. Rather, that will occur in connection with the second advent, still future from our day. (e.g., Zechariah 14; Matthew 24-25; Acts 1:6-11)

7 And of the angels he saith, WHO
MAKETH HIS ANGELS SPIRITS, AND HIS
MINISTERS A FLAME OF FIRE.

In contrast to God's decree in Psalm 2 to the Son, and
His promise in 2 Samuel 7 to the Son, we have what God
said in Psalm 104:4 **of the angels**. A little more context
from Psalm 104 is helpful here:

> Psalm 104:1 Bless the LORD, O my soul. O
> LORD my God, thou art very great; thou
> art clothed with honour and majesty. 2
> Who coverest *thyself* with light as *with* a
> garment: who stretchest out the heavens
> like a curtain: 3 Who layeth the beams of
> his chambers in the waters: who maketh
> the clouds his chariot: who walketh upon
> the wings of the wind: 4 Who maketh his
> angels spirits; his ministers a flaming fire: 5
> *Who* laid the foundations of the earth,
> *that* it should not be removed for ever.

The Psalmist glorifies God, who is "clothed with honour
and majesty," and in particular, glorifies God as creator.
Of course, the author told us earlier that it was the Son
"by whom also he made the worlds," and so the glory due
the creator God in Psalm 104 is likewise due the Son.
And the point drawn out from Psalm 104:4 is that the
angels are only servants of the creator: **Who maketh his
angels spirits; his ministers a flaming fire.** In other
words, God created the world through the Son, and the
angels were merely servants, doing God's bidding, and
not a Son.

**8** But unto the Son *he saith*, THY THRONE, O GOD, *IS* FOR EVER AND EVER: A SCEPTRE OF RIGHTEOUSNESS *IS* THE SCEPTRE OF THY KINGDOM. **9** THOU HAST LOVED RIGHTEOUSNESS, AND HATED INIQUITY; THEREFORE GOD, *EVEN* THY GOD, HATH ANOINTED THEE WITH THE OIL OF GLADNESS ABOVE THY FELLOWS.

In contrast to the angels who are referred to by God as his servants, God said **unto the Son** the words captured in Psalm 45:6-7. As with the prior quotes, we do well to look to the fuller context of Psalm 45, which is a royal wedding Psalm. In his excellent commentary, Derek Kidner describes Psalm 45 in these words: "The outward splendor of the event [the wedding] is evoked in every line, and beneath the surface we can sense the momentous event that it is for the two central characters: both an end and a beginning (10f., 16f.), pivotal not only for them but for the kingdom, whose future is bound up with the sons they will produce. Above and beyond this, the psalm is Messianic. The royal compliments suddenly blossom into divine honours (6f.), and the New Testament will take them at their full value." [1]  Of verses 6 and 7 quoted in Hebrews, Kidner remarks that it "is an example of the Old Testament language bursting its banks, to demand a more than human fulfillment..." [2]

What happens in Psalm 45 is that the acclamations turn from an earthly king to the king to come, and there is a

---

[1] Derek Kidner, *Tyndale Old Testament Commentaries: Psalms 1-72* (Downers Grove: InterVarsity Press 2008), pp. 187-88.
[2] *Ibid.*

contrast between the reference to "O God" in Psalm 45:6
and "God, even thy God" in 45:7. The author of Hebrews
understands the Psalmist to address the Son with the
words, **Thy throne, O God, is for ever and ever.** Just as
Hebrews 1:5-6 looked forward to the second advent of
the Son, so also do these verses from Psalm 45. The Son
will be given the throne of David, and he will rule
righteously: **a scepter of righteousness is the scepter of
thy kingdom.** This pictures the kingdom Jesus offered
Israel during the first advent, which they rejected, that
will be instituted when Jesus returns. The Psalmist
continues in characterizing the Son's future reign as a
righteous king, **Thou hast loved righteousness, and hated
iniquity,** and for this reason **God, even thy God,** in other
words God the Father, **anointed thee with the oil of
gladness above thy fellows.** Obviously, since the Son is
called God and made a king with a throne that **is for ever
and ever,** the Son is superior to angels.

The Son also achieves an exalted position **above thy
fellows.** The Greek term translated **fellows** in Hebrews
1:9 is *metachoi* and means a "mutual sharer" (see Luke 5:7
where it is translated "partners"). This is another
important term for understanding the argument of
Hebrews, occurring in Hebrews 1:9, 3:1, 3:14, 6:4, and 12:8.
The Son's **fellows** are the "many sons unto glory" through
Jesus referred to in Hebrews 2:10-11. The writer of
Hebrews comments in 3:14 that "we are made partakers
[Gr. *metachoi*] of Christ...." Believers are mutual sharers
or companions or partners with the Son, who will be
anointed king of the earth. We are companions of the
King, and as Paul wrote in Romans 8:17, co-heirs with
him: "And if children, then heirs; heirs of God, and
joint-heirs with Christ; if so be that we suffer with him,
that we may be also glorified together."

10 And, THOU, LORD, IN THE BEGINNING
HAST LAID THE FOUNDATION OF THE
EARTH; AND THE HEAVENS ARE THE
WORKS OF THINE HANDS: 11 THEY SHALL
PERISH; BUT THOU REMAINEST; AND THEY
ALL SHALL WAX OLD AS DOTH A GARMENT;
12 AND AS A VESTURE SHALT THOU FOLD
THEM UP, AND THEY SHALL BE CHANGED:
BUT THOU ART THE SAME, AND THY YEARS
SHALL NOT FAIL.

These verses quote Psalm 102:25-27 and continue the
focus on God as creator. Based on the author's
understanding that creation was accomplished through
Jesus, he understands the words he quotes as applicable
to the creator Son. And the point made here is a simple
one. The creation is temporal and **shall perish** but the
Son **remainest**. The Son has *eternality*, an attribute
unique to God, whereas the created universe is
temporary. Not only that, when the universe grows **old
as doth a garment**, the Son **shalt...fold them up, and they
shall be changed**. As simply as folding up a sheet, the Son
will retire the universe and change it, implying the
creation of a new one. But the Son will never change; he
will remain **the same** and will never die, for his **years shall
not fail**. The end of the present material universe and
creation of the new heavens and new earth is described in
Revelation 21, an event that occurs one thousand years
into the Son's reign on David's throne.

13 But to which of the angels said he at any
time, SIT ON MY RIGHT HAND, UNTIL I
MAKE THINE ENEMIES THY FOOTSTOOL?
14 Are they not all ministering spirits, sent

forth to minister for them who shall be
heirs of salvation?

Finally, the author quotes from Psalm 110:1, a psalm
authored by King David, again asking the rhetorical
question, **to which of the angels said he at any time...?**.
In Psalm 110, we have David, inspired by the Holy Spirit,
capturing the divine conversation between God the
Father and God the Son: "The LORD said unto my Lord,
Sit thou at my right hand, until I make thine enemies thy
footstool." The author of Hebrews leaves out "The
LORD said unto my Lord" because his audience knows
well the passage, but it is important for us to catch this
point as it makes clear that the Father is speaking to the
Son, David's Lord. Note that Jesus also interpreted this
verse as applying to himself. In Matthew 22, while with
the Pharisees, Jesus asked them, "What think ye of
Christ? Whose son is he?" (Matthew 22:42) They
answered that the Christ (the Messiah) was "the son of
David," but Jesus corrected them by pointing to Psalm
110: "He saith unto them, How then doth David in spirit
call him Lord, saying, The LORD said unto my Lord, Sit
thou on my right hand, till I make thine enemies thy
footstool? If David then call him Lord, how is he his
son? And no man was able to answer him a word..."
(Matthew 22:42-46) And thus Jesus himself construed
Psalm 110:1 to capture God the Father addressing His
Son, which is how the author of Hebrews takes it. And
his point is that God did not address the angels with a
promise to **make thine enemies thy footstool**, but
addressed this promise to the Son. Recall that in
Hebrews 1:2 the Son is "appointed heir of all things" and
in 1:3 "sat down on the right hand of the Majesty on
high." Thus, at this time, Jesus continues to sit at the

right hand of the Father until he asks (Psalm 2) to take his inheritance, an event we see play out in Daniel 7:9-14 and Revelation 5.

The chapter closes with a question about the angels that demands the answer, "yes." The question is, **are** the angels **not all ministering spirits**, and of course that is exactly what angels are, namely ministers or servants (consider also Psalm 103:20) and spirits. And their specific task is **to minister for them who shall be heirs of salvation**, namely believers. So if angels serve believers, then the Son—who recall is **anointed ...above thy fellows**—is necessarily superior to them. Note that this is one of the key verses appealed to for the idea of "guardian angels," but that pushes it too far. We need to understand that angels are spirits (so we typically cannot see them) that are serving believers today. We spend most of our lives oblivious to what they do, but the Bible affirms their service.

The **salvation** in view here is not justification, but the future salvation, for justification is now for the believer and would not be referred to as something to be inherited in the future. There can be a tendency to always take the term save and salvation in the sense of justification, but nearly half the time these terms are used they are not talking about that at all. The noun salvation is a generic term that means deliverance, and context must determine the nature of the deliverance. The immediate context is pointing to the future deliverance of the Son from his enemies, which will occur as the Son's kingdom is initiated, and thus the salvation in view for the **heirs of salvation** is their participation with the Son in his kingdom as his "fellows" (or partakers, companions, partners). This is consistent with Hebrews 9:28, which frames the salvation in view as eschatological: "So Christ was once offered to bear the sins of many; and unto them that look for him shall he appear the second time without sin unto salvation." (see also, e.g., Romans 13:11; 1 Peter 1:5) While the chapter closes at this point, the argument that Jesus is better than angels continues in chapter 2 after a parenthetical "warning passage" that we will take up in the next lesson.

## Closing

Modern culture is infatuated with angels. There are songs about them, television shows and movies, and Christian bookstores peddle various trinkets that are supposed to look like angels. Many people believe that people who die become angels, and even embrace notions of angels earning their wings or staying on earth as guardians for their loved ones. What we know of angels we must take from the Bible, not Hollywood or speculation. That said, the Scriptures do paint angels as powerful beings who move in the presence of God himself. Yet the author of Hebrews points us not to angels but to the Son, for whom the angels are merely servants. And indeed, he points out that angels are servants of believers as well. It is difficult for us to grasp all the implications of this, or to understand all that angels do, but we are reminded that it is the Son who is due the glory. The Son is better than angels, and the revelation of God in His Son is better than the revelation of God in the Law of Moses. And this has serious implications for anyone who would consider turning away from Jesus and back to first century Judaism.

## Application Points

- **MAIN PRINCIPLE:** Angels are merely servants, but the Son is superior because he is God and will reign forever.

- We need a complete view of who Jesus is and to understand our position as his *metachoi* (partakers, companions) and the implications that relationship has for our decisions and actions.

## Discussion Questions

1. What is the role of angels as described in Hebrews 1:5-14?

2. What things do we learn about Jesus in Hebrews 1:5-14 that show he is superior to angels?

3. If Jesus' will reign on David's throne forever and we are mutual shares (*metachoi*) with him, what does that suggest about our future? How should that knowledge affect what we do now?

4. Could Jesus be an angel?

5. Is it acceptable to worship angels? Or pray to angels?

6. How might angels minister (serve) believers today?

# Chapter 3

# Better than Angels - Part 2

If you have ever examined a *Where's Waldo?* picture book, you know how finding Waldo, with his distinctive red and white striped shirt, becomes extraordinarily difficult when he is blended in with hundreds of other people in a scene. The pictures contain so many people in such confused arrangements that they look like a homogeneous blend of people and Waldo is lost. Sometimes church can look pretty homogeneous as well, with no one standing out, but it is not. Superficially, it may appear homogeneous in that people may wear similar clothes, sing the same songs, join in the same prayers, listen to the same sermon, etc. But it is great mistake to assume that because these externalities look similar that each individual's experience of God is the same. To make matters worse, many people are confused about the world to come, some imagining that all believers go to heaven, are assigned a cloud, a pair of wings and a harp. Others think dead Christians become angels and have to earn their wings. The reality, however, is far different from these Hollywood notions of heaven. As the writer of Hebrews will show us, there is a world to come where Jesus will rule and reign and, in varying degrees, believers will rule and reign with him. The sobering reality is that while the externalities of our Christian walks may look alike on Sunday mornings, there will be a future accounting for how each believer personally utilized his/her time, talent and energy. Our lives now are training grounds for the world to come, and how we live now will affect our experience in the world to come. God appeals to us to live a life of faithful obedience to the Word. Some will say, "Well, I don't want to be concerned about that. As long as I'm in, that's good enough for me." But the writer to the Hebrews warns of such a lackadaisical attitude as leading to dire consequences, including a loss of the blessings that could be ours in the world to come. Real life is serious business, and our Christian walk has both temporal and eternal consequences.

### Scripture and Comments

As we begin to look at chapter 2, it is important to keep the chapter 1 context in view. Remember that the chapter divisions are not part of the inspired text, but came later as a help to us in locating verses. The chapter 2 break comes in the middle of the author's argument (1:5 – 2:18) that Jesus is better than angels. That said, we can think of the argument in 1:5 – 14 as part 1 of the argument (focusing on the deity of Jesus and his exalted position as heir and sovereign) and 2:5 – 18 as part 2 (focusing on Jesus' role as head of a new humanity that will exercise dominion over the earth). Between parts 1 and 2 we have the first of the five so-called "warning passages" in

Hebrews, which will be addressed below. It is important to see that the immediate context for the first warning passage is focused on the world to come. In Hebrews 1:6, the author quotes from last verse of the Song of Moses (Deuteronomy 32:43), which culminates the Song with a Messianic prophecy of a future deliverer / conqueror. In Hebrews 1:8-9, the author quotes Psalm 45:6-7, verses that look to the future kingdom reign of Messiah. In Hebrews 1:13, the author quotes Psalm 110:1, which looks forward to the future reign of the priest-king after he is delivered from his enemies. And in Hebrews 1:14, the author refers to believers as "heirs of salvation," not in reference to justification but our future participation in the Lord's kingdom. Then immediately after the warning passage in 2:1-4, the author in 2:5 references "the world to come, whereof we speak." And thus we see that the contextual focus within the argument that Jesus is superior to angels is decidedly on the eschatological world to come, i.e., the future kingdom of the Son, and we should allow this context to inform our interpretation of the first warning passage.

> <u>Hebrews 2:1</u> Therefore we ought to give the more earnest heed to the things which we have heard, lest at any time we should let *them* slip. <u>2</u> For if the word spoken by angels was stedfast, and every transgression and disobedience received a just recompence of reward; <u>3</u> How shall we escape, if we neglect so great salvation; which at the first began to be spoken by the Lord, and was confirmed unto us by them that heard *him*; <u>4</u> God also bearing *them* witness, both with signs and wonders,

and with divers miracles, and gifts of the
Holy Ghost, according to his own will?

Again, these four verses constitute the first of the five
"warning passages" in Hebrews. The **therefore** looks
back to the content of Chapter 1: the superiority of the
revelation of God in His Son, the Son's exalted position
as heir and sovereign of all things, the Son's superiority to
angels, and the contextual focus on the future kingdom.
In view of these things, **we ought to give the more
earnest heed to the things which we have heard**. The
entire book of Hebrews has a strong focus on the Word
of God, and not just from the perspective of what we
know, but what we do with what we know, and so there
is an emphasis on giving **the more earnest heed** to it, in
other words, believing and living it. The superiority of
the Son and his exalted status has serious implications
concerning what his audience (and we today) does with
what the Son had to say. The phrase **the things which we
have heard** refers to **so great salvation; which at the first
began to be spoken by the Lord, and was confirmed unto
us by them that heard him**. To understand the point of
the warning passage, we need to understand the **so great
salvation** in view here, a teaching that was first taught by
Jesus, then by the apostles to the audience of Hebrews
(this does not mean that none of them heard Jesus, but
many or most are second generation believers). There
can be a tendency to read every New Testament use of
"save" or "salvation" in terms of heaven and hell, and
certainly that is sometimes the meaning, but nearly half
of the time, it is not.

The verb "save" is the Greek *sozo*, and the noun
"salvation" is the Greek *soteria*. The general meaning is

simply "to deliver or rescue" (verb) or "deliverance" (noun), and context determines from what one is being delivered. Without trying to be exhaustive, a handful of examples will illustrate the point that these terms are not always used in reference to our justification (deliverance from sin's penalty or hell). The verb form is used to reference deliverance from drowning (Matthew 14:30), physical deliverance (Matthew 24:13), and from sickness, i.e., healed (Mark 5:23), and the noun form is used to reference a deliverance from hunger (Acts 27:34), deliverance from the power of sin (Philippians 2:12), and a physical deliverance from a flood (Hebrews 11:7). Thus, we must ask what **great salvation** is in view based on the context. As shown above, there is a focus throughout chapter 1 on the "world to come", i.e., the Lord's kingdom. And the nearest antecedent use of **salvation** was just a few verses earlier in Hebrews 1:14, where on the heels of referencing Psalm 110:1 ("Sit at my right hand, until I make thin enemies thy footstool?") and Jesus' deliverance from enemies, the author refers to believers as "heirs of salvation." In connection with Jesus' inheriting his kingdom in the future, believers will participate as his "fellows" (1:9, the Son's *metachoi* or partners) and thus inherit blessings and privileges in the Son's kingdom. Notably, the phrase "heirs of salvation" suggests a deliverance to be obtained or inherited later, consistent the salvation in view in Hebrews 9:28 (Jesus "shall appear the second time without sin unto salvation"), whereas the concept of being justified is an immediate deliverance from sin's penalty and present possession of peace with God upon placing faith in Christ. Paul made this clear in Romans 5:1: "Therefore, since we have been declared righteous by faith, we have

44

peace with God through our Lord Jesus Christ." The **great salvation** in view then relates to the **world to come**, as further confirmed by verse 5.

With the future deliverance into the blessings of the kingdom in view, the author urges his audience **to give the more earnest heed** to this "Son revelation" (see Hebrews 1:2 and 2:3) **lest at any time we should let them slip**. What I refer to as "Son revelation" here may also be thought of as New Covenant teaching, a concept the author will devote much attention to beginning in chapter 8. The term **slip** has the idea of carelessly drifting away, like falling asleep in a raft and waking up miles away from where you started. The certainty of the consequences of drifting away is explained first by illustrating from the Law of Moses. In reference to the Law, the author argues that **if the word spoken by angels was stedfast, and every transgression and disobedience received a just recompence of reward**, so much more should we expect that every transgression of the New Covenant teaching from the Son would likewise have strict consequences for disobedience.

Note that the Old Testament does not say that God delivered the Law to Moses through angels, but that is confirmed in the New Testament. (see Galatians 3:19) And under the Law, infractions had specified penalties, including in some instances the death penalty. Since the revelation of God through the Son is superior to the revelation through the angels, and since disobedience to the latter had consequences, so also must disobedience to the former. Next, the author reminds his audience that when the "Son revelation" was spoken, God vindicated the veracity of the messengers (**bearing them witness**) through **signs and wonders, and with divers miracles, and gifts of the Holy Ghost**. Often in John's Gospel, Jesus would tell people that if they did not believe his Words, they should believe because of the works. (e.g., John 10:38, 14:11) This was also the case when the apostles accompanied their doctrine with signs. It is not the case that these men had "healing ministries" or "prophetic ministries" the way some snake oil peddlers claim today (none of whom seem able to verifiably raise dead folks), but they preached the Son and God vindicated what they had to say about the Son. Based on these arguments, the author asks the rhetorical question **how shall we escape...?**, meaning, of course, that we cannot escape the consequences of neglecting the Son revelation. But what are those consequences?

There are three primary views about the meaning of the warning passages, with various "subsets" of these views: (1) the author is warning believers about the possibility of losing their salvation (some expositors posit a variation on this view suggesting that the author was making empty warnings to scare them, knowing it was not actually possible); (2) the author speaks to the unbelievers in the group and warns them that their conduct reveals their being lost; and (3) the author warns believers who are contemplating turning away from the teachings of Jesus back to Judaism about negative consequences that do not include a loss of their justification. A cautionary note should be made at this point. The book of Hebrews is a single unit of thought, and it is beneficial to read the book through in its entirety several times before wrestling with the hard passages so that they can be understood within the flow and argument of the entire book as well as their immediate context. As already indicated, what we see is that in chapter 1, the argument that Jesus is better than angels relies on Old Testament verses looking forward to his return, his kingdom, and believers' participation in the kingdom, and in that context, believers are called in 1:14 "heirs of salvation." In 2:5, the author says his subject matter is still the "world to come" that will be put in subjection to Jesus, and in the balance of chapter 2, believers will participate with Jesus in the world to come. Further, as we shall see, in the extended warning passage in 3:7-4:13, the author's focus will be on potential loss of blessings in the future kingdom when the Lord returns and subdues his enemies. Indeed, as already shown in the prefatory materials, there is an eschatological focus throughout the book, and when the author transitions from setting out his theological foundation in the first ten chapters to the "application" material that follows, the emphasis is living out lives of faith with our focus on the world to come, to wit, the new Jerusalem or heavenly country.

Accordingly, the first two views do not fit because, contextually, the **great salvation** in view is a future deliverance into the world to come, which excludes their justification being in view. The first view also fails because numerous New Testament verses affirm that one's justification cannot be lost. (e.g., John 3:16; Romans 8:30, 11:29) The second view is the result of theological presuppositions contrary to the text, which affirms over and again that the author addresses only believers. Obviously, a non-believer might read the book, but the author's often highly technical message is written only to believers with a solid Old Testament background, who are called "partakers of the heavenly calling" (3:1), "partakers of Christ" (3:14), and "partakers of the Holy

Ghost") (6:4). The author says his audience "tasted of the heavenly gift" (6:4) and "tasted the good word of God" (6:5) in the same way "that he [Jesus] by the grace of God should taste death for every man" (2:9). Tasted here is an expression. Jesus did not nibble around the edges of death, but died on that cross, just as the audience "tasted" (possessed) the heavenly gift and indwelling of the Holy Spirit. We are left with the third view, which is that the author is warning his audience of negative consequences not affecting their justification.

Even within this third view, some expositors interpret the warning passages collectively as warnings about temporal judgment for disobedience, while others take all the passages as addressing eschatological consequences (i.e., loss of inheritance and rewards), but neither approach works well for all of the warnings. The better view is that through the several warning passages, the author warns his audience of both. Contextually, the focus here in chapter 2 is the negative eschatological consequences that will affect their experience (rewards) in the world to come. The possibility of temporal judgment will be made explicit, for example, in Hebrews 10:27, where the audience is warned of "a certain fearful looking for of judgment and fiery indignation, which shall devour the adversaries," a fairly clear reference to the judgment that fell on Jerusalem in A.D. 70. The reality is that prolonged disobedience will result in both immediate consequences and a loss of inheritance, which does not sit well with many today who would forget that "God is not mocked: for whatsoever a man soweth, that shall he also reap." (Galatians 6:7)

Importantly for the warning in this chapter, the concept that how believers live now will affect their experience in the world to come is consistent with other New Testament passages on the issues of rewards and inheritance. In 2 Corinthians 5:10, Paul taught about the future judgment of believers, sometimes referred to as the bema judgment: "For we must all appear before the judgment seat of Christ; that every one may receive the things *done* in *his* body, according to that he hath done, whether *it be* good or bad." Paul is referencing believers appearing before the judgment seat (bema) of Christ to be recompensed based on their works. In 1 Corinthians 3:11-15, Paul elaborated on this future judgment for believers:

> <u>1 Corinthians 3:11</u> For other foundation can no man lay than that is laid, which is Jesus Christ. <u>12</u> Now if any man build upon this foundation gold, silver, precious stones, wood, hay, stubble; <u>13</u> Every man's work shall be made manifest: for the day shall declare it, because it shall be revealed by fire; and the fire shall try every man's work of what sort it is. <u>14</u> If any man's work abide which he hath built thereupon, he shall receive a reward. <u>15</u> If any man's work shall be burned, he shall suffer loss: but he himself shall be saved; yet so as by fire.

The stuff of our lives is pictured as being tested by fire, and either it burns away like wood, hay and stubble, or it survives into eternity with eternal consequence and value. This judgment is not about heaven and hell, nor about whether they have trusted Christ for the forgiveness of sins, but about faith works, which will determine whether rewards are received. This is clear because Paul contemplates a hypothetical man whose life has nothing of eternal value to show for it (it all burns up), but he "shall be saved; yet so as by fire."

This teaching on rewards for faithful service was taught not only by Paul, but in fact Jesus taught on the subject. On the heels of Peter's great confession in Matthew 16:16 ("Thou art the Christ, the Son of the living God"), Jesus addressed rewards for discipleship:

> <u>Matthew 16:24</u> Then said Jesus unto his disciples, If any *man* will come after me, let him deny himself, and take up his cross, and follow me. <u>25</u> For whosoever will save his life shall lose it: and whosoever will lose his life for my sake shall find it. <u>26</u> For what is a man profited, if he shall gain the whole world, and lose his own soul? or what shall a man give in exchange for his soul? <u>27</u> For the Son of man shall come in the glory of his Father with his angels; and then he shall reward every man according to his works.

The Bible teaches that justification is by faith alone in Christ alone, but to be a faithful disciple will cost us. To his audience Jesus said, "If any man will come after me...." He was not speaking figuratively, but of literally pursuing after him in his earthly ministry as disciple, as Peter did. The disciple must deny himself, subjecting his will to Jesus' will, his plans to Jesus' plans, etc. When Jesus speaks in verse 25 of "save" and "lose," he is speaking to his believing apostles (except Judas Iscariot), and the point Jesus makes is that a disciple chooses between (life no. 1) the life Jesus has for him or her and (life no. 2) the life they might otherwise pursue to serve their own self-interest. You cannot have both, Jesus explains, and indeed "whosoever will save his life [no. (2)] shall lose it [no. (1)]." And in contrast, "whosoever will lose his life [no. (2)] for my sake shall find it [shall save no. (1)]." One life can be saved or delivered into eternity, being rewarded and having eternal value, while the other will last no longer than our short time here. The word "soul" in verse 26 is the same Greek term translated "life" in verse 25 and has the same meaning. The term "soul" almost always refers to the contents of our lives, and the point simply is that a man that lives life no. 2 to the fullest during his time on earth, even to the point of gaining the whole world, will profit nothing from it in the kingdom. In the kingdom, when "the Son of man shall come in the glory of his Father with his angels... he shall reward every man according to his works." This is exactly what Paul said, and it is no surprise the author to Hebrews tells us that their doctrine came from the apostles who received it from Jesus. Jesus often taught about rewards. (e.g., Matthew 5:12, 6:1, 10:42, 19:21; Mark 9:41, 10:21; Luke 6:23, 12:33-34, 18:22)

With this bit of background in mind, which will be more fully developed by the author later in Hebrews, we see contextually one sense in which those who neglect the New Covenant teaching will not **escape** consequences. Again, the focus in chapters 1 and 2 is on the world to come, the fact that the Son is heir and sovereign of all things, will have the victory over his enemies, will rule the world in righteousness, and that believers are his partners and brethren. As we see in Revelation 5:10 of Jesus' work for us: "And hast made us unto our God kings and priests: and we shall reign on the earth." Some believers assume that everyone in heaven will be sitting on clouds with harps and wings, enjoying the same experience, but the New Testament rejects that view. There is a world to come, in subjection to Jesus our Lord and King, and we are privileged to have the opportunity to participate in positions of authority as kings and priests. Our lives now are the training ground for the world to come, and our faithfulness will determine our role later. Accordingly, it is fitting that the author of Hebrews warns his readers (and by application, us) of the dire consequences in the kingdom for a believer to drift away from the Word into disobedience, thus forfeiting those future privileges. While what we read in chapter 1 may seem rather "theological" in the sense that we may not immediately grasp the implications for our lives, the warning passage not only provides a transition but grounds us in the reality of just how practical the argument of Hebrews is. Life is serious business and our faithfulness (or lack thereof) has consequences.

> 5 For unto the angels hath he not put in subjection the world to come, whereof we speak. 6 But one in a certain place testified, saying, WHAT IS MAN, THAT THOU ART MINDFUL OF HIM? OR THE SON OF MAN, THAT THOU VISITEST HIM? 7 THOU MADEST HIM A LITTLE LOWER THAN THE ANGELS; THOU CROWNEDST HIM WITH GLORY AND HONOUR, AND DIDST SET HIM OVER THE WORKS OF THY HANDS: 8 THOU HAST PUT ALL THINGS IN SUBJECTION UNDER HIS FEET. For in that he put all in subjection under him, he left nothing *that is* not put under him. But now

we see not yet all things put under him. 9 But we see Jesus, who was made a little lower than the angels for the suffering of death, crowned with glory and honour; that he by the grace of God should taste death for every man.

Having provided the first "warning passage" as both a transition between the two arguments that Jesus is superior to angels, and also as a means of pushing along his technical argument by drawing out some practical implications, the author now returns to the issue of angels. God **hath... not put in subjection the world to come** to angels. First, note again that the focus in what follows is on the **world to come.** Second, his point, by implication, is that God DID **put in subjection the world to come** to the Son, and that is key to understanding what follows. He quotes from Psalm 8:4-6, but for context, shown below is the entire psalm:

1 O LORD our Lord, how excellent *is* thy name in all the earth! who hast set thy glory above the heavens. 2 Out of the mouth of babes and sucklings hast thou ordained strength because of thine enemies, that thou mightest still the enemy and the avenger. 3 When I consider thy heavens, the work of thy fingers, the moon and the stars, which thou hast ordained; 4 What is man, that thou art mindful of him? and the son of man, that thou visitest him? 5 For thou hast made him a little lower than the angels, and hast crowned him with glory and honour. 6 Thou madest him to

have dominion over the works of thy hands; thou hast put all *things* under his feet: 7 All sheep and oxen, yea, and the beasts of the field; 8 The fowl of the air, and the fish of the sea, *and whatsoever* passeth through the paths of the seas. 9 O LORD our Lord, how excellent *is* thy name in all the earth!

In Psalm 8, King David is meditating on the greatness of the Creator God of the universe, and as he ponders God's glory looking up at the stars in the sky and in light of God's sovereignty, David is beside himself in how God has acted in unexpected ways in dealing with humanity. What strikes David as odd is that God made humanity **a little lower than the angels** yet **crownedst him with glory and honour** by making him in God's image, and in addition, **didst set him over the works of thy hands.** Indeed, God **put all things in subjection under his feet.** At this point, the author of Hebrews stops his quote of Psalm 8 and adds commentary, but if we continue reading Psalm 8, we see David explain what God put under the dominion of man, namely "all sheep and oxen... the beasts of the field; the fowl of the air, and the fish of the seas...." To understand David's perspective, and what the author of Hebrews is doing, we need to go back to Genesis 1. When God made man, he made him in his image *and* placed the planet under man's authority:

Genesis 1:26 And God said, Let us make man in our image, after our likeness: and let them have dominion over the fish of the sea, and over the fowl of the air, and over the cattle, and over all the earth, and

over every creeping thing that creepeth
upon the earth. 27 So God created man in
his *own* image, in the image of God created
he him; male and female created he them.

We see this dominion play out as Adam is placed in
God's garden "to dress it and to keep it" (Genesis 2:15)
and then God "brought [the animals] to Adam to see
what he would call them: and whatsoever Adam called
every living creature, that was the name thereof" (Genesis
2:19). However, there was one angel (demon / Satan) that
believed he had authority over the planet, and yet this
new creation (man), lower than angels, is granted
dominion and probably is seen by Satan as a usurpation
of his authority. There can be some reasonable debate
about when Satan rebelled and fell, based on such
passages as Ezekiel 28:11 ff., but what is important to
understand here is that when we read Genesis 3 and the
deception of Eve, we are reading about Satan going on
the attack because Adam is an affront to his authority.

When Eve is deceived and Adam chooses his wife over
God by partaking in the fruit of the tree of knowledge,
they both know death and are expelled from the Garden.
God tells Adam, "Because thou has hearkened unto the
voice of thy wife, and has eaten of the tree...in sorrow
shalt thou eat of it all the days of thy life; thorns also and
thistles shall it bring forth to thee...in the sweat of thy
face shalt thou eat bread, till thou return unto the
ground...." (Genesis 3:17-19) As Adam and Eve were
expelled from God's Garden, they lost dominion to
Satan. Yet in pronouncing the curse, God pronounced
the good news also, "And I will put enmity between thee
and the woman, and between they seed and her seed; it

shall bruise thy head, and thou shalt bruise his heel."
(Genesis 3:15) We see Satan's claim of dominion after
that in various places such as Satan's response to God in
Job 1:7 that he has been "going to and fro in the earth,
and [] walking up and down in it" and his offer to Jesus in
Matthew 4:8 ff. of "all the kingdoms of the world."
Indeed, Paul refers to Satan as the "god of this world" in
2 Corinthians 4:4. Yet there remains the promise God
made in Genesis 3:15 of a coming "seed" of the woman,
i.e., a human that would deal a mortal blow to Satan. As
Genesis unfolds, God is explaining the "seed," which will
come through Abraham.

Abraham is promised in Genesis 15:2-6 that he will have a
child and a lineage as numerous as the stars of the Milky
Way, "So shall thy seed be." And many years later, after
Isaac is born and grows to his teen years, Abraham obeys
God's command to take him on the mountain as a
sacrifice, but of course God stops him and provides his
own sacrifice. Following Abraham's demonstration of
faith, God clarifies the "seed" promise:

> Genesis 22:17 That in blessing I will bless
> thee, and in multiplying I will multiply thy
> seed as the stars of the heaven, and as the
> sand which *is* upon the sea shore; and thy
> seed shall possess the gate of his enemies;
> 18 And in thy seed shall all the nations of
> the earth be blessed; because thou hast
> obeyed my voice.

Centuries later, God further clarifies that the seed will
come through the lineage of King David as God makes
David a house and "will set up thy seed after thee, which
shall proceed out of thy bowels, and I will establish his

kingdom...I will stablish the throne of his kingdom for ever." (see 2 Samuel 7:4 ff) So in Genesis 22:17 we have the "seed" (plural) and in 22:18 the "seed" (singular) that we are later told will come through David. As the gospels open, we are told that Jesus is the "son of David, the son of Abraham" (Matthew 1:1), "he shall be great, and shall be called the Son of the Highest: and the Lord God shall give unto him the throne of his father David" (Luke 1:32), and God "hath raised up an horn of salvation for us in the house of his servant David" (Luke 1:69). Further, God "hath holpen his servant Israel, in remembrance of his mercy; as he spake to our fathers, to Abraham, and to his seed for ever" (Luke 1:54-55) and is remembering "his holy covenant; the oath which he sware to our father Abraham...." (Luke 1:72-73). The Apostle Paul also explains the fulfillment of the "seed" promise in Jesus Christ with specific reference to the "seed" (singular) of Genesis 22:18: "Now to Abraham and his seed were the promises made. He saith not, And to seeds, as of many; but as of one, And to thy seed, which is Christ." (Galatians 3:16)

With this background in mind, we can see how the author of Hebrews relies upon but adds content to David's words of Psalm 8. David reflects on how God placed the world under the dominion of Adam, but as we saw in Genesis 3, the first Adam failed and God promised a "seed" of the woman that would defeat Satan with a mortal blow, taking back what was lost there. The Bible is woven around the "seed" promise, fulfilled in Christ. Thus, although David followed Psalm 8:6 and the reference to putting "all things in subjection to man" with references to the animals, the author of Hebrews focuses on the "all things" and explains, **For in that he**

put all things in subjection under him, he left nothing
that is not put under him. But remember, that authority
was lost in Genesis 3, so he continues, But now we see
not yet all things put under him, that is, under the first
Adam. However, where the first Adam failed to exercise
dominion, the last Adam (Jesus) will prevail. He explains,
But we see Jesus, who was made a little lower than the
angels... In his incarnation, Jesus was the unique God-
man, fully God and fully human, and as man he was like
Adam and Eve, made lower than the angels. One of the
purposes of Jesus' incarnation was for the suffering of
death on a cross, but Jesus was also crowned with glory
and honour when God vindicated his Messianic claims
and raised him from the dead. This phrase crowned with
glory and honour in verse 9 is the same we read in verse 7
in reference to humanity. The point is that what man
lost in Genesis 3, Christ regained at the cross, and not for
himself only. In fact, Jesus by the grace of God... when
he died on the cross taste[d] death for every man. Jesus
took the death penalty we deserved, and by doing so
removed the separation from God that began in Genesis
3 for all those who would identify with him by faith. As
we shall see, the cross and the resurrection fulfilled
Genesis 3:15, and so where the first Adam failed the last
Adam triumphed over Satan and wrested back dominion
of all things so that the world to come will be placed in
subjection to the Son.

> 2:10 For it became him, for whom *are* all
> things, and by whom *are* all things, in
> bringing many sons unto glory, to make the
> captain of their salvation perfect through
> sufferings. 11 For both he that sanctifieth
> and they who are sanctified *are* all of one:

> for which cause he is not ashamed to call
> them brethren, 12 Saying, I WILL DECLARE
> THY NAME UNTO MY BRETHREN, IN THE
> MIDST OF THE CHURCH WILL I SING
> PRAISE UNTO THEE. 13 And again, I WILL
> PUT MY TRUST IN HIM. And again, BEHOLD
> I AND THE CHILDREN WHICH GOD HATH
> GIVEN ME.

What we will see is that Jesus is the leader of a new
humanity that will exercise dominion of the **world to
come**. We read that **it became him, for whom are all
things, and by whom are all things...**, in other words, it
**became** the creator God **in bringing many sons unto
glory, to make the captain** or leader **of their salvation,**
namely Jesus, **perfect through sufferings.** The **salvation**
in view here is the entire spectrum of salvation from
justification to glorification, and **bringing many sons unto
glory** has a view to the world to come, when humanity
will once again exercise dominion over creation exhibiting
the **glory and honour** that God crowned humanity with in
the Garden (see verse 7). He explains that Jesus (**he that
sanctifieth**) and believers (**they who are sanctified**) are **all
of one,** meaning **all of one** Father, so that Jesus the Son **is
not ashamed to call them** (the **many sons**) his **brethren.**
The term sanctified is the Greek *hagiazo*, which means
to make holy, and so Jesus and the **many sons unto glory**
are united as holy **brethren** in a new humanity that will
triumph over the creation where the first Adam failed.
The exercise of this authority will be during the **world to
come** when the "appointed heir of all things" (Hebrews
1:2) Jesus Christ takes what is his (Hebrews 10:13), and as
his **brethren** we will share in that. But in what sense
could Jesus be made **perfect through sufferings**?

In Jesus' incarnation, he set aside the independent use of his divine attributes (see Philippians 2:5 ff; e.g., "made himself of no reputation, and took upon him the form of a servant, and was made in the likeness of men") and learned experientially what it is to be human, so that we read in Luke 2:52 that "Jesus increased in wisdom and stature, and in favour with God and with man." The Bible teaches us that God matures believers through trials and suffering. (e.g., Romans 5:1-5; James 1:2-4) The idea of **perfect** means completion or finished. Thus, in his humanity, Jesus was made **perfect** or complete **through sufferings** just as God does in the lives of maturing believers. (see James 1:4, "let patient have her perfect work, that ye may be perfect and entire, wanting nothing") This point will be a critical one as the author introduces Jesus' role as a high priest, which requires that he be human and that he understands the infirmities of being human.

When the author says that Jesus calls believers **brethren**, he attributes to Jesus the words of Psalm 22:22: "I will declare thy name unto my brethren: in the midst of the congregation will I praise thee." We do well to remember that Jesus himself quoted from Psalm 22:1 from the cross: "My God, my God, why hast thou forsaken me?" (see Matthew 27:46, Mark 15:34) When Jesus did so, he was claiming Psalm 22, not just his momentary experience of separation form the Father, but the entirety of Psalm 22, which moves from sorrow to the triumph Jesus will experience after his resurrection. Looking to that triumph, the words of David in Psalm 22 become the words of Jesus, **I will declare thy name unto my brethren, in the midst of the church will I sing praise unto thee.** This pictures Jesus in the presence of his

**brethren** in the kingdom singing praise to the Father. The author then quotes from Isaiah 8:17-18 (in the LXX). In Isaiah 8:17, Isaiah trusted the Lord to deliver a remnant of Israel (the same **brethren** in view in Hebrews since the focus is Jewish believers), and in the same way, Jesus looks to the Father to deliver the remnant (**I will be put my trust in him**). Similarly, in Isaiah 8:18, Isaiah and his sons are presented as a sign to Israel of what God will do in delivering a remnant, and in the same way Jesus and the **brethren** are signs of what God will do and the future blessings to come.

> 2:14 Forasmuch then as the children are partakers of flesh and blood, he also himself likewise took part of the same; that through death he might destroy him that had the power of death, that is, the devil; 15 And deliver them who through fear of death were all their lifetime subject to bondage. 16 For verily he took not on *him the nature of* angels; but he took on *him* the seed of Abraham. 17 Wherefore in all things it behoved him to be made like unto *his* brethren, that he might be a merciful and faithful high priest in things *pertaining* to God, to make reconciliation for the sins of the people. 18 For in that he himself hath suffered being tempted, he is able to succour them that are tempted.

At this point, the author will bring to a close his argument that Jesus is superior to angels and introduce the concept of Jesus as High Priest. He notes that **the children**, that is, the **sons** or **brethren** that are **sanctified** (made holy) by Jesus, are **partakers of flesh and blood,** or in other words, human (the term **partakers** is the Greek *koinonia*, meaning "to have in common with"). And in the same way, Jesus **himself likewise took part of the same,** meaning he took on human flesh in his incarnation, and he did so not only to experience life as a human, but to experience death, **that through death he might destroy him that had the power of death, that is, the devil.** So we were told above that one reason for the incarnation was so that God could bring many sons to glory. Here, we are given a second reason, namely to triumph over **the devil,** in fulfillment of Genesis 3:15. The term **destroy** is the Greek *katargeo*, meaning "to render inoperative." Remember that by Satan's deception sin entered the human experience, and with it, death. Death means separation, and the death of Adam and Eve included both their separation from God (expulsion from the Garden) and later their physical separation of body and spirit (or physical death). From Genesis 3 forward, Satan **had the power of death,** meaning physical death, subject of course to God's restrictions (e.g., Job 1:10). But the God-man Jesus took the death we all deserved, yet lives, rendering Satan's **power of death** inoperative as to all those (the **brethren**) who identify with Jesus by faith, experiencing the benefit both of Jesus' substitutionary death and Jesus' substitutionary life.

Whereas Satan had authority over death, Jesus brings eternal life (e.g., John 3:16) to those who trust him. Thus, we read the third reason for the incarnation and the cross, namely to **deliver them who through fear of death were all their lifetime subject to bondage.** It is not just that believers are freed from death (see prior paragraph) but from the **fear of death.** For the believer, physical death is not an ending but a beginning and so the bondage of mortality is gone. And to accomplish all of this, Jesus did not take **on him the nature of angels**, but of humans, indeed, of **the seed of Abraham**. This, of course, again shows the superiority of the God-man Jesus to angels. Moreover, and as we have seen in the analysis above, this also brought fulfillment to Genesis 22:18.

But yet more can be said about the incarnation, for **in all things it behoved Jesus to be made like unto his brethren** (i.e., human) so that **he might be a merciful and faithful high priest in things pertaining to God**. The author will have a great deal to say about Jesus' role as High Priest, but note here that a fourth reason for the incarnation was so that Jesus could be a suitable High Priest. Jesus **himself hath suffered being tempted**. Jesus knows the human experience and so can minister on our behalf. He can **succour** or help **them that are tempted** because he can sympathize with what it is to be **tempted**. And in his role as High Priest, he **make[s] reconciliation for the sins of the people**. The term **reconciliation** means a propitiation, a satisfaction of the wrath of God. In the Old Testament, the High Priest in the line of Aaron made atonement for the sins of the people once a year in the Feast Day of Atonement. The author will develop the idea later of how Jesus fulfilled this role once and for all in the heavenly tabernacle.

## Closing

On July 21, 1969, Neil Armstrong became the first man to walk on the moon. The event was televised live to the world, and as Neil Armstrong stepped onto the moon, he described the event as "one small step for [a] man, one giant leap for mankind." Human history paints a picture of such "giant leap[s] for mankind" and many people believe that our academic and technological achievements render belief in God obsolete. They believe that we can work together to solve the dire problems of disease, poverty, racism, violence, pollution, etc. But in fact, mankind has never taken a step forward that was not followed with taking two steps back. The more and more enlightened we convince ourselves we are, the more capable we think we are to solve our problems, the more skillful we become at killing on grander and grander scales. And while so many claim to have outgrown the theistic superstitions of the past, their lives are consumed by the material and sensual snares of the world. In short, humanity has not subdued the creation, but bowed down in obeisance to it. Humanity in the first Adam failed its fundamental task of subduing creation as God's image-bearers, but there is good news. There is a new humanity, whose leader is Jesus, who will subdue all things and flourish in righteousness as God's image dwellers. Jesus' triumph is the only true "giant leap for mankind," but it is only for the mankind in Christ by faith.

## Application Points

- **MAIN PRINCIPLE:** Angels are merely servants, but the Son is superior because he is the head of the new humanity who will exercise dominion in the world to come.

- There will be severe consequences affecting our experience now and in the world to come if we fail to endure in obedience to Jesus.

## Discussion Questions

1. What is the "salvation" at issue in the first warning passage (2:1-4)?

2. If the first warning passage means that believers can through disobedience lose their salvation, how can they get it back? And what is the relationship between what we can do to lose our salvation with what we did to obtain salvation in the first place?

3. What objections can you think of to the view that the author is warning his audience they can lose their salvation even though he knows they cannot?

4. If the first warning passage is addressed to non-believers (professors of Christ and not possessors of Christ) in a mixed audience, why is the audience referred to in 3:1 as "holy brethren, partakers of the heavenly calling..."?

5. Articulate the four reasons given in Hebrews 2 for the incarnation.

6. Is every believer's experience in the world to come identical?

7. Is every believer's present experience of salvation identical?

8. What is the role of the Word of God in these experiences?

# Chapter 4

# Better than Moses

In the ancient world, a rich man built a "household," which was much more than the physical home, but included his family, employees, property and business. The efficient operation of the household required many servants, and chief among those would be a lead servant. We see this in the Old Testament example of Joseph, first in Potiphar's household, and later in Pharaoh's household in his prime minister role. The lead servant position was one of great responsibility and honor, but always submissive to the owner and builder of the household. The owner's son was not a servant, but a son, and in due time the household would become his. When we look back in the Old Testament at Moses and other great heroes of the faith, we must remember that all of them were servants of God, and not a son. Amidst so many diverse views of Jesus, all of which make him out in one way or another to be a mere servant, the author of Hebrews exalts Jesus as a son over his own house. That being the case, his glory and his Word are superior to anything associated only with servants. Our privilege as believers is that Jesus made us children of God and partners with him. As Paul wrote in Romans 8:17: "And if children, then heirs; heirs of God, and joint-heirs with Christ; if so be that we suffer with him, that we may be also glorified together."

## Scripture and Comments

Hebrews 3 begins with a **wherefore**, signaling us that the author is looking back to what he already said as he presses forwarded in his argument that Jesus is better. Having established Jesus as the ultimate revelation of God, who is superior to all angels and to whom the world to come will be completely subjected, he will now argue that Jesus is better than Moses. Like the angels, who are only servants, Moses also was a servant, not a Son. Moreover, just as chapters 1 and 2 have a heavy focus on the world to come—with the admonition that how we live now affects our experience in the world to come— chapter 3 will continue and further explain the connection of our present obedience to Jesus with our experience in the world to come. If disobedience to the revelation of God through Moses had dire consequences, how much more so will disobedience to the revelation of God through Jesus Christ.

> Hebrews 3:1 Wherefore, holy brethren, partakers of the heavenly calling, consider the Apostle and High Priest of our profession, Christ Jesus; 2 Who was faithful to him that appointed him, as also Moses *was faithful* in all his house. 3 For this *man* was counted worthy of more glory

than Moses, inasmuch as he who hath
builded the house hath more honour than
the house. 4 For every house is builded by
some *man*; but he that built all things *is*
God. 5 And Moses verily *was* faithful in all
his house, as a servant, for a testimony of
those things which were to be spoken
after; 6 But Christ as a son over his own
house; whose house are we, if we hold fast
the confidence and the rejoicing of the
hope firm unto the end.

Critical to understanding the argument of Hebrews is
seeing that the author is speaking to a saved (justified)
audience. Many expositors deal with the warning
passages by insisting—against the weight of all the
evidence—that the audience is a mixed group of saved
and lost, and the warnings are to the lost within the
group. But if we are to be guided by the text, then we
must take at face value the author's description—and in
reality, God the Holy Spirit's description—of the
audience as **holy brethren**. The audience of Hebrews is
both **holy** and **brethren**. This description excludes the
possibility that the message is addressed to a mixed
audience. And if such a description were not enough,
they are not only **holy brethren** but also **partakers of the
heavenly calling**. The term **partakers** is the Greek
*metachoi* that we previously saw in reference to Jesus'
"fellows" (Hebrews 1:9) and has the sense of mutual
sharers or partners. The audience is composed of mutual
sharers in **the heavenly calling**, which is no doubt the
calling of the gospel into the family of God. (see 2
Thessalonians 2:14) The author calls upon his audience
to **consider...Christ Jesus**. The term **consider** (Greek

*katanoeo*) means to observe fully. The author draws our complete attention to **Christ** (Messiah) **Jesus,** who is both **Apostle and High Priest of our profession.** The term **apostle** means an envoy or someone sent with authority, thus indicating that Jesus represents God before people. But he is also the **High Priest of our profession** of faith (e.g., Hebrews 4:14, 10:23), and in that role represents the redeemed before God.

Our attention is called to **consider... Jesus** because he **was faithful to him** (i.e., God the Father) **that appointed him** over the Father's house, **as also Moses was faithful in his** (God's) **house.** The latter statement reflects the idea of Numbers 12:7: "My servant Moses... is faithful in all mine house." God spoke to Moses in a burning bush (Exodus 3) and used Moses, a faithful servant, to lead Israel out of captivity and to the Promised Land. But Jesus **was counted worthy of more glory than Moses.** The reason, as with Jesus' superiority to angels argued in chapter 1, is rooted in the distinction between a servant and a Son. The author explains that **he who hath builded the house hath more honour than the house,** and of course, **every house is builded by some man,** but ultimately, **he that built all things is God.** Thus, **Moses verily** (truly) **was faithful in all** God's **house, as a servant, for a testimony of those things which were to be spoken after.** The idea of this latter phrase is reflected in 10:1 when the author refers to the Law of Moses as "a shadow of good things to come." God owns the household and appointed Moses as a servant or steward of the house to lead the people of Israel, and this foreshadowed what would occur when Jesus is over God's house as the Son who will lead in his kingdom. By implication, the new order in Jesus is superior to the older order in which Moses was a servant.

In contrast to Moses' role as a servant over God's household, Jesus is **a son over his own house**, which reflects that the Father's house becomes the Son's by inheritance. (Hebrews 1:2) The **holy brethren, partakers of the heavenly calling** of verse 1 comprise the Son's house...**if we hold fast the confidence and the rejoicing of the hope firm unto the end.** The **if** here means that maybe they will **hold fast** and maybe they will not. This verse transitions the reader to the second warning passage that begins to be developed in the next verse. Note that the summary warning is essentially repeated in 3:14: **For we are made partakers** (partners, companions) **of Christ, if we hold the beginning of our confidence stedfast unto the end.** This is a clarion call to steadfast endurance—which is the central exhortation of the whole book—and the plain sense of the warning to these believers is that the drifting away the author warned about in 2:1-4 may affect their place in the Son's house (verse 6) or as the Son's partners / companions / fellows (verse 14). Consistent with the notes on chapter 2, what the author will explain as the second warning is fully developed in chapters 3 and 4 is not that they are in danger of losing their justification as some teach (deliverance from sin's penalty – eternal separation from God) but loss of their inheritance or rewards that will be referred to as rest. As indicated in chapter 2, the warnings overall in Hebrews include temporal consequences, but the passage here seems focused on the privilege accorded those in Jesus' house during the kingdom. Some expositors assume anyone not in the Son's house is lost, but the imagery here is of enjoying the exalted status of those who are members of the king's household sharing in his authority as compared to those under the king's authority that are not members of his household. (e.g., Genesis 12:17, 41:40, 45:2, 50:7) The Son is presently seated at the right hand of the Father waiting for the time when he will take his inheritance (Hebrews 1:2-4, 1:13, 10:13), and when the Son does take his inheritance, the Son's house will rule and reign over the coming kingdom (Hebrews 1:8-9), and believers who persevere in obedience will share in that authority. (see Revelation 1:6, 5:10)

Before examining 3:7-11 carefully, it will be helpful to get more context. Like other books of the Bible, the questions raised tend to be answered within the book. Hebrews as a book (or epistle) is a single unit and the author anticipates our meditating on the entire book as a single unit rather than zeroing in on a verse in a vacuum. As we have already seen in chapters 1 and 2, there is a pronounced eschatological focus on the kingdom, which carries forward in subsequent chapters. (e.g., Hebrews 9:28, 10:16, 37) The author writes in Hebrews 11:1-2 a description of what faith looks like, which itself looks to the future: "Now faith is the substance of things hoped for, the evidence of things not seen. For by it the elders obtained a good report." Today we have many teaching a so-called prosperity gospel—that believers with sufficient faith (faith in what is not well answered) will receive material blessings in this life. But the Bible says such a doctrine is the antithesis of faith in that it lacks content and is all about immediate (fleshly) gratification. In contrast, the faith at issue for believers in Hebrews is living with one foot in heaven's door, living in the *now* on the basis of the certainty of God's promised future blessings. This is what Paul refers to in 2 Corinthians 5:7 as walking by faith, not by sight. Thus, the author refers in his description of faith to "things hoped for" (i.e., future blessings) and "things not seen" (i.e., not yet seen), which is consistent with the focus on the "world to come" and on the heavenly city (e.g., Hebrews 13:14, "For we have no continuing city, be we seek one to come.").

With this faith in mind, consider these examples of living in the present based on God's Word about the future:

> Hebrews 11:7 By faith Noah, being warned of God of things not seen as yet, moved with fear, prepared an ark to the saving of his house; by the which he condemned the world, and became heir of the righteousness which is by faith. 8 By faith Abraham, when he was called to go out into a place which he should after receive for an inheritance, obeyed; and he went out, not knowing whither he went. 9 By faith he sojourned in the land of promise, as *in* a strange country, dwelling in tabernacles with Isaac and Jacob, the heirs with him of the same promise: 10 For he looked for a city which hath foundations, whose builder and maker *is* God..13 These all died in faith, not having received the promises, but having seen them afar off, and were persuaded of *them*, and embraced *them*, and confessed that they were strangers and pilgrims on the earth....16 But now they desire a better *country*, that is, an heavenly: wherefore God is not ashamed to be called their God: for he hath prepared for them a city.

We see that Noah was warned of "things not seen" (i.e., a flood) and by faith started swinging a hammer in the construction of the ark. Similarly, God told Abraham "to go" and Abraham left his home for the Promised Land, but he considered it a temporary dwelling as he looked forward beyond his lifetime to the heavenly city. The author explains how these people "died in faith," that is, died living in obedience and without receiving all of God's promises, but only having "seen them afar off" (through eyes of faith), yet fully persuaded of them. And not only were they persuaded, they "embraced" the reality of God's promises and lived in the now on that basis as mere "strangers and pilgrims on the earth" as they looked beyond their lifetimes to the heavenly city. With this orientation to the sort of "life of faith" at issue in Hebrews, it will be helpful to next get an Old Testament orientation about the events of Numbers 13-14. But first, we do well to remind ourselves that the historic events of the Old Testament like those in Numbers 13-14 are examples for us to teach us spiritual matters:

> 1 Corinthians 10:1 Moreover, brethren, I would not that ye should be ignorant, how that all our fathers were under the cloud, and all passed through the sea; 2 And were all baptized unto Moses in the cloud and in the sea; 3 And did all eat the same spiritual meat; 4 And did all drink the same spiritual drink: for they drank of that spiritual Rock that followed them: and that Rock was Christ. 5 But with many of them God was not well pleased: for they were overthrown in the wilderness. 6 Now these things were

> our examples, to the intent we should not
> lust after evil things, as they also lusted....
> 11 Now all these things happened unto
> them for ensamples: and they are written
> for our admonition, upon whom the ends
> of the world are come.

Not only is the Old Testament history of Israel (and in
particular of the Exodus) instructive to us, but we are
reminded that these ancient people were believers
following the "cloud" of God, having by faith left Egypt
and walked through the walls of water as God split the
Red Sea ("baptized unto Moses"). They even drank the
living water in the wilderness, which was a type of Christ
(1 Corinthians 10:4), yet the generation that left Egypt by
faith ultimately failed in faith to enter the Promised
Land. This particular failure is recorded in Numbers 13-
14 and is the background for Hebrews 3-4, and the reader
is encouraged to read the entirety of Numbers 13-14. For
our purposes here, we consider some excerpts below.
First, God told Moses to send spies into the land of
Canaan:

> Numbers 13:1 And the LORD spake unto
> Moses, saying, 2 Send thou men, that they
> may search the land of Canaan, which I
> give unto the children of Israel: of every
> tribe of their fathers shall ye send a man,
> every one a ruler among them. 3 And
> Moses by the commandment of the LORD
> sent them from the wilderness of Paran: all
> those men *were* heads of the children of
> Israel.

Note that God refers to the land as that "which I give unto the children of Israel." This is, to use the concepts of Hebrews applied to Numbers 13-14, the promise of future blessing by God that should affect how they live in the present. Moses, of course, obeys and sends spies into Canaan, including the faithful Caleb and Joshua. Observe the contrasting reports that the people receive back from the spies:

> Numbers 13:26 And they went and came to Moses, and to Aaron, and to all the congregation of the children of Israel, unto the wilderness of Paran, to Kadesh; and brought back word unto them, and unto all the congregation, and shewed them the fruit of the land. 27 And they told him, and said, We came unto the land whither thou sentest us, and surely it floweth with milk and honey; and this *is* the fruit of it. 28 Nevertheless the people *be* strong that dwell in the land, and the cities *are* walled, *and* very great: and moreover we saw the children of Anak there. 29 The Amalekites dwell in the land of the south: and the Hittites, and the Jebusites, and the Amorites, dwell in the mountains: and the Canaanites dwell by the sea, and by the coast of Jordan. 30 And Caleb stilled the people before Moses, and said, Let us go up at once, and possess it; for we are well able to overcome it. 31 But the men that went up with him said, We be not able to go up against the people; for they *are* stronger than we. 32 And they brought up

an evil report of the land which they had
searched unto the children of Israel,
saying, The land, through which we have
gone to search it, *is* a land that eateth up
the inhabitants thereof; and all the people
that we saw in it *are* men of a great stature.
33 And there we saw the giants, the sons of
Anak, *which come* of the giants: and we
were in our own sight as grasshoppers, and
so we were in their sight.

The spies confirm that God was true when He told them
the land flowed with milk and honey. But all the spies
except Caleb and Joshua focus on what they saw in the
land, i.e., fortified cities and strong peoples that will not
simply leave. In contrast, Caleb says they should go take
it at once. It is apparent who is living in the present
based on God's promised future blessings, or in Paul's
terminology, who is walking by faith and who is walking
by sight. Unfortunately, the other spies prevail upon the
people and even warn of giants in the land so that the
people of Israel are mere "grasshoppers" before them.
The nation has God's promises on the one hand (faith)
and the unfaithful spies' report on the other (sight), and
they choose poorly:

Numbers 14:1 And all the congregation
lifted up their voice, and cried; and the
people wept that night. 2 And all the
children of Israel murmured against Moses
and against Aaron: and the whole
congregation said unto them, Would God
that we had died in the land of Egypt! or
would God we had died in this wilderness!

> 3 And wherefore hath the LORD brought
> us unto this land, to fall by the sword, that
> our wives and our children should be a
> prey? were it not better for us to return
> into Egypt? 4 And they said one to
> another, Let us make a captain, and let us
> return into Egypt.

So here we have the people of God, who saw the plagues
fall on Egypt, who in faith placed the blood on their
doorposts when the death angel passed over, who in faith
left Egypt and fled Pharaoh through the sea, who ate and
drank daily from God's provision in the wilderness, now
ready to return to slavery in Egypt rather than remain in
the care of God because they *do not believe they can
take the land even though God said it was a done deal.*
At this point, we should note that in order for many
expositors to accommodate their "mixed audience"
presupposition about Hebrews they must insist either
that the rebellious generation of Israel in Numbers 13-14
consisted entirely of lost people (except Moses, Caleb
and Joshua) or of believers who through sin lost their
salvation. That is not only contrary to Paul's description
in 1 Corinthians 10 seen above, and the testimony of
Hebrews 11:29 ("By faith they passed through the Red sea
as by dry land: which the Egyptians assaying to do were
drowned."), but also the testimony in Numbers. Moses
asked God to forgive them and He did, but that did not
mean that their rebellion would have no consequences:

> Numbers 14:19 Pardon, I beseech thee, the
> iniquity of this people according unto the
> greatness of thy mercy, and as thou hast
> forgiven this people, from Egypt even until

now. 20 And the LORD said, I have
pardoned according to thy word: 21 But *as*
truly *as* I live, all the earth shall be filled
with the glory of the LORD. 22 Because all
those men which have seen my glory, and
my miracles, which I did in Egypt and in
the wilderness, and have tempted me now
these ten times, and have not hearkened to
my voice; 23 Surely they shall not see the
land which I sware unto their fathers,
neither shall any of them that provoked me
see it: 32 But *as for* you, your carcases, they
shall fall in this wilderness.

God forgave them of their rebellion and allowed them to
live out their lives in the wilderness enjoying the benefits
of His gracious provisions, but they died in the
wilderness. Their disbelief resulted in their loss of the
privilege of entering into the Promised Land. And one
final observation before we turn back to Hebrews 3 is
that what they lost because of their disobedience—the
land—is referred to by God as **rest**:

Joshua 1:13 Remember the word which
Moses the servant of the LORD
commanded you, saying, The LORD your
God hath given you **rest**, and hath given
you **this land**.

Deuteronomy 3:18 And I commanded you
at that time, saying, The LORD your God
hath given you **this land** to possess it: ye
shall pass over armed before your brethren
the children of Israel, all *that are* meet for
the war. 19 But your wives, and your little

ones, and your cattle, (*for* I know that ye have much cattle,) shall abide in your cities which I have given you; 20 Until the LORD have given **rest** unto your brethren, as well as unto you, and *until* they also possess **the land** which the LORD your God hath given them beyond Jordan: and *then* shall ye return every man unto his possession, which I have given you.

With this Old Testament background in mind, the author of Hebrews sets about the task of explaining his concern that his audience might, in the face of persecution and trials, return to religious Judaism and lose future kingdom blessings. He begins by quoting from Psalm 95.

7 Wherefore (as the Holy Ghost saith, TO DAY IF YE WILL HEAR HIS VOICE, 8 HARDEN NOT YOUR HEARTS, AS IN THE PROVOCATION, IN THE DAY OF TEMPTATION IN THE WILDERNESS: 9 WHEN YOUR FATHERS TEMPTED ME, PROVED ME, AND SAW MY WORKS FORTY YEARS. 10 WHEREFORE I WAS GRIEVED WITH THAT GENERATION, AND SAID, THEY DO ALWAY ERR IN *THEIR* HEART; AND THEY HAVE NOT KNOWN MY WAYS. 11 SO I SWARE IN MY WRATH, THEY SHALL NOT ENTER INTO MY REST.)

If you look at Psalm 95 you will not see an ascription of authorship, but of course, as with all of the Bible, the one author is the **Holy Ghost** who recorded the very Words of God for us through the written Word. Psalm 95 is an intense call to worship and praise of the Creator God, and in the midst of the call to worship and acknowledgement that "we are the people of his pasture, and the sheep of his hand," the psalmist beckons the reader of his psalm to hear the voice of God: **Today if ye will hear his voice.** The call is for **today** because we cannot change yesterday and are not promised tomorrow; it is a call with urgency to **hear** God's **voice** and by implication, to respond in obedience. We **hear** the **voice** of God in His written Word (for us today, the Bible) and the Holy Spirit uses that **voice** to change us if we yield to it (e.g., Colossians 3:16, Ephesians 5:18). The psalmist issues the call to obedience **today**, which by implication of the warning that follows is coupled with the promise of a future blessing / rest. At the same time, the Holy Ghost appeals to them not to refuse to hearken to God's Word, after the example of that generation that listened to the spies' report about the giants and did not enter into the Promised Land / rest. He says, **Harden not your hearts, as in the provocation, in the day of temptation in the wilderness.** Of course, this is the sin (disbelief) we examined above from Numbers 13-14, for which God forgave that rebellious generation, but they still faced the consequence that they died in the wilderness and did not enter the rest. God says of that **generation** that **I was grieved** and **they do always err in their heart**, and as a result, **they shall not enter into my rest.**

> 12 Take heed, brethren, lest there be in any of you an evil heart of unbelief, in departing from the living God. 13 But exhort one another daily, while it is called TO DAY; lest any of you be hardened through the deceitfulness of sin. 14 For we

are made partakers of Christ, if we hold
the beginning of our confidence stedfast
unto the end; 15 While it is said, TO DAY IF
YE WILL HEAR HIS VOICE, HARDEN NOT
YOUR HEARTS, AS IN THE PROVOCATION.

In view of the example in Psalm 95, based on the events
of Numbers 13-14, the author warns his audience to **take
heed, brethren.** Note again, he speaks to them as
**brethren**, that is, fellow believers, people who with the
author are in the family of God. His warning to his
fellow believers is not to be like the believers in Numbers
13-14 that failed in faith and lost the blessing of entering
the rest (land) God had for them. They did not enter
because of unbelief, and so he says to **take heed...lest
there be in any of you an evil heart of unbelief, in
departing from the living God.** His concern is that in the
face of the persecution and trials they face, they might
turn from Christ Jesus back to Judaism, falling as
grasshoppers before giants, as it were. (e.g., Hebrews
10:23-27, 13:10-14) We are reminded that he is writing to
believers that are no doubt participants in local church
(see also 10:25) when he encourages them to **exhort one
another daily.** Christians are not to shoot their wounded,
but to build them up daily, especially in times of
persecution or other trials. Just as the call to faith is
urgent, so also is the call to build up one another, **while it
is called today, lest any of you be hardened through the
deceitfulness of sin.** The episode in Numbers 13-14
demonstrates how deceitful sin is that after all of the
special revelation, provisions, and signs from God, they
not only were unwilling to enter the land but were ready
to return to Egypt. In the same way, the author is
concerned here that some in his audience may return to

the old system of Temple worship and synagogues (their Egypt) and lose out on the future blessings God has for them (typified by the Promised Land). The **deceitfulness** is the idea that you could turn away from Jesus back to the old Judaism without dire consequences.

The author reminds his audience that they are **partakers** (mutual sharers or partners with) **of Christ, if we hold the beginning of our confidence stedfast unto the end.** Just as the generation in the wilderness lost out on the physical rest available to them in the Promised Land at that time, so also will the audience of Hebrews lose out on future blessings if they turn back in disbelief from the teachings of the new order in Jesus Christ. In Hebrews 4, the author will explain more about the nature of the "rest" that remains for believers today. For now, he applies the clarion call of Psalm 95 to his audience, **Today if ye will hear his voice, harden not your hearts, as in the provocation.** In other words, **today** hear the revelation of God in His Son of the blessings of the world to come and press on / endure / labor in faith in the now of daily living. The author knows they face genuine challenges, struggles and affliction, but they pale in comparison to the future blessings God has for them.

> 16 For some, when they had heard, did provoke: howbeit not all that came out of Egypt by Moses. 17 But with whom was he grieved forty years? *was it* not with them that had sinned, whose carcases fell in the wilderness? 18 And to whom sware he that they should not enter into his rest, but to them that believed not? 19 So we see that they could not enter in because of unbelief.

He reminds his audience that **some** in the wilderness, **when they had heard, did provoke: howbeit not all that came out of Egypt by Moses.** As we have seen from Numbers 13-14, Caleb and Joshua believed God's promise that they would take the land and were ready to enter the rest. Others provoked God in disbelief. And the question is asked, **with whom was** God **grieved forty years? was it not with them that had sinned, whose carcasses fell in the wilderness?** And of course, we know that God was **grieved** with those who accepted the report of the spies that the land could not be taken and rejected not only the urging of Caleb and Joshua, but the promise of God Himself that the land was theirs for the taking. And as a result of this sin of disbelief, that generation died in the wilderness. God did not allow them to **enter his rest** (the land) because they **believed not** His Word that they would be able to take it. These things, as Paul reminds us in 1 Corinthians 10, are an example to us. The author will explain in Chapter 4 that a rest remains for the people of God if they will labor in faith for it. The alternative for the disobedient believer, as he warned in 3:6 and 3:14, is loss of the future blessings as the partners or companions of Christ in the world to come, a loss of the rest that remains for Christians to labor to enter.

## Closing

Being a child is a relationship that once established is fixed, but the quality of the relationship (the fellowship or intimacy of the relationship) is subject to change. The expectation of parents is that children will grow to maturity and be productive adults able to raise their own children to maturity. Some children, however, seem to lapse again and again, perhaps with the inability to keep a job, handle their finances, maintain normal relationships, entanglement with substance abuse, etc. They never cease to be children, but continually regressing creates obstacles to the intimacy of the relationship and even forgiveness within the relationship cannot always remove the consequences. Choices result in the forfeiture of blessings that were available because of the relationship and at some point the blessings may be lost forever. In this way, God's dealings with His children parallels earthly parents' dealings with their children. Whether and to what extent, as children of God, that we live in obedience and steadfast endurance can translate into permanent consequences. The relationship is never severed but the intimacy and benefits of the relationship can be diminished.

## Application Points

- **MAIN PRINCIPLE:** It is the privilege of believers who walk in obedience and steadfast endurance to be a part of Jesus' household and partners with Jesus in the future blessings.

- Jesus, as a Son over his own house, is superior to Moses, who was a servant in God's house.

- The generation of Israel in Numbers 13-14 lacked faith in God's promise to them that they could obtain the land (rest), and though they were forgiven they forfeited the land (rest), and this historical episode exemplifies how disobedience in believers now can result in forfeiture of their inheritance.

## Discussion Questions

1. Why did Moses not get to enter the Promise Land? Does this mean he was not "saved" (justified)?

2. What are the reasons we know the generation of Numbers 13-14 (and referenced in Psalm 95) were believers who forfeited the land (rest) but did not forfeit their justification?

3. If a believer can forfeit their justification, is there any place in the Bible that teaches how a person can regain their justification?

4. How do believers hear the voice of God?

5. Why is there so much emphasis on hearing God's voice "today"?

6. In Hebrews 3:13, we are told to exhort or encourage one another daily? What are some of the other "one another" exhortations in the New Testament?

7. Is other believers' spiritual well-being my business, and is my spiritual well-being their business?

# Chapter 5

# A Better Rest

Our world is all about immediate gratification, and people will give up so much to achieve that gratification. Students give up the future material blessings of an education to have fun today. Young people give up future marriage blessings for momentary fleshly gratification. In the spheres of the home, marriage, school, jobs, and relationships, people are all too willing to forfeit future blessings for short-lived immediate gratification, and all of this is contrary to God's will. Some today are teaching that sufficient faith results in material blessings now, but what they are touting as faith is just the world's carnal counterfeit with a misplaced Biblical label on it. This carnal doctrine is exactly the opposite of Biblical faith, for the faith / life of a believer in Jesus Christ is to live a life of obedience and steadfast endurance in view of God's promised future blessings. This is the clarion call of Hebrews that is to change the entire outlook we have on our lives now. The faith / life we are called to entails laboring now in view of God's promised future rest, and in the face of adversity God provides grace enablement to press forward. Maturity is not a lack of failures in life, but maturity is seen in how we respond to our failures and press forward in obedience.

## Scripture and Comments

Chapters 3 and 4 comprise a unit but are treated separately because the length of a typical sermon or Bible study lesson will not allow sufficient time to teach both chapters. In chapter 3, the author argued that Jesus as a Son over his own house was superior to Moses as a servant in God's house, with the application that just as disobedience to the revelation of God through Moses met with consequences, so much more will disobedience to the Son. The author leaves no doubt that he is only addressing believers, "holy brethren, partakers of the heavenly calling." And he illustrates the negative consequences to disobedient believers by quoting from Psalm 95, which itself recalls the events of Numbers 13-14, wherein the generation of Israel in the wilderness believed the majority report of the spies that the land could not be taken. Moses interceded and God forgave that generation, but they still faced the consequence of a lost inheritance, namely they lost the right to enter into the Promised Land, which is referred to as "rest." This was an example for the audience of Hebrews (and for us) that disobedience to the Word of Christ can result in a lost inheritance. In chapter 4, the author further explains why the generation in the wilderness lost their inheritance (the rest / land) and the "rest" that remains for the people of God that his audience is at risk of losing if they drift away in disobedience in the face of their current trials.

Hebrews 4:1 Let us therefore fear, lest, a promise being left *us* of entering into his rest, any of you should seem to come short of it. 2 For unto us was the gospel preached, as well as unto them: but the word preached did not profit them, not being mixed with faith in them that heard *it*. 3 For we which have believed do enter into rest, as he said, AS I HAVE SWORN IN MY WRATH, IF THEY SHALL ENTER INTO MY REST: although the works were finished from the foundation of the world. 4 For he spake in a certain place of the seventh *day* on this wise, AND GOD DID REST THE SEVENTH DAY FROM ALL HIS WORKS.

As we saw in Hebrews 2:1, 3:1 and 3:7, the author here begins with a **therefore**. Throughout these chapters the general argument that "Jesus is Better" is being built up one block at a time. As described above, the immediate context for this **therefore** is the author's example from Psalm 95 of how the generation in the wilderness lost their inheritance of the land / rest when they believed the spies that said the land could not be taken instead of the promise of God that it was theirs. The life of faith for believers is living in the present based on God's Word, including His promised future blessings. In light of the example of failed faith in Psalm 95, the author issues a warning inclusive of himself: **Let us** (the author and his audience and by implication us) **therefore fear, lest, a promise being left of us of entering into his rest, any of you should seem to come short of it**. Just as the generation in the wilderness lost the promised rest because they did not believe God's promise to give them the land, so also the present generation is at risk of losing their promised **rest**, which obviously is not the same land / rest.

The issue for the generation in the wilderness was not lack of revelation from God. They saw God bring the plagues on Egypt, God led them out of Egypt through Moses with much of Egypt's riches, then made a way for their escape through the Red Sea, led them through the wilderness with a cloud by day and fire by night, and sustained them with food and water in the wilderness. The author explains that **unto us was the gospel preached, as well as unto them**. The term **gospel** simply means "good news" and context must always determine what good news is at issue. Based on the context from chapter 3 that the author is building on, the **gospel** preached to the wilderness generation was the promise that God would lead them to the Promised Land and give them the land to dwell there in security. Of course, God revealed a great deal more to them through Moses, but the promise of future blessing in the land is what is at issue in this context, which is why the author explains that **the word preached did not profit them, not being mixed with faith in them that heard it**. Again, based on chapter 3 and the reliance by the author there on Psalm 95, the good news from God that was not believed and thus **did not profit them** was God's promise that they could take the land. And again, the author draws the parallel to his audience, to whom was also **the gospel preached**. Just as justification (salvation from sin's penalty) was not at issue in the example, it is not under consideration for the current generation, for whom the author already explained were "holy brethren, partakers of the heavenly calling."

We must keep in mind that what we might often think of as "the gospel" (the death, burial and resurrection of Jesus Christ for lost sinners) is not the entirety of the good news about Jesus Christ revealed in the Bible. We also know, for example, that Jesus ascended to the Father, remaining at his right hand until his enemies are made his footstool (Hebrews 1), and will return and institute the kingdom, subjecting the world to himself (Hebrews 2). Indeed, the prologue proclaimed that God "in these last days [has] spoken unto us by his Son" and the author has this new "Son revelation" in mind. It is the "good news" God delivered in Jesus His Son in view for these believers to whom a future rest is promised as they participate as "partners" (companions or partakers) with Christ (Hebrews 1:9, 3:14). Thus, the author writes that in contrast to the generation in the wilderness who lost out on the promised rest, **we which have believed do enter into rest.** The verb tense for **have believed** is Greek perfect, indicating past action with continuing consequences (here, the point is they still believe), and it is having believed the fuller orb of the good news revealed in the Son, including the kingdom promises, that is in view. And by continuing to believe those promises, the author does not mean head knowledge or acquiescence but obedience and steadfast endurance (see Hebrews 11). Those who do that will **enter into rest.**

At this point, he will begin to explain how it is a new rest in view and not the land, by again quoting from Psalm 95: **As I have sworn in my wrath, if they shall enter into my rest.** Note here that the KJV translation is of the same Greek language as in 3:11 but takes a very literal sense ("if they shall enter into my rest") instead of the idiomatic understanding ("They shall not enter into my rest") in reliance on Psalm 95. We need to understand that author is quoting Psalm 95 and the sense is, **they shall** not **enter into my rest.** Thus, the consequences faced by that unfaithful generation in the wilderness foreshadowed (was a type of the) consequences for his first century audience of what they might lose if they continue down the road of disobedience rather than living in steadfast endurance.

The author then adds to this warning, **although the works were finished from the foundation of the world.** Remember that Genesis 1 records six literal days of creation (the description of each day ends with "and the evening and the morning were the... day") and then a seventh day when God ceased his creative activities. This seventh day does not contain the familiar statement that "the evening and the morning were the [seventh] day" because the "day" of rest from creating would not end. Thus, the author quotes from Genesis 2:2, **And God did rest the seventh day from all his works.** His point is that while the "rest" available to that generation of Israel in the wilderness is obviously not available to believers now (we are not being told to enter a physical Promised Land), there is still a "rest" available that partakes in the seventh day rest of God.

> 5 And in this *place* again, IF THEY SHALL ENTER INTO MY REST. 6 Seeing therefore it remaineth that some must enter therein, and they to whom it was first preached entered not in because of unbelief: 7 Again, he limiteth a certain day, saying in David, TO DAY, after so long a time; as it is said, TO DAY IF YE WILL HEAR HIS VOICE,

HARDEN NOT YOUR HEARTS. <u>8</u> For if Jesus had given them rest, then would he not afterward have spoken of another day. <u>9</u> There remaineth therefore a rest to the people of God. <u>10</u> For he that is entered into his rest, he also hath ceased from his own works, as God *did* from his. <u>11</u> Let us labour therefore to enter into that rest, lest any man fall after the same example of unbelief.

The author continues to build on the notion of another type of rest that remains, returning again to Psalm 95 with the phrase, **If they shall enter into my rest**, and again the idiomatic sense from Psalm 95 is, **They shall** not **enter into my rest**. Since the Psalmist warns his audience of the danger of not entering into **my rest** centuries after the events of Numbers 13-14, the author of Hebrews concludes that a different rest must remain for believers, **seeing therefore it remaineth that some must enter therein**. Concerning the events of Numbers 13-14, **they to whom it was first preached entered not in** the rest **because of unbelief**, namely that generation did not believe God's message that the land was theirs to take. Yet after these events, God **limiteth** or fixed **a certain day, saying in David** (this may mean David wrote Psalm 95 or may simply being referencing the Psalter as **in David** since he wrote so much of the Psalter), **To day**, after so long a time. Again, the point is that the call to hear the voice of God **To day** came centuries after the events of Numbers 13-14, meaning that the call to God's rest remains. Thus, the psalmist made the call to enter God's rest to people who could not possibly enter in the same way as those of Numbers 13-14 (i.e., entering the

Promised Land physically since they were already there), indicating that a different rest remains, **To day if you will hear his voice, harden not your hearts.** The author makes the point that if Joshua (note that **Jesus** is the Greek equivalent of the Hebrew name Joshua, and contextually here Joshua is indicated) **had given them** the **rest** that remained in view in Psalm 95 when he led the people into the Promised Land centuries earlier, **then** the psalmist in Psalm 95 **would... not afterward have spoken of another day.** And the conclusion is that **there remaineth therefore a rest to the people of God**, and that rest remains available to the audience of Hebrews, and by application, to us **today.**

The message to the Hebrews and by application to us is that **he that is entered into his** (God's seventh day) **rest...hath ceased from his own works, as God did from his.** With this, the author ties the instruction on **rest** to the larger argument that is the thrust of the entire book, namely a call to believers who are experiencing adversity and trials to continue in steadfast obedience with a view to a future when the trials are past and blessings come. Nowhere in the Bible are Christians promised an easy life, nor is it taught that sufficient faith guarantees material or physical blessings during our earthly sojourn. Rather, the Bible presents the reality that the Christian life will have trials (e.g., James 1:2-4; Romans 5:3-5, 8:18; 2 Corinthians 1:5-7) and the faith / life God calls us to is maintaining steadfast endurance and obedience now in view of the reality (or confident hope) of God's promised future blessings (e.g., Hebrews 3:6, 14). Or in the language at hand in this passage, we are to **work** now (steadfast endurance and obedience) so that we can enjoy God's seventh day **rest** (blessings) later. The seventh day rest lost to humanity in the Fall is made available again in Christ. Thus, he exhorts them, **Let us labour** (work) now **therefore to enter into that rest** that remains.

If salvation from sin's penalty (justification) were in view, then the instruction would be to go earn your justification by works. When we read verses like this it is critical that we read in view of the immediate and larger context of Hebrews, a message to believers facing adversity who are tempted to fall back into Judaism. Justification is not in view here, but instead, the author is stressing the relationship between living in steadfast endurance and obedience now and their enjoyment (or forfeiture) of future blessings. And thus the warning to these believers is to **labour** (endure in obedience in this life) **lest any man fail** or forfeit their rest **after the same example of unbelief** as the generation of Israel in Numbers 13-14. That generation of believers was forgiven and sustained by God throughout their lives but forfeited the physical rest of the Promised Land God offered. So we may summarize, "God promises that if you live a life of steadfast endurance and obedience you will inherit future blessings (rest), but if you do not steadfastly endure you will forfeit the future blessings."

> 12 For the word of God *is* quick, and powerful, and sharper than any twoedged sword, piercing even to the dividing asunder of soul and spirit, and of the joints and marrow, and *is* a discerner of the thoughts and intents of the heart. 13 Neither is there any creature that is not manifest in his sight: but all things *are* naked and opened unto the eyes of him with whom we have to do.

In view of the heavy focus on believing the Word of God, the author makes some of the most powerful statements in the whole of the Bible about the effectiveness of God's Word, which he describes as **quick, and powerful, and sharper than any twoedged sword.** This is reminiscent of God's Words through Isaiah, "So shall my word be that goeth forth out of my mouth: it shall not return unto me void, but it shall accomplish that which I please, and it shall prosper in the thing whereto I send it." God's Word is viewed as a living organism (**quick** or living) that is **powerful**, meaning it has the ability to accomplish God's purposes. To be sure, God's Word always accomplishes His purposes. In the most fundamental of examples, God said in Genesis 1:3, "Let there be light: and there was light." When we speak of the Bible, we are talking about a written record of God's Word, and that record through the ministry of the Holy Spirit will be **quick and powerful** in our lives. So for example, in Colossians 3:16, Paul wrote: "Let the word of Christ dwell in you richly in all wisdom, teaching and admonishing one another in psalms and hymns and spiritual songs, singing with grace in your hearts to the Lord." Paul captured the same idea in Ephesians encouraging them to "be filled with the Spirit," and the point is to be influenced or controlled by the Spirit who uses the Word of God to affect change in us. (see also Ephesians 4:20 ff.)

The **word of God** has the ability, analogous to a **twoedged sword,** to cut **even to the diving asunder of soul and spirit, and of the joints and marrow**. Of course, the best of swords can cut exceedingly fine in the physical realm but God's Word is like such a sword in spiritual matters. And thus the **word of God...is a discerner of the**

**thoughts and intents of the heart.** The term **discerner** is the Greek *kritikos* from which we get the English term "critique." It looks beyond the merely physical and examines and reveals our internal heart motivations. We do well to remember that we have three enemies: Satan, the world, and our flesh. And with all of these the fight occurs between our ears (in our minds), as Paul wrote in 2 Corinthians 10:1-5:

> 10:1 Now I Paul myself beseech you by the meekness and gentleness of Christ, who in presence *am* base among you, but being absent am bold toward you: 2 But I beseech *you*, that I may not be bold when I am present with that confidence, wherewith I think to be bold against some, which think of us as if we walked according to the flesh. 3 For though we walk in the flesh, we do not war after the flesh: 4 (For the weapons of our warfare *are* not carnal, but mighty through God to the pulling down of strong holds;) 5 Casting down imaginations, and every high thing that exalteth itself against the knowledge of God, and bringing into captivity every thought to the obedience of Christ;

When we are tempted to disobey, we can blame neither God nor the devil, however, because in reality we are responding to our own internal lust patterns, and when we follow those thoughts they lead to sin and our net experience is not what sin promised but death:

> James 1:13 Let no man say when he is tempted, I am tempted of God: for God

> cannot be tempted with evil, neither tempteth he any man: 14 But every man is tempted, when he is drawn away of his own lust, and enticed. 15 Then when lust hath conceived, it bringeth forth sin: and sin, when it is finished, bringeth forth death.

The Hebrews are facing trials and the possibility of returning to Judaism to avoid further persecution hangs over them. On the other hand, they are presented with the call that **Today if ye will hear** God's **voice** (God's Word in His Son), do not **harden...your hearts**, which is a response that begins in the mind. They are reminded that God's Word cuts through it all and reveals their hearts, whether they are oriented to God or disbelief. And thus the warning that **there** is no **creature that is not manifest in** God's **sight: but all things are naked and opened unto the eyes of him** (God) **with whom we have to do.**

The thing about this sin of disbelief in the face of adversity is we may fool ourselves into believing that a small step is an insignificant step. But think of a couple of examples from the book of Daniel. In Daniel 1, Daniel and his three friends are set apart from all the other kidnapped children of that generation because they would not eat the king's meat. How easy it would have been to justify eating the king's steak. This was not a question of murder or some sexual sin, but simply of eating the king's meat, yet Daniel and his three friends drew a line they would not dare cross. Likewise in Daniel 3, on the heels of the dream in Daniel 2, the king built a statue to his own greatness and demanded that everyone bend the knee when the music stopped playing. Daniel's friends refused, but how easy, how small a thing it would have been to just bend the knee that one time. They might reason that they would do it with their fingers crossed, or that their bending the knee was only superficial and not representative of their hearts, but they refused. The temptation to compromise to avoid adversity begins in the mind and how we respond determines whether it gives rise to sin, but to be sure, no matter how small a step the lure of compromise may seem, in God's eyes the step is a mile in the wrong direction every time. And so the Hebrews, with adversity on their left and God's Word on their right, must know that God's Word is making manifest the intents of their hearts and there is no such thing as an insignificant compromise.

Finally, the author says that all things are manifest **with whom we have to do**. This last phrase means to give an account. The teaching that believers will give an account for how they used their time, talent and energy is taught elsewhere in the New Testament in relation to the rewards (promised future blessings) at issue in the passage under consideration. Paul wrote in 2 Corinthians 5:10: "For we must all appear before the judgment seat of Christ; that every one may receive the things done in his body, according to that he hath done, whether it be good or bad." As Paul makes clear elsewhere, the bema judgment is with a view to our faith being approved and rewarded, and has nothing to do with the question of our justification, for even the believer whose life burns up completely is saved. (1 Corinthians 3:10-15) The connection between the living Word and this judgment is that our obedience and our motives will be tested for approval, and approval will translate into rewards, or in the language of chapters 3 and 4, rest. In this sense, portions of our lives can have eternal consequence and be translated into eternity. This is why, when Jesus taught on rewards, he said: "For whosever will save his life shall lose it: and whosoever will lose his life for my sake shall find it...For the Son of man shall come in the glory of his Father with his angels; and then he shall reward every man according to his works." (Matthew 16:25-27) We choose between our plan and Jesus' plan, and choosing Jesus' plan (losing our life) results in a rewarded life that has eternal consequence and rewards (will save it). Those rewards are part of the promised **rest** that the author exhorts his audience to **labour** for.

> 14 Seeing then that we have a great high priest, that is passed into the heavens, Jesus the Son of God, let us hold fast *our* profession. 15 For we have not an high priest which cannot be touched with the feeling of our infirmities; but was in all points tempted like as *we are, yet* without sin. 16 Let us therefore come boldly unto the throne of grace, that we may obtain mercy, and find grace to help in time of need.

The author returns to the idea that closed chapter 2, namely the role of Jesus as high priest, which will become even more prominent later in the book. This is a reminder that we must view Hebrews all the way through as a single unit of tightly woven and highly organized ideas, and one of the most critical to the author is Jesus' role as high priest. In light of the promise that remains of a rest for the people of God, he encourages his audience, **seeing then that we have a great high priest,** that is passed into the heavens, Jesus the Son of God, let us hold fast our profession. Again, the encouragement is to a life of steadfast endurance and obedience, and here the encouragement relates to our having a **great high priest** that we know is seated at the right hand of the Father (Hebrews 1:13), having **passed into the heavens**. The reason Jesus is **a great high priest** is because of his incarnation. He experienced being human, so that **we have not an high priest which cannot be touched with the feeling of our infirmities**. In the incarnation, Jesus was **in all points tempted** (or tested) **as we are, yet without sin**. This does not mean that Jesus' experience was identical to every experience you have had, but that he faced the trials and tribulation that are common to humanity (see 1 Corinthians 10:13) and therefore can sympathize with us as he fulfills his role as **high priest**, our representative before the Father.

In the next several chapters the author will build on this idea of Jesus as our **great high priest** after the order of Melchisedec, but for now his point is that we are not alone in our trials. Of course, we can and should minister to one another within the local church body (Hebrews 3:13, "exhort one another daily"; 10:24, "consider one another to provoke unto love and to good works"; and 10:24, "exhorting one another: and so much the more, as ye see the day approaching"), but we need to turn in prayer to Jesus. He says, **Let us therefore come boldly unto the throne of Grace, that we may obtain mercy, and find grace to help in time of need**. The knee jerk reaction of many Christians when trials come along is to first abandon going to church (cf. Hebrews 10:25) and then to withdraw from God. But if we are to maintain steadfast endurance and obedience, we must minister to one another and we must learn to pray to God the Father through our **great high priest** the Son for mercy. And here is a great promise to claim – God will provide **grace to help in time of need**. One believer does not endure better than another because he or she is just stronger, but because they have learned to endure by the grace enablement of God to do so, and this is a benchmark of spiritual maturity.


## Closing

We find a story recorded in Matthew 29:29-34 about two blind men sitting beside the road out of Jericho, no doubt begging for alms. One day Jesus was passing by, and "when they heard that Jesus passed by, cried out, saying, Have mercy on us, O Lord, thou Son of David." (Matthew 20:30) For crying out to Jesus for mercy, "the multitude rebuked them....but they cried the more, saying, Have mercy on us, O Lord, thou Son of David." (Matthew 20:31) At that point, Jesus stopped and spoke to them, "What will ye that I shall do unto you?" (Matthew 20:32) Their response was, "Lord, that our eyes may be opened," and "Jesus had compassion on them, and touched their eyes: and immediately their eyes received sight, and they followed him." (Matthew 20:33-34) There is a simple principle here. In American churches, we can get "too dignified" to fall on our faces before Christ and plead for mercy. The reality of our High Priest is that we can set aside the self-help books and learn to pray earnestly. We do not have to wait for the trials to pray, but when the trial comes **do not** stop going to church, **do not** stop communicating with Christian friends and **do not** stop reading God's Word daily. But **do** pray for mercy to endure the trial. You are not strong enough to handle it alone, any more than these two blind men could fix their blindness. The crowd rebuked them but Jesus invites your prayer, and he will stop in the way and respond.

## Application Points

- **MAIN PRINCIPLE:** Labor now to enjoy a future inheritance (rest), and do not forfeit your inheritance by falling into the pattern of disobedience of that generation of Israel in the wilderness as recorded in Numbers 13-14.

- God's Word is able to accomplish His purposes in our lives and does so by making manifest the intents of our hearts.

- As we endeavor to obey and steadfastly endure in the face of adversity, we can approach God though our High Priest Jesus for mercy in our times of need.

## Discussion Questions

1. What was the "good news" that the generation in Numbers 13-14 received?

2. What is the "good news" received by the Hebrews and what does it mean to hear the "good news" in faith?

3. In what sense did God rest on the seventh day?

4. What is the rest that remains today for the people of God?

5. What does it mean that the Word of God is living and powerful and sharper than any two-edged sword?

6. At what point in the trial should we pray for mercy?

# Chapter 6

# Regression to Immaturity

There is a natural progression in the growth process of small children. Parents know well the questions always asked after a baby is born. How much did he weigh when he was born? How long was she? What percentile is he in for this or that attribute? How long were her feet? Most infants grow fairly rapidly and their diet moves from milk to cereal and pureed foods, then later to solid food. By the by, they sit up for themselves and then some learn to crawl or scoot around, and eventually there are those precious first steps and (praise the Lord) getting potty trained, and parents (at least moms) remember all the dates these great events occurred. At certain ages we expect certain milestones to have been met. We expect a 1-year old to eat baby food and not just milk. And by 2 years we expect most children to be walking, etc. But what would we think if we observed a healthy teenager still in diapers and drinking from a baby bottle? Such an occurrence is contrary to the natural order of physical development of children. Concerning spiritual matters, there is also an intended progression that begins with a state of spiritual infancy and progresses forward to adulthood with milestones along the way as God uses various events in our life to grow us in our faith. And just as we would be shocked to see a teenager still in diapers and drinking from a baby bottle, so also we should be surprised by a 15-year believer (a person who has been a Christian for 15 years) who knows little of the Word of God and the life of faith. Even more disconcerting is seeing someone who had grown to maturity in his or her knowledge and application of the Word of God to life and then regressed back to living by sight and not by faith. Such is the issue the author of Hebrews takes up in Hebrews 5 in his concern about how the adversity his audience faced from non-believing Jews was affecting their faith.

## Scripture and Comments

In chapters 3 and 4 the writer spoke of the rest that remains a promised hope to believers who live in obedience to the Word of God and steadfastly endure in the face of affliction and trials. He closes chapter 4 with the promise that believers have a great High Priest who can sympathize with their struggles, and from whom they may receive mercy and grace in their time of need so they may endure. The writer now wishes to begin building on this doctrine of Jesus as our faithful high priest, but as we shall see, he will take a detour and provide an enlightening parenthesis in the argument in 5:11 through 6:20 to address the relationship between spiritual maturity and the capacity to assimilate God's Word.

Hebrews 5:1 For every high priest taken from among men is ordained for men in things *pertaining* to God, that he may offer both gifts and sacrifices for sins: 2 Who can have compassion on the ignorant, and on them that are out of the way; for that he himself also is compassed with infirmity. 3 And by reason hereof he ought, as for the people, so also for himself, to offer for sins. 4 And no man taketh this honour unto himself, but he that is called of God, as *was* Aaron. 5 So also Christ glorified not himself to be made an high priest; but he that said unto him, THOU ART MY SON, TO DAY HAVE I BEGOTTEN THEE. 6 As he saith also in another *place*, THOU *ART* A PRIEST FOR EVER AFTER THE ORDER OF MELCHISEDEC.

Two fundamental requirements of a High Priest are that he be human and appointed to the post. In order to develop an argument that Jesus is a High Priest after the order of Melchisedec, the author must first argue that Jesus meets these two basic requirements for being the High Priest. To do so, he calls upon his audience's knowledge of the office of High Priest under the Law of Moses. Under the Law, **every high priest taken from men is appointed to service to God for the people.** The first High Priest was Moses' brother Aaron, who was selected by God, along with his sons, to act as priests in Exodus 28:1, and this was reconfirmed in Numbers 17:1-8. Those who would reject God's selection or otherwise usurp the office must face God's wrath. (e.g., Numbers 16:1-15; 1 Samuel 13:5-14; 2 Chronicles 26:16-23) Thus, the author states that **no man taketh this honour unto himself, but he that is called of God, as was Aaron.** The tasks of the high priest are to **offer both gifts** (offerings other than animals) **and sacrifices** (animals) **for sins.** Most notably among these tasks, and the one the author will focus on later, is the High Priest's role in the annual Feast Day of Atonement (or Yom Kippur), wherein a sacrifice is made for the sins of Israel. (e.g., Leviticus 23:27 ff.) Because of the humanity of the High Priest, he **can have compassion on the ignorant, and on them that are out of the way; for that he himself also is compassed with infirmity.** The High Priest and those he serves are sinners who all face struggles in the flesh, and thus he can empathize with the people for whom he helps make the sacrifices. And since he is himself a sinner, **he ought, as for the people, so also for himself, to offer for sins.**

Jesus did not usurp the position of High Priest, but was instead appointed by God. Thus, the author explains that **Christ glorified not himself to be made an high priest**, but instead, just as God appointed Jesus heir and sovereign of all things in Psalm 2:7 (cf. Acts 13:33 showing this was fulfilled at the resurrection), **Thou art my Son, to day have I begotten thee**, God also appointed him a priest **in another place**, i.e., Psalm 110:4, with the proclamation, **Thou art a priest for ever after the order of Melchisedec.**

> 7 Who in the days of his flesh, when he had offered up prayers and supplications with strong crying and tears unto him that was able to save him from death, and was heard in that he feared; 8 Though he were a Son, yet learned he obedience by the

things which he suffered; 9 And being
made perfect, he became the author of
eternal salvation unto all them that obey
him; 10 Called of God an high priest after
the order of Melchisedec.

The author turns to proving Jesus' humanity and ability
to sympathize with people in the role of a priest. He
begins with a reference to Jesus' prayer at Gethsemane
on the evening he was arrested. To understand what the
author of Hebrews is telling us, it is helpful to first
compare Jesus' prayer immediately before and after the
Last Supper:

(BEFORE) John 12:27 Now is my soul
troubled; and what shall I say? Father, save
me from this hour: but for this cause came
I unto this hour. 28 Father, glorify thy
name. Then came there a voice from
heaven, *saying*, I have both glorified *it*, and
will glorify *it* again. 29 The people
therefore, that stood by, and heard *it*, said
that it thundered: others said, An angel
spake to him. 30 Jesus answered and said,
This voice came not because of me, but for
your sakes.

(AFTER) Matthew 26:38 Then saith he
unto them, My soul is exceeding sorrowful,
even unto death: tarry ye here, and watch
with me. 39 And he went a little further,
and fell on his face, and prayed, saying, O
my Father, if it be possible, let this cup
pass from me: nevertheless not as I will,
but as thou *wilt*.

We see that immediately before the Last Supper, Jesus says that he will *not* pray, "Father, save me from this hour." Then shortly after the Last Supper, he prays, "O my Father, if it be possible, let this cup pass from me." A common understanding is that Jesus, in his humanity, prayed that he would not have to go to the cross. This interpretation is out of accord with what Jesus said just hours before, and if this interpretation is correct, then it is the one prayer of Jesus that the Father rejected. The better position, and the one that makes sense of our passage in Hebrews, is not that Jesus was praying to avoid the cross (the John 12 passage makes that clear). Rather than praying that the "cup" (of God's wrath) would never come, he was praying that it would pass, which is not the same. The thing about sacrifices is that they always die and stay dead. Jesus was willing to go there, but prayed that the wrath would pass, and the writer to the Hebrews says that **when he had offered up prayers and supplications with strong crying and tears unto him that was able to save him from death**, he was **heard** for his piety. Note that the KJV says "in that he feared" but the translator's margin notes indicate the alternative "for his piety" (or submissiveness) that better fits the context. God answered that prayer, the wrath passed and the Son did not stay dead, as Peter said in Acts 2:32 ("This Jesus hath God raised up"); see also 4:10 ("whom ye crucified, whom God raised from the dead"), 10:40 ("Him God raised up the third day"), and 13:30 ("But God raised him from the dead").

The point the author intends here is simply that the human experience entails trials, and Jesus knew trials. **Though he were a Son, yet learned he obedience by the things which he suffered**. It is a fact that God uses affliction to mature believers (e.g., Hebrews 12; James 1:2-4), and in his humanity, Jesus experienced this part of being human, to the point of going to the cross. And because of his obedience to the cross, **he was perfected,** his growth was brought to completion, which implies his resurrection that followed the cross, so that **he became the author of eternal** or perpetual **salvation unto all them that obey him.** Jesus was the **author** or source of **eternal salvation** as the final and complete sacrifice for humanity's sin, an issue the author will address explicitly later, and the deliverance in view is **eternal,** meaning perpetual, so that it is the fuller orb of salvation is in view that extends forever and includes the future eschatological blessings. This **eternal salvation** is not through obedience of works, but of faith, as in Romans 1:5, 6:17, 10:16 and 16:25-27. Not only was Jesus the source **of eternal salvation,** but after his resurrection God declared Jesus **an high priest after the order of Melchisedec.** The author will pick up on the topic of Melchisedec in chapter 7, but beginning in 5:11, takes a detour to deal with the issue of spiritual maturity and whether his audience is ready for deeper doctrinal teaching, of which the priesthood of Melchisedec is an example.

> 11 Of whom we have many things to say, and hard to be uttered, seeing ye are dull of hearing. 12 For when for the time ye ought to be teachers, ye have need that one teach you again which *be* the first principles of the oracles of God; and are become such as have need of milk, and not of strong meat. 13 For every one that useth milk *is* unskillful in the word of righteousness: for he is a babe. 14 But strong meat belongeth

to them that are of full age, *even* those who by reason of use have their senses exercised to discern both good and evil.

The author has **many things to say** about Melchisedec, but finds the subject matter **hard to be uttered, seeing you are dull of hearing.** The Greek *gegonate* translated **are** is in the perfect tense, which indicates a completed past action with continuing consequences. The KJV captures the point that they are presently **dull of hearing,** but the Greek and the context of what follows indicates they became dull of hearing and remain so. In other words, his audience regressed from a previous state of maturity; they could hear before and now they cannot. What the author has to say about Melchisedec is not **hard** for him to say, but for them to comprehend. **For when for the time you ought to be teachers, ye have need that one teach you again.** He is not speaking here of teaching in the sense of a public ministry (e.g., leading a Bible study), but that given the length of time they have been believers, they should have grown to a position of maturity where they are able both to sit down with another person and explain the Christian faith as well as live out the Christian life of faith. But instead, he says, **ye have need that one teach you again which be the first principles of the oracles of God.** The point is not necessarily that they forgot what they learned, but knowing what the Book says and living life on the basis of the Book are not the same. The Bible has rules but is much more than that, for it tells us from God's biased view what reality is and implores us to live on that basis, and the audience of Hebrews is no longer living as mature believers. They have regressed from a position of relative maturity back to immaturity and it is reflected in their lives.

As the author continues to explain, they have **become such as have need of milk, and not of strong meat.** We see here that **milk** and **meat** are metaphors for the basics of the Christian faith and the deeper doctrines. By implication, since the author for the first time here in chapter 5 suggests a weakness of their capacity to grasp what he desires to teach, what he explained in the prior chapters was, more or less, fundamentals, and the deeper matters about Melchisedec are **strong meat.** The point made here is the same as Paul made in 1 Corinthians 3:1-4, where he says that the believers in Corinth, because of their carnal lifestyles (i.e., their lives look no different than those of unbelievers), have no more capacity for the Word of God than unsaved people:

> 1 Corinthians 3:1 And I, brethren, could not speak unto you as unto spiritual, but as unto carnal, *even* as unto babes in Christ. 2 I have fed you with milk, and not with meat: for hitherto ye were not able *to bear it*, neither yet now are ye able. 3 For ye are yet carnal: for whereas *there is* among you envying, and strife, and divisions, are ye not carnal, and walk as men? 4 For while one saith, I am of Paul; and another, I *am* of Apollos; are ye not carnal?

Unlike the Corinthians, who generally lived carnal lifestyles, the audience in Hebrews is flirting with a return to Judaism in the face of persecution, but the result is the same. In both cases, a turning away from God results in a temporal loss of capacity for the deeper things of God. Probably, the point is not that they cannot understand the words on the page, but they cannot grasp the implications for their lives and execute on them in daily living. As he explains, **every one that useth milk is unskillful in the word of righteousness: for he is a babe.** Physically, all people are getting older no matter what they do. Whether they are living productive lives or wasting their time, talent and energy, they are physically aging. But it is not so with spiritual life. Every believer must of necessity begin as a spiritual baby, feeding on **milk**, but God's plan is for every child to grow into a mature adult who is sustained on **strong meat.** Thus he continues, **strong meat belongeth to them that are of full age, even those who by reason of use have their senses exercised to discern both good and evil.** At this juncture, a number of observations about this issue of spiritual maturity can be derived from this critically important passage:

1. Maturity is not equivalent to knowledge of the Bible, but maturity presupposes knowledge of the Bible.

2. Our learning of the Bible can far outpace our spiritual growth.

3. Maturity is knowing the Word and living life on the basis of what God says reality is.

4. In the spiritual growth process, you are either moving forward or back.

5. Milk is not so much about the topic under consideration, but the depth to which the topic is explored. The author introduced the doctrine of Melchisedec earlier and that introduction was milk. The deeper content about this doctrine to be covered later in the book is meat.

The writer says, **strong meat belong to them that are full age**, i.e., are spiritually all grown up or mature. He then elaborates on what maturity is, namely that maturity describes **those who by reason of use have their senses exercised to discern both good and evil.** The word **senses** means their perception or discernment, and the mature person has his **senses exercised.** The term exercised is the Greek verb *gumnazo*, from which we get the English term "gymnasium." The term had its root in the sporting games of the time and referenced the training for those games. And finally, the goal of this training is that they may **discern both good and evil.** Putting all of this together, maturity is not merely knowing **strong meat** but applying it in the arena of life regularly so that one's senses—perception and judgment of reality—become in line with God's view of the world around us, thus enabling us to discern (call balls and strikes) reality and make life decisions on the basis of the Word of God (point 3 above). To do this we must be able to feed on **strong meat**, but that alone is not maturity, which is point 1 above. To exercise our senses in the crucible of life will take time, and this is why our head knowledge can outpace our ability to skillfully apply what we know to the decisions of life (point 2). What happened to the Hebrews is that they (or some of them) stopped enduring in obedience to God's Word, and the result was a regression back to a state of being spiritual babies again. The Christian walk is one of obedience and steadfast endurance toward the prize, and when we fail to endure, by the by we will regress (point 4). This is why it is so critical that—especially in the face of affliction—we press on. Maturity does not mean we never fail, but maturity is seen in how we respond when we do fail. The mature believer gets back up and keeps pressing forward by the grace enablement of God. (Hebrews 4:16)

## Closing

There are certain things every child loves to do, and among them is running up the escalator on the down side. If you run vigorously you can make it to the top, but if you stop running you will be ferried back down to the bottom. It is nearly impossible to just "tread water" on the moving escalator for a prolonged period. The spiritual life is like that. You are either pressing forward toward the promised blessings in faith or you are being pushed back. A great deception many have accepted is that you can stand still in the spiritual walk for a prolonged period. Those people regress back to immaturity regardless of whether they are conscious of their regression, and if they stay there they will forfeit the promised blessings. The life of obedience and faithful endurance is a progression forward as God by His Word and the ministry of the Spirit in our lives changes us to be more holy, more like His Son. God implores all His children to this life, and at times it will seem like running up the down side of the escalator, and in those times of adversity God teaches us the most about faithful endurance and also provides grace for the moment if we ask for it.

## Application Points

- **MAIN PRINCIPLE:** Jesus qualifies as a High Priest because he is fully human and able to sympathize with us and because God the Father appointed him a priest forever after the order of Melchisedec.

- Learn the Word of God and consistently strive to apply it both to properly perceive the world and your particular circumstances from God's perspective and to live on the basis of God's Word.

## Discussion Questions

1. What are the qualifications for being a High Priest?

2. What is the function of a High Priest?

3. How does Jesus' incarnation help qualify him as a High Priest?

4. How was Jesus' final prayer in Gethsemane, following the Last Supper, answered?

5. Contrast by examples how a spiritual babe might respond to affliction and how a mature Christian ought to respond. Consider not just the decision, but the perception of the significance and purpose of the affliction.

6. What are examples of doctrines in the Bible that are milk? Meat?

7. Define spiritual maturity in your own words.

8. Can you mature without knowing the Word of God? What are the implications for your life—regardless of the excuse—if you never learn enough Bible to explain the sanctification process? Or to explain how a believer is to walk in the Spirit? Or to explain generally when Christ will return and what he will do after that and what we as believers will do after that?

# Chapter 7

# Pressing Forward to Maturity

The Bible has a great deal to say about some issues and almost nothing to say about others, with a lot of issues falling somewhere in between the extremes. It stands to reason that professed "Bible preaching churches" would give time to the doctrines of the Bible in proportion to the amount of attention the Bible itself gives those doctrines. Often that is not the case, and as a result there is often confusion among people that have been in church for a long time as to what constitutes the "fundamentals" of the faith and what constitutes the "deeper issues." The doctrines that get the most attention are assumed to be the fundamentals we all should know well, when in fact it may be that the doctrines that get little or no attention are the fundamentals. For example, in many churches the doctrine of rewards (or the bema judgment for believers) is rarely or never addressed, but I would submit that based on the frequency of attention given this doctrine in the New Testament that it is a fundamental of the faith critical to our Christian walk. Indeed, this doctrine is central to Hebrews and, in particular, to the material in chapters 2 through 4 that we have already covered. Interestingly, when you get to chapter 5 the author suggests he wants to now cover a deeper issue that his audience may not be ready for, which implies the material covered before chapter 5 was in the author's mind the basics (or milk), including the issue of rewards. In chapter 6, the author is encouraging his audience to leave behind the basics and press on to maturity. Getting a true Biblical perspective on the ABC's of the faith is critical to the progress of our spiritual growth. But at the same time, we cannot stay there forever. It is also imperative we move on to the deeper matters.

## Scripture and Comments

Chapters 5 and 6 comprise a unit but are treated separately here because of the length of a typical sermon or Bible study. In chapter 5, the writer explained that he desired to teach his audience about the priesthood of Melchisedec but was concerned that they would not be able to grasp it because of their regression back to a state of immaturity. He then explained the relationship between spiritual maturity and the ability to understand the Word of God. In chapter 6, he will sound the warning that prolonged immaturity can result in being confirmed in that state. In other words, the opportunity to press forward to maturity is in God's control, and after a period of prolonged immaturity, especially as a result of drifting away, God may close that opportunity permanently. But there is hope for the Hebrews, for the author is confident that God will allow them to press forward and return to maturity.

> Hebrews 6:1 Therefore leaving the principles of the doctrine of Christ, let us go on unto perfection; not laying again the foundation of repentance from dead works, and of faith toward God, 2 Of the doctrine of baptisms, and of laying on of hands, and of resurrection of the dead, and of eternal judgment. 3 And this will we do, if God permit. 4 For *it is* impossible for those who were once enlightened, and have tasted of the heavenly gift, and were made partakers of the Holy Ghost, 5 And have tasted the good word of God, and the powers of the world to come, 6 If they shall fall away, to renew them again unto repentance; seeing they crucify to themselves the Son of God afresh, and put *him* to an open shame.

The author begins with **therefore**, signally that he is building on what he just explained about spiritual maturity and his desire to teach them "strong meat," namely the doctrine of the priestly order of Melchisedec. He then lists some of what he would label as the basics of the faith, expressing his desire to press forward to deeper issues, saying, **let us go on unto perfection** or maturity, **not laying again the foundation** principles. These basics are important, but they are a place to begin, and in the growth process explained at the end of chapter 5, the "babe" is supposed to press on to adulthood or spiritual maturity, which means moving out of the kindergarten basics. Thus, they must **leav[e] the principles of the** doctrine of Christ... repentance from dead works, and of faith toward God, of the doctrine of baptisms, and of the laying on of hands, and of resurrection of the dead, and of eternal judgment. At this point comes what is probably the strongest warning in the New Testament for believers: **And this we will do**, that is, press on to maturity, **if God permit**.

The obvious warning he is making is that God may permit them to press forward from their regressed state back to maturity, and He may not. Bible expositor J. Dwight Pentecost referred to this as a warning of being confirmed in a state of "spiritual senility." To use the author's words, it is a warning of being confirmed permanently in the state of being a spiritual "babe" in Christ, and the problem is that (1) babies make messes where adults (spiritually mature believers) would because of their trained perception properly discern and deal with the issues of life, and (2) babies run a risk of forfeiting their inheritance. Whereas chapters 2 through 4 emphasized the eschatological consequences (rewards and inheritance) of disobedience to Christ, this passage emphasizes the temporal consequences. But it is important that we see the book of Hebrews as a unit where the author is warning of the reality of both temporal and eschatological consequences stemming from the same conduct, so that the book is not about one or the other, but both. The good news is that in verse 9, the author will indicate that he is "persuaded" that God will allow his audience to press forward to maturity. But that is not always a guarantee, and the point of the warning is that a believer can regress to a point and remain there too long so that pressing back to maturity is taken off the table. Thus, he writes, **For it is**

**impossible... to renew them again unto repentance.** We will deal with all the words in the middle, but note the magnitude of this warning. There comes a point where turning around is **impossible.** And for this reason we need to understand the warning and heed it with all seriousness.

First of all, we need to understand that here, as with the other warning passages, the author is addressing and warning believers! Note how he describes them in terms that could never be applied to unbelievers. First, they **were once enlightened.** The term **enlightened** is the same Greek word (*photizo*) used, for example, in Ephesians 1:18 ("The eyes of your understanding being **enlightened**; that ye may know what is the hope of his calling...."). The author will use it again in Hebrews 10:32 when he says, "But call to remembrance the former days, in which, after ye were **illuminated**, ye endured a great flight of affliction." This likely refers to the regeneration of the Holy Spirit, and in any event is a past spiritual event by which their minds were opened to the truths of God. Importantly, note that the author does not simply say they "were enlightened" but that they **were once enlightened.** The term **once** is the Greek *hapax* and here means that their being **enlightened** was a one-time event, in the same way the term is used to indicate that Jesus died once for our sins. (e.g., Hebrews 9:28, 1 Peter 3:18) Those who teach that you can lose, throw away or forfeit salvation, amidst a myriad of other problems, also face the problem that our justification is a one-time event and the Bible nowhere describes how to be "re-justified." They were **once enlightened**, a one-time event that is only true of believers.

There is more, for they **tasted of the heavenly gift**. Contextually, their **enlightenment** as well as their having **tasted of the heavenly gift** should be read in conjunction with their being **made partakers** (mutual sharers) **of the Holy Ghost.** At this point someone may say, "They only tasted the heavenly gift." Back in Hebrews 2:9, the author used the same term to express the truth that Jesus "by the grace of God should taste death for every man." Jesus did not nibble around the edges of the cross when he tasted death for every man, and in the same way, the author is not suggesting his audience had one nibble of the indwelling of the Holy Spirit, but is using a figure of speech to express their receipt of **the heavenly gift**, which is a reference to the indwelling Holy Spirit, and by that indwelling they became mutual sharers **of the Holy Ghost.** Moreover, they also **tasted of the good word of God, and the powers of the world to come.** As we saw in chapter 5, the audience had attained to a state of relative maturity before many of them regressed. They had heard the great truths of the future blessings in the **world to come** for those who endure as Christ endured, and they lived on that basis. Again, they did not merely "nibble" but **tasted** (devoured, fully assimilated) **the good word of God.** The term translated "word" here is not the usual Greek *logos* but *rhema*, which means a specific utterance of God, which contextually are the teachings about the **world to come.** They had heard and accepted the truth of these teachings and on the basis of God's promised future blessings were obedient in lives of steadfast endurance. (see Hebrews 6:10, 10:32-34) But at some point many began to regress.

The warning is that for believers who grew to a point of relative maturity, **if they shall fall away**, then it is

**impossible...to renew them again unto repentance.** As will be made clear, he is not saying they have all fallen away and cannot be renewed, but is sounding the ominous warning that they are in danger of doing so and being confirmed in a regressed state. The term **renew** is the Greek verb *anakainizo*, used only here in the New Testament. The related noun *anakainosis* is used only in Romans 12:2 ("but be ye transformed by the **renewing** of your mind") and Titus 3:5 ("and **renewing** of the Holy Ghost"). These terms are not used outside the New Testament. The meaning is a complete "brick by brick" renovation. Also note that the term **repentance** is a much-confused term in our day. To "repent" does not mean to turn from sinning, for otherwise we would not have Bible verses about God repenting or not repenting. (e.g., Exodus 32:12, Deuteronomy 32:36) Indeed, in Hebrews 7:21 we have the statement that "The Lord sware and will not repent, Thou art a priest for ever after the order of Melchisedec," in other words, God the Father appointed Jesus a priest and will never change His mind. The Greek term is *metanoia* and means a change of thinking or change of mind. Context determines the thinking that is to be changed (or not changed as the case may be). Necessarily, repenting is the flip side of believing, for to change one's mind from one belief to another entails believing something we did not believe before, and this in turn may entail acting on that change of thinking by trusting Christ or stopping a particular sin. Thus, the warning in context here in Hebrews 6:6 is that at some point it becomes impossible to do the "brick by brick" renovation process of moving believers from a regressed state of spiritual immaturity back to **repentance**, i.e., back to spiritual maturity, a state which reflects a renewed mind. To grow up, as the author carefully explained at the end of chapter 5, is to move from living on milk to living on meat. This group regressed back to milk and back to thinking like babies in Christ, and he wants to see them return back to thinking like adults or mature believers, and thus uses the term **repentance** to indicate this change of thinking.

We do well to pause here and connect the warning of chapter 6 with the warnings in chapters 2 through 4. The earlier warnings were focused on eschatological consequences, a loss of inheritance and rewards, or in the language of chapters 3 and 4, a loss of future rest. Here in chapter 6, however, the warning is about temporal or immediate judgment in the form of being confirmed a spiritual babe. These warnings are flip sides of a coin, for the one confirmed as a baby will never mature and lead a life of steadfast endurance that is the sort of life for which future rewards are contemplated. The message in these warnings, and the remaining warnings later in the book, is that continued disobedience has both temporal and eschatological consequences, and for a time in our lives God will allow us to right the ship or get back on track, but if the disobedience continues for too long a time, the door of opportunity closes, just as it did for the disobedient generation of Israel in Numbers 13-14 that the author used as a backdrop for the extended warning passage in Hebrews 3 and 4.

What the audience is contemplating, in the face of affliction, is a return to Judaism. Remember, it is the Judaism of Jesus' day that labeled him a blasphemer and cried out, "crucify him." In the moment, compromise often seems like a small step with no harm done, but in

God's eyes the step is a mile wide. And here, they are flirting with re-identifying with the group that said, "give us Barabbas" (my paraphrase). This is no small step, but is tantamount to **crucify[ing] to themselves the Son of God afresh, and put[ting] him to an open shame.** Since what they are contemplating doing is spitting in the face of Jesus (although surely none of them would articulate it that way), the warning of the consequences of doing so is severe, to wit, being permanently confirmed in a state of spiritual senility. As we will see, the result of such a confirmation, among other things, will be a forfeiture of their inheritance.

> 7 For the earth which drinketh in the rain that cometh oft upon it, and bringeth forth herbs meet for them by whom it is dressed, receiveth blessing from God: 8 But that which beareth thorns and briers *is* rejected, and *is* nigh unto cursing; whose end *is* to be burned.

In an allegory that uses similar imagery to the famous Parable of the Soils (Matthew 13), the author pictures the Word of God as **the rain** falling down **the earth**, which represents believers. Some believers will respond to the Word in obedience and others will not, and obedience will be evident by the fruit of their lives. Thus, **the earth** that **bringeth forth herbs** (vegetation)... **receiveth blessing from God.** In contrast, **the earth...which beareth thorns and briers is rejected, and is nigh unto cursing; whose end is to be burned.** The believers **(the earth)** that produce useful vegetation are blessed of God because the fruit of their lives is **meet** (useful) **for them by whom it is dressed,** in other words, their lives are fruitful and a blessing to others. In contrast, other believers' "fruit" consists of useless **thorns and briers** that is no benefit to anyone else, and that "fruit," such as it is, **is to be burned.** It is NOT the earth (the believers) that is burned, but the useless fruit. What is in view here, as with so much of Hebrews, is the same as what Paul addressed in 1 Corinthians 3:11-15 where Jesus looks at the fruit of the believer's life and tests the fruit by fire, with a view to rewarding the life of faithfulness. There, as here, the useless produce (wood, hay, stubble) is burned but the person without lasting fruit (gold, silver, precious stones) is "saved, yet so as by fire." The audience of Hebrews runs the risk of being confirmed in their regressed state of immaturity, and the "fruit" of their Christian lives being destroyed in the sense that it will not translate into future rewards.

> 9 But, beloved, we are persuaded better things of you, and things that accompany salvation, though we thus speak. 10 For God *is* not unrighteous to forget your work and labour of love, which ye have shewed toward his name, in that ye have ministered to the saints, and do minister. 11 And we desire that every one of you do shew the same diligence to the full assurance of hope unto the end: 12 That ye be not slothful, but followers of them who through faith and patience inherit the promises.

Against the backdrop of the severe warning about being confirmed in their regressed state, the author shares his confidence that they have not yet reached that point.

Thus, he says, **beloved, we are persuaded** of **better things of you...though we thus speak** in terms of this severe warning. The **better things** he is convinced of are **things that accompany salvation**, that is, things connected with or related to **salvation**, but what salvation is in view here? Again, the focus of Hebrews to this point has consistently been on the relationship between how you live now and the blessings associated with the "world to come" or future kingdom, including in the immediate context of verse 5 (**have tasted... the powers of the world to** come), which is why he refers to believers in 1:14 as those "who shall be *heirs* of salvation" and encourages them in 9:28 that Jesus will "appear the second time...unto salvation." The warning earlier in the chapter is of the possibility of being confirmed as a result of failing to live obediently with steadfast endurance, thus never reaching spiritual maturity, and by implication, losing rewards associated with the believer's participation in the kingdom. The warning of the allegory in 6:7-8 is likewise a warning about loss of future rewards. Consequently, the **salvation** in view here is not justification, but looks to the salvation they stand to inherit in the future. Despite the severe warning the author gave them, he is **persuaded** that they are not going to be confirmed in a regressed state but will get back on track toward maturity, and thus obtain those **things** (blessings or rewards) **that accompany** the **salvation** they stand to inherit when Christ returns.

Part of the reason the author is so confident God will permit them to press forward toward maturity is that **God is not unrighteous to forget your work and labour of love, which ye have shewed toward his name, in that ye have ministered to the saints, and do minister.** We are again reminded that his audience is believers who reached a level of relative maturity and were walking with God, as seen in their service to other believers (relate this back to the allegory of 6:7-8) in the past and their continuing service. This is hardly a picture of weak-kneed "professors" of Jesus who made an empty profession but are not "possessors," which will be further confirmed in 10:32-35 where they are reminded of their faithful endurance through "a great fight of afflictions...reproaches and afflictions...." Just as they were historically diligent in their walk with God through the sorts of trials most of us in churches in the United States have never endured because of our faith, the author says **we desire that every one of you do shew the same diligence to the full assurance of hope unto the end.** Since we cannot be sure who is the author, we also cannot identify the **we**, but the message is clear. He calls to remembrance their former diligence (or eagerness) and urges them to show **the same diligence** (eagerness) for the rest of their lives (**unto the end**) so that they will return to maturity and gain the rewards for a life of faithfulness.

To this point, he urges them not to be **slothful** or lazy in terms of obedience to God and service to others, but instead, be **followers of them who through faith and patience inherit the promises.** The word **followers** is the Greek *mimetes* and means **followers** in the sense of imitators. Most of chapter 11 will be devoted to a survey of believers of the past (e.g., Enoch, Moses) who provide us with faith examples to imitate. Here, the author generally points their thinking back to such examples of faithful believers that through obedience and endurance will in the future **inherit the promises.** In 11:13, the author writes, "These all died in faith, not having received the promises, but having seen them afar off, and were persuaded of them, and embraced them...." He wants his audience to follow their example, living with one foot in the world to come so that they may also inherit the promises.

13 For when God made promise to Abraham, because he could swear by no greater, he sware by himself, 14 Saying, SURELY BLESSING I WILL BLESS THEE, AND MULTIPLYING I WILL MULTIPLY THEE. 15 And so, after he had patiently endured, he obtained the promise. 16 For men verily swear by the greater: and an oath for confirmation *is* to them an end of all strife. 17 Wherein God, willing more abundantly to shew unto the heirs of promise the immutability of his counsel, confirmed *it* by an oath: 18 That by two immutable things, in which *it was* impossible for God to lie, we might have a strong consolation, who have fled for refuge to lay hold upon the hope set before us: 19 Which *hope* we have as an anchor of the soul, both sure and stedfast, and which entereth into that within the veil; 20 Whither the forerunner is for us entered, *even* Jesus, made an high priest for ever after the order of Melchisedec.

While many examples of lives of faith await us in chapter 11, the author here focuses on Abraham as the sort of proto-typical example of a life of faith they should imitate. **God made promise to Abraham** in Genesis 12:1-3 and Genesis 15 of a child (and a nation) and Abraham responded to the promise in Genesis 15 with the question, "whereby shall I know that I shall inherit it?" (Genesis 15:8) In an accommodation to Abraham's human weaknesses (doubts), God added to his Word an oath or covenant (Genesis 15:9-16) and sealed it as a blood covenant based solely on the veracity of God (Abraham was unconscious at the time of the oath) insofar as only the manifestation of God in the form of "a burning lamp" passed between the portions of the sacrificed animals (Genesis 15:17) used to inaugurate the blood covenant. These promises were re-confirmed and expanded in Genesis 17. Years later Abraham and Sarah had the promised child Isaac and when Isaac was a teen, God told Abraham to sacrifice him. Abraham was obedient but before sacrificing Isaac, God stopped him and provided an animal sacrifice. At this point God re-affirmed and clarified the covenant promises through the angel of the LORD:

> Genesis 22:15 And the angel of the LORD called unto Abraham out of heaven the second time, 16 And said, **By myself have I sworn**, saith the LORD, for because thou hast done this thing, and hast not withheld thy son, thine only *son*: 17 That in blessing I will bless thee, and in multiplying I will multiply thy seed as the stars of the heaven, and as the sand which *is* upon the sea shore; and thy seed shall possess the gate of his enemies; 18 And in thy seed shall all the nations of the earth be blessed; because thou hast obeyed my voice.

In this re-affirmation, God says, "By myself have I sworn," and thus the author of Hebrews says that God **sware by himself** since **he could swear by no greater** person and then quotes from Genesis 22:17. After years of Abraham's obedience and endurance, **he obtained the promise** of Isaac. Of course, Isaac was born years earlier, but having passed the test of his obedience, the certainty of the future blessings was made sure by the oath of Genesis 22:15-17. Just as in human dealings, people **swear by the greater**, such as swearing by a king or by God, and such an **oath** provides a **confirmation....to them** and **an end of all strife** or dispute. In other words, an oath settles the matter because it makes certain from a human perspective their future dealings. In a like way, **God, willing more abundantly to shew unto the heirs of promise the immutability** (never changes) **of his** promises **confirmed** His promises **by an oath**. Note the he refers to what **God** will **shew unto the heirs**, which like so much of the book reflects a future orientation. God's promises to Abraham would inure to the benefit both of the nation that would come from Abraham and the nations through the "seed" (singular), that is, through Jesus Christ. (Galatians 3:16-18)

The author says **that by two immutable things**, namely God's promise and His oath, **in which it was impossible for God to lie, we might have a strong consolation** or encouragement. God's promises to the Hebrews are as certain as those to Abraham, and indeed are a fulfillment of the promises to Abraham in the seed that is Jesus Christ. The author refers to his audience as persons **who have fled for refuge** to the Son / Messiah about whom he has been arguing the superiority to the old order. The notion of **refuge** is reminiscent of the cities of refuge

under the Law (e.g., Numbers 35:6 ff.). In the face of
affliction, rather than drifting back into Judaism, they
should see the certainty of the great promises of God to
Abraham being fulfilled in His Son and take **refuge** in the
Son—he is their city of refuge—**to lay hold upon the
hope set before us**, that is, their Messianic hope
concerning the future kingdom and the kingdom
blessings. Their hope in Jesus should radically change
their perspective and their living in the now, and in this
way the promises of pressing forward in faithful
endurance to maturity and inheriting the future blessings
are **an anchor of the soul, both sure and steadfast**,
tethering them as an anchor tethers a boat so that they
do not drift away from Jesus.

This Messianic hope goes **within the veil**, that is, in the
very presence of God. The hope they have entails a
future living in the presence of God. We are reminded
that **even Jesus**, as **the forerunner**, already **for us entered**
into the very presence of God in his priestly function as
**an high priest for ever after the order of Melchisedec**.
This latter point will be more fully developed in chapters
9 and 10, but in short, Jesus entered the heavenly
tabernacle and offered his blood once for all time for all
believers in all ages. Pulling all of this together, the
author warns his audience of the possibility of
confirmation in a state of regression and loss of future
blessings, but then says he is confident of better things
for them and urges them to press forward on the basis of
the certainty of those promised blessings and the fullness
of their Messianic hope in Jesus Christ. In the next
chapter, he will begin a thorough development of the
priestly order of Melchisedec, which the author views as
constituting part of the "meat" of the Word of God.

## <u>Closing</u>

Life is serious business. As one of my professors always reminded us, life is not a 50-yard sprint but a marathon, and as Paul told the Corinthians in 1 Corinthians 9:24, we must run to win. Some folks will say that it is good enough for them to get into heaven and they are unconcerned with rewards. Others say that aspiring to rewards is only rooted in bad motives so we should not do so. But the Bible says we should run to win, and in the language of Hebrews, we should "go on unto perfection." God never says the marathon will be easy, but He implores us to press on with vigor to maturity and "lay hold upon the hope set before us." And the warning is that if we spend long enough at the starting line unwilling or too slothful to engage in the race and move on to maturity, we may get confirmed there. The writer says more than once to the Hebrews to take heed—to take the warnings seriously. We need to catch hold of this notion that not all believers enjoy the same experience of God in their lives now because of the choices they make, and neither will they have the same experience in the kingdom. Future blessings are promised to those who live in obedience and steadfast endurance, and God never really details the downside of what life in the kingdom will be like for those who refuse to steadfastly endure, but God minces no words on the seriousness of the issue that we should all be amply motivated to press forward in our walks until God takes us home. The promised future blessings should comfort, motivate and invigorate our living now.

## Application Points

- **MAIN PRINCIPLE:** Prolonged immaturity places a believer in danger of being confirmed in that state and thus forfeiting their inheritance.

- Pressing forward to maturity requires embracing the deeper doctrines, the meat of the Word of God, like the priestly order of Melchisedec.

## Discussion Questions

1. What are some examples of doctrines that are the fundamentals (or milk)?

2. What are some examples of doctrines that are the deeper issues (or meat)?

3. How can we tell milk from meat?

4. How long should it take a new believer to reach a state of maturity?

5. What does immaturity look like in practical terms in the life of a believer?

6. What does maturity look like in practical terms in the life of a believer?

7. If a person has been a church-going believer for 30 years, is that any guarantee that person is mature?

8. If two people are church-going believers for 30 years at the same church, does that mean their Christian experience and maturity are essentially equivalent?

# Chapter 8

# A Superior Priesthood

I have to think that the faithful saints for centuries were perplexed as they came to Genesis 14:18 and met the mysterious Melchisedec, a character that appears out of nowhere then quickly exits left, then is not mentioned for centuries until King David penned Psalm 110, then again exited the scene for a thousand years until God's fuller revelation of Melchisedec in the book of Hebrews. In God's progressive revelation, He left trails of breadcrumbs, as it were, in every direction you could look, leading to Jesus Christ. The Old Testament feasts and sacrifices pointed to Christ. The many prophecies about his birth, life, death and resurrection pointed to him as well. The promise of a New Covenant in the prophets pointed to the new age that would dawn in the future inaugurated by Jesus' blood. The tabernacle itself was a sketch of the future atoning work of Christ. Some trails are more faint than others, and so it is with Melchisedec, yet now in Hebrews 7, what was dimly suggested before comes full circle as we come to understand the priesthood for which the Son of God is

High Priest. The reason for the crumbs is at least two-fold. For those in the past, there was something to look forward to, something great God would do, and the faithful were watchful. For us, we see the fulfillment then look back at the trail of crumbs that remind us that God was always in control, not surprised, not learning as the journey of time progressed, but knowing the end from the beginning, propelling history forward on His timing to the culmination in Christ. That presentation of the shadowy figure of Melchisedec in Genesis 14 was not out of place, nor unnecessary, but surgically placed in time and space, the deliberate fingerprint of the Creator to become not only clear, but reassuring, to future generations.

## Scripture and Comments

In Hebrews 5, the author wished to dive into the topic of the priesthood of Melchisedec, to whom he previously alluded but about which he had not shared in any detail yet. Indeed, he said that "we have many things to say" about Melchisedec, but he realized that many in his audience had regressed so that his subject matter was "hard to be uttered, seeing" that they had become "dull of hearing." (Hebrews 5:10-11) The author then inserted a detour or parenthetical in the balance of chapter 5 and all of chapter 6 to address the relationship between the process of maturing spiritually and our capacity to understand the deeper things (the meat as opposed to milk) of the Word of God. He warned his audience of the danger of spending a prolonged period in infancy and becoming confirmed in that state rather than moving on to maturity, then expressed his confidence that God would move them to maturity. Having completed his detour and expressed confidence of better things for his audience, the author returns to the doctrinal topic about which he said "we have many things to say," namely the person and ministry of Melchisedec. As we will see, the priestly order of Melchisedec is more ancient than that of the Levites (or that of Aaron), is superior to the Aaronic or Levitical priesthood, administrates a superior covenant (the New Covenant) and most importantly, it is this Melchisedecan priesthood of which God the Son is High Priest, under whom we serve.

> <u>Hebrews 7:1</u> For this Melchisedec, king of Salem, priest of the most high God, who met Abraham returning from the slaughter of the kings, and blessed him; <u>2</u> To whom also Abraham gave a tenth part of all; first being by interpretation King of righteousness, and after that also King of Salem, which is, King of peace; 3 Without father, without mother, without descent, having neither beginning of days, nor end of life; but made like unto the Son of God; abideth a priest continually. 4 Now consider how great this man *was*, unto whom even the patriarch Abraham gave the tenth of the spoils. 5 And verily they that are of the sons of Levi, who receive the office of the priesthood, have a commandment to take tithes of the people according to the law, that is, of their brethren, though they come out of the loins of Abraham: <u>6</u> But he whose descent is not counted from them received tithes

of Abraham, and blessed him that had the promises. 7 And without all contradiction the less is blessed of the better. 8 And here men that die receive tithes; but there he *receiveth them*, of whom it is witnessed that he liveth. 9 And as I may so say, Levi also, who receiveth tithes, payed tithes in Abraham. 10 For he was yet in the loins of his father, when Melchisedec met him.

The author draws on an episode from the life of Abraham where Sodom and Gomorrah had been attacked by Chedorlaomer and other kings and, in addition to robbing these cities, kidnapped Lot, Abraham's nephew. Abraham armed his servants and recovered Lot, and on his way home was met by the king of Sodom and the mysterious King of Salem, as recorded in Genesis 14:

> Genesis 14:17 And the king of Sodom went out to meet him after his return from the slaughter of Chedorlaomer, and of the kings that *were* with him, at the valley of Shaveh, which *is* the king's dale. 18 And Melchizedek king of Salem brought forth bread and wine: and he *was* the priest of the most high God. 19 And he blessed him, and said, Blessed *be* Abram of the most high God, possessor of heaven and earth: 20 And blessed be the most high God, which hath delivered thine enemies into thy hand. And he gave him tithes of all.

The author explains that the name **Melchisedec** means **King of righteousness**, and the title **King of Salem** (what would later be Jerusalem) means **King of peace**. These are fitting names for the priest that is a type for Jesus, the one whose "name shall be ...Prince of Peace, of the increase of his government and peace there shall be no end" (Isaiah 9:6-7), and who "with righteousness shall he judge...and righteousness shall be the girdle of his loins" (Isaiah 11:4-5). This mysterious king **met Abraham returning** from battle **and blessed him**, and to honor this king, **Abraham gave** Melchisedec **a tenth part** of the spoils. It is not our author's point to teach anything concerning tithing for church age believers in this passage, but to use the fact of Abraham's tithe to Melchisedec to make a technical but compelling argument that the priesthood of Melchisedec is superior to the priesthood of Levi. Remember that Abraham had a child of promise, Isaac, who in turn had a child named Jacob, from whose sons the tribes of Israel came (e.g., Judah, Ephraim, Levi, etc.). The tribe of Levi became the tribe of priests who administered the Law or Covenant of Moses at the Tabernacle and later the Temple.

When you read Genesis 14, Melchisedec comes out of nowhere and quickly exits the scene. After that, the Bible is silent about the man for centuries until he is mentioned in Psalm 110:4, and then centuries later here in Hebrews. For explaining the type, the author views the brief episode in Genesis 14 like a snapshot that contains everything we know of the man, and we are to make no assumptions. Viewed on such a limited canvas, Melchisedec is **without father, without mother, without descent**, meaning he has no genealogy. This is important because being a Levitical priest is based on genealogy—a man is a priest because he is of that tribe and his parents were of that tribe. But the basis for Melchisedec being a priest is not genealogy, because he has none. Further, he has **neither beginning of days, nor end of life** (remember, we are viewing the snapshot in Genesis 14 without no assumptions about other information), which is like Jesus, who is eternal (no beginning, no end). Thus, Melchisedec is **made like unto the Son of God**, that is, he is a type or picture of Jesus, and for the reason that he pictures eternality (**neither beginning of days, nor end of life**), he **abideth a priest continually.** Levitical priests are mortal and die, but this priest **abideth** or lives and serves his role forever.

With the type clearly in mind, consider the author's argument. First, Melchisedec **blessed** Abraham who **had the promises** from God (e.g., Genesis 12:1-3), and it is obvious that **the less is blessed of the better**, in other words, the person of greater position blesses the person of lesser position. So we can draw as a first conclusion from Genesis 14 that Melchisedec is greater than Abraham since Melchisedec gave the blessings to Abraham. Second, the **sons of Levi** or the Levitical priests **take tithes of the people according to the law**, in other words, by command of the Law of Moses they administered (e.g., Numbers 18:21, 26). But before there were Levites to collect tithes from their Jewish **brethren, the patriarch Abraham** paid or tithed **the tenth of the spoils** to Melchisedec, who **liveth** forever (again, as a type, based on looking at Genesis 14 as a snapshot that represents all we know of the man). And when **Abraham** tithed to the greater person Melchisedec, the lineage from his great grandson Levi, who came **out of the loins of Abraham**, are seen to have **paid tithes in Abraham** when **he** (Levi) **was yet in the loins of his father** Abraham. In other words, just as Abraham paid tithes to the superior person Melchisedec, so also the Levites *seminally in Abraham* paid tithes to the superior person Melchisedec. And if the Levites who receive tithes from the people in turn pay tithes to the priest Melchisedec who lives forever, then the continuing priesthood of Melchisedec is superior to the priesthood of Levi.

11 If therefore perfection were by the Levitical priesthood, (for under it the people received the law,) what further need *was there* that another priest should rise after the order of Melchisedec, and not be called after the order of Aaron? 12 For the priesthood being changed, there is made of necessity a change also of the law. 13 For he of whom these things are spoken pertaineth to another tribe, of which no man gave attendance at the altar. 14 For *it is* evident that our Lord sprang out of Juda; of which tribe Moses spake nothing concerning priesthood.

Having argued that the priestly order of Melchisedec is superior to that of Levi, the author considers why centuries after the Genesis 14 reference to the priesthood of Melchisedec—and thus centuries after the Levitical priesthood was established—there is a reference in Psalm 110 to another priest being appointed a priest after the order of Melchisedec. He asks the rhetorical question, if **perfection** (made right with God) **were by the Levitical priesthood...what further need was there that another priest should rise after the order of Melchisedec, and not be called after the order of Aaron** (the first high priest)? The required answer is there was not

**perfection...by the Levitical priesthood** or the Law they administered. We know from other Bible passages that the Law was not designed to make people right (or justified) before a Holy God, but to show them they are sinners. (e.g., Romans 3:19-28, 5:20, 7:5-12) The author will make a similar point in 7:18-19. But note what he next points out, **for the priesthood being changed** from Levitical to Melchisedecan, **there is made of necessity a change also of the law.** In other words, a priesthood and the Law administered by the priests are a unit, so that if the one is changed, the other is also. His point is that the appointment of a new permanent priest after the order of Melchisedec to replace the Levitical priesthood implies that the Law of Moses is also replaced. This new priest is Jesus who **pertaineth to another tribe...for it is evident that our Lord sprang out of Juda.** Again, the priests under the Law of Moses all came from the tribe of Levi, but Jesus is from the tribe of Judah (through Jacob's son Judah) and therefore cannot serve as a Levitical priest. Indeed, **Moses spake nothing concerning priesthood** to suggest any priestly role for Judah.

> 15 And it is yet far more evident: for that after the similitude of Melchisedec there ariseth another priest, 16 Who is made, not after the law of a carnal commandment, but after the power of an endless life. 17 For he testifieth, THOU *ART* A PRIEST FOR EVER AFTER THE ORDER OF MELCHISEDEC. 18 For there is verily a disannulling of the commandment going before for the weakness and unprofitableness thereof. 19 For the law made nothing perfect, but the bringing in of a better hope *did*; by the

which we draw nigh unto God. 20 And inasmuch as not without an oath *he was made priest:* 21 (For those priests were made without an oath; but this with an oath by him that said unto him, THE LORD SWARE AND WILL NOT REPENT, THOU *ART* A PRIEST FOR EVER AFTER THE ORDER OF MELCHISEDEC:) 22 By so much was Jesus made a surety of a better testament. 23 And they truly were many priests, because they were not suffered to continue by reason of death: 24 But this *man*, because he continueth ever, hath an unchangeable priesthood.

The author argues that **it is yet far more evident** that there is another priest **after the similitude of Melchisedec.** Again, we know this from Psalm 110:4, **for** God **testifieth, Thou art a priest for ever after the order of Melchisedec.** Unlike the Levites who become priests **after the law of a carnal commandment,** in other words, a rule based on physical descent or genealogy, the new priest is established **after the power of an endless** (or eternal) **life.** The contrast is between those who become temporary priests of the Mosaic Law to replace those before them who died and the One who becomes a permanent priest by God's direct appointment. And since the priesthood and the administered law go together as a unit, the designation of a new priesthood **is verily a disannulling of the commandment going before,** that is, the **disannulling of the** Mosaic Law. The reason for the **disannulling of the** Mosaic Law is **the weakness and unprofitableness thereof.** We must remember that the Law is the Word of God, good and holy and pure, and the **weakness** at issue here does not at all take an improper dig at the Law. Rather, the Law of Moses was weak because of the flesh of people, which manifested in their inability to keep it perfectly. The Law was unprofitable because it could not make anyone right before God. As our author explains, **the law made nothing perfect**, but in contrast, **the bringing in of a better hope did, by the which we draw nigh unto God.** What no one could do under the Law, the Son did, offering a **better hope** to those who identify with him by faith, and are consequently able to **draw nigh unto God.**

The author emphasizes the point that the Levitical **priests** became priests by genealogy, not by **an oath from God.** In contrast, Jesus was designated a priest **with an oath by** God **that said unto** Jesus, **The Lord sware and will not repent** (will never change His mind), **Thou art a priest for ever after the order of Melchisedec.** Remember again that a priesthood and a covenant or law administered by the priesthood are a unit, so that through the superior means by which Jesus became a priest, we get a superior covenant. In this way, that is, by an oath from God Himself, **was Jesus made a surety** or guarantee **of a better testament.** And another key reason the covenant associated with the priesthood of Melchisedec is better is that the Levitical priests were mortal and had to be replaced. He explains that **they truly were many priests, because they were not suffered to continue by reason of death.** In contrast, **this** Jesus, **because he continueth** or lives **ever** (forever) and has been designated in Psalm 110:4 to be a priest **for ever, hath an unchangeable** or permanent **priesthood.**

25 Wherefore he is able also to save them to the uttermost that come unto God by him, seeing he ever liveth to make intercession for them. 26 For such an high priest became us, *who is* holy, harmless, undefiled, separate from sinners, and made higher than the heavens; 27 Who needeth not daily, as those high priests, to offer up sacrifice, first for his own sins, and then for the people's: for this he did once, when he offered up himself. 28 For the law maketh men high priests which have infirmity; but the word of the oath, which was since the law, *maketh* the Son, who is consecrated for evermore.

The author now draws a most practical conclusion from his technical argument, namely that the priest that serves forever **is able also to save them to the uttermost that come unto God by him, seeing he ever liveth to make intercession for them.** In this book with its heavy focus on the world to come and our future deliverance into the kingdom, we are to understand that Jesus does not just save (justify), he completely saves in the sense of the entire salvation of believers, past (justification), present (sanctification) and future (glorification). He is ever available **to make intercession for them** that **come unto God by** faith in **him.** The concept of **intercession** means to interpose or plead on behalf of another person, and in context, means to pray to God the Father on behalf of us. Elsewhere in the New Testament, we are taught that part of Jesus' high priestly role is to intercede on our behalf as he is seated at the right hand of the Father. (see Romans 8:34) Also, the Holy Spirit intercedes for us when we do not know quite how to pray. (Romans 8:26) And, we should note, as believers and especially in our local church context, we need to intercede in prayer for others. (1 Timothy 2:1)

Jesus is perfectly matched to our needs in a **high priest** in that he is **holy, harmless** (or innocent)**, undefiled, separate from sinners, and made higher than** or exalted above **the heavens.** The author argued earlier in the book that we have a great high priest because in his incarnation he learned what it is to be human and can thus sympathize with our trials and struggles. Here, he focuses on Jesus' deity, expressing that we have a superior priest that is fully human and fully God in a superior exalted position. Moreover, unlike **those high priests** under the Law of Moses who had to **offer up** an animal **sacrifice, first for** their **own sins, and then for the people's,** our High Priest Jesus only offered a sacrifice **once, when he offered up himself.** The contrast is between sinful priests that must offer sacrifices (note the plural) for their own sins and the sins of those they serve and Jesus who made one sacrifice. **For the law** of Moses **maketh men high priests which have infirmity,** in other words, that are sinners. **But the word of the oath** that we find in Psalm 110:4, which came centuries **since** or after **the law** of Moses, **maketh the Son** a priest, **who is consecrated** (completed or perfected in his role as the High Priest; see the use of this term in 2:10, 5:9, 7:19, 9:9, 10:1, 10:14, 11:40, 12:23) **for evermore.**

Bringing this all together to its practical implication, the author established that Jesus is a priest after the order of Melchisedec, which priesthood is superior to the priesthood associated with the Mosaic Law because the priesthood of Melchisedec is permanent and is founded on a better sacrifice that needed to only be made once. Moreover, the Mosaic Law could never make anyone right with God, but the law associated with the priestly order of Melchisedec is built on a better hope and the priest lives and serves in his priestly role forever. The author will in chapter 8 emphasize that there is a superior New Covenant associated with this priesthood and in chapter 9 he will speak of the superior sacrifice and superior tabernacle associated with this priesthood. But getting down to the brass tacks, only a fool would flirt with going back to the old order, which is done away since the change of priesthood necessarily means a change of covenant. To believers today, a natural application would be a warning against legalism and mindless ritual as a means of sanctification. The old covenant built on works was weak and unprofitable and so was replaced. So why do many Christians view their faith as simply a new list of rules to keep that will make them spiritual, rather than a way to draw near to God in Christ?

## Closing

I love antiques but I recognize that older is not always better. Technology becomes obsolete and gets replaced by something better. I have an old phonograph that you have to wind up by hand and it plays one song before you need to wind it up again and turn the record over, a far cry from our modern mp3 players in sound quality and convenience. I have a 1963 automobile that has no a/c, no fuel injection, no power steering, and no power brakes, a far cry from the comforts of my newer truck.

In my office I have a device called a stereoscope that in the early 1900's, at a time when few people were able to do any extensive travel, allowed folks to see three dimensional photos from around the world, but a far cry our modern media and the ease with which so many of us can travel to the places people used to only see in books (and on stereoscopes or glass slides). While I am all for nostalgia and like my antiques, I am not ready to trade in the new for the old. In Hebrews, God systematically compares the ministry and priesthood associated with the New Covenant to the old, and no analogy can really capture the stark differences because so much of the comparison is the heavenly to the earthly. The point God makes is this: Why would you dream of trading the new for the old? And to a modern audience, I would ask, why would you trade the grace of God in His Son for any alternative?

## Application Points

- **MAIN PRINCIPLE:** The priesthood of Melchisedec is superior to the Levitical priesthood because it alone is designed to make people perfect.

- The priesthood of Melchisedec is superior to the Levitical priesthood because the High Priest Jesus was appointed by an oath from God Himself and now serves in his priestly role forever.

## Discussion Questions

1. What does Hebrews 7 teach about tithing in a church context?

2. Where does the Bible first mention Melchisedec and what does the Old Testament teach us about him?

3. Based on verse 12, at what point was the Mosaic Covenant terminated?

4. In what way was the Mosaic Covenant weak and unprofitable?

5. Is the Old Testament Law inferior to the New Testament? Stated another way, does it have the same authority as the New Testament? Should Christians study the Old Testament?

6. What is the significance to the argument of Hebrews that Jesus can "save them to the uttermost that come unto God by him"? (verse 25)

# Chapter 9

# A New Covenant

From 1912 to 1929, Thomas Edison marketed a phonograph that played records thicker than 78's with a reproducer that used a diamond, rather than a steel needle, to contact the records and produce sound, which were often referred to as Diamond Discs. Only Edison produced records for these players, and the record sleeves read: "COMPARISON WITH THE LIVING ARTIST REVEALS NO DIFFERENCE". In publicity campaigns, a live performer would be presented alongside their recorded song to bolster the claimed quality of the recording, which was in fact far superior to the less expensive 78s of that time. But the reality was that neither the Edison discs nor any recording fully captures the live sound. Despite Edison's marketing, his fine records were at best a sketch or shadow of the live performer. And as we shall see, as beautiful and tremendous as the Temple in Jerusalem was, in all its splendor, it was but a sketch or shadow of the genuine article, the heavenly Temple, which is associated with a superior priesthood and the ministration of a superior covenant. To his Jewish Christian audience flirting with a return to Judaism, the author points out that it was always God's plan to inaugurate a New Covenant based on a one-time sacrifice of the Son's blood in the heavenly temple. He calls on them to quit looking back at the mere shadow of the heavenly, which is no good to them now, and get on board with what God is doing with the ministry of the New Covenant.

## Scripture and Comments

In chapter 7, the author of Hebrews argued from the recorded meeting of Abraham and Melchisedec in Genesis 14 and from Psalm 110 that the priesthood of Melchisedec is superior to the priesthood of Aaron (or the Levitical priesthood). He now argues from the Old Testament that there is not only another priesthood, but associated with the Melchisedecan priesthood is a heavenly temple and a New Covenant. The author wants his Jewish Christian audience to understand that this is not some new doctrine, but that it was plainly foretold in the Old Testament that God would implement the New Covenant and it would accomplish what the Mosaic Covenant could not.

> Hebrews 8:1 Now of the things which we have spoken *this is* the sum: We have such an high priest, who is set on the right hand of the throne of the Majesty in the heavens; 2 A minister of the sanctuary, and of the true tabernacle, which the Lord pitched, and not man. 3 For every high priest is ordained to offer gifts and sacrifices: wherefore *it is* of necessity that

this man have somewhat also to offer. 4 For if he were on earth, he should not be a priest, seeing that there are priests that offer gifts according to the law: 5 Who serve unto the example and shadow of heavenly things, as Moses was admonished of God when he was about to make the tabernacle: for, SEE, saith he, *THAT* THOU MAKE ALL THINGS ACCORDING TO THE PATTERN SHEWED TO THEE IN THE MOUNT.

Having set forth the very technical arguments concerning the priesthood of Melchisedec in chapter 7, the author gives us **the sum** or the main point, namely that **we have such an high priest, who is set on the right hand of the throne of the Majesty in the heavens; a minister of the sanctuary, and of the true tabernacle, which the Lord pitched, and not man.** This hearkens back to the profound statement made of Jesus in the prologue, that "when he had by himself purged our sins, sat down on the right had of the Majesty on high." (Hebrews 1:3) This Jesus is not only the High Priest, but also the Son to whom the Father said, "Sit on my right hand, until I make thine enemies thy footstool." (Hebrews 1:13) This point is so important that he will make it again in 10:12 and 12:2. Jesus completed the work of providing a once for all sacrifice for sins, a point to be elaborated on in chapter 9, and then **set on the right hand** of the Father in fulfillment of Psalm 110:1, waiting for the Father to give him his inheritance, which points to the coming kingdom. The author demonstrated in chapter 7 that Jesus belongs to the superior priesthood, and now introduces us to the fact that Jesus' priestly duties are performed in a superior sanctuary in heaven. Thus, he says that Jesus is **a minister of the sanctuary, and of the true tabernacle.** Of course, the Levitical priests ministered in the tabernacle and later the Temple, both constructed by men on the earth. In contrast, the **true tabernacle** where Jesus is a **minister** was **pitched** or built by **the Lord** himself, **and not man.** More will be said about this greater heavenly tabernacle in chapter 9.

The priestly function within the greater tabernacle is also superior. The role of **every high priest** is to **offer gifts and sacrifices,** and accordingly, Jesus **may have somewhat also to offer.** But there is a tremendous difference between what the earthly High Priest offers and what Jesus offered in the heavenly tabernacle. Indeed, **if** Jesus **were on earth, he should not be a priest** at all because there **are** already **priests** under **the law** tasked with offering **gifts.** The author is drawing a sharp distinction between the earthly and the heavenly. The earthly Levitical priests **serve unto the example and shadow** (sketch, prototype, outline) **of heavenly things.** In other words, what is done by the High Priest and the Levitical priests within the earthly tabernacle provides a picture of the heavenly. Indeed, with regard to the construction of **the tabernacle,** the author reminds us of what we read in Exodus 25:40: "And look that thou make them after their pattern, which was shewed thee in the mount." When we read the specifications for the tabernacle, the precision provided in the Scripture is because the earthly is the picture of the heavenly, and therefore must be constructed with great care and exacting detail. Naturally, the real thing (the heavenly tabernacle) is superior to that which is only a sketch of it, and Jesus ministers in the heavenly tabernacle.

<u>6</u> But now hath he obtained a more excellent ministry, by how much also he is the mediator of a better covenant, which was established upon better promises. <u>7</u> For if that first *covenant* had been faultless, then should no place have been sought for the second. <u>8</u> For finding fault with them, he saith, BEHOLD, THE DAYS COME, SAITH THE LORD, WHEN I WILL MAKE A NEW COVENANT WITH THE HOUSE OF ISRAEL AND WITH THE HOUSE OF JUDAH: <u>9</u> NOT ACCORDING TO THE COVENANT THAT I MADE WITH THEIR FATHERS IN THE DAY WHEN I TOOK THEM BY THE HAND TO LEAD THEM OUT OF THE LAND OF EGYPT; BECAUSE THEY CONTINUED NOT IN MY COVENANT, AND I REGARDED THEM NOT, SAITH THE LORD. <u>10</u> FOR THIS *IS* THE COVENANT THAT I WILL MAKE WITH THE HOUSE OF ISRAEL AFTER THOSE DAYS, SAITH THE LORD; I WILL PUT MY LAWS INTO THEIR MIND, AND WRITE THEM IN THEIR HEARTS: AND I WILL BE TO THEM A GOD, AND THEY SHALL BE TO ME A PEOPLE: <u>11</u> AND THEY SHALL NOT TEACH EVERY MAN HIS NEIGHBOUR, AND EVERY MAN HIS BROTHER, SAYING, KNOW THE LORD: FOR ALL SHALL KNOW ME, FROM THE LEAST TO THE GREATEST. <u>12</u> FOR I WILL BE MERCIFUL TO THEIR UNRIGHTEOUSNESS, AND THEIR SINS AND THEIR INIQUITIES WILL I REMEMBER NO MORE. <u>13</u> In that he

saith, A new *covenant*, he hath made the first old. Now that which decayeth and waxeth old *is* ready to vanish away.

Jesus is a priest of a superior order in a better (heavenly not earthly) sanctuary than the Levitical priests, and hence the author fittingly says that Jesus **hath...obtained a more excellent ministry.** The author suggested in chapter 7 the issue he now takes up, namely that a priesthood and a covenant are a unit so that a change of one necessitates a change of the other: "For the priesthood being changed, there is made of necessity a change also of the law." (Hebrews 7:12) Returning to this issue, he says that Jesus **is the mediator of a better covenant** than the Mosaic Covenant, **which was established on better promises.** As he explained in chapter 7, the **better covenant** is better because "the law made nothing perfect" and the new covenant brings in a "better hope...by the which we draw nigh unto God" (7:19). The New Covenant is also better because it is associated with a better (permanent) high priest and better (one time) sacrifice. He also said the old covenant (the Law) is terminated because of its inability to make people right before God: "there is verily a disannulling of the commandment going before for the weakness and unprofitableness thereof." (Hebrews 7:18)

Returning to this critical point, he writes that **if that first covenant had been faultless, then should no place have been sought for the second.** We need to keep in mind that the author is not saying the Law is bad or anything less than the holy Word of God, for as Paul wrote, "Wherefore the law is holy, and the commandment holy, and just, and good." (Romans 7:12) The problem is that people are sinners by nature and so a covenant of rules just shows how sinful they are rather than leading them to holiness. (Romans 7:22-23) Before moving to verse 8, we have to remember that the author cannot make such grand claims about the Law being set aside without strict proof—chapter and verse—that his audience will accept. Therefore, he continues here, **for finding fault with them,** that is, with God's people because they could not consistently keep the Law, then he quotes "chapter and verse" from Jeremiah 31, **for finding fault with them, he saith, Behold, the days come, saith the Lord, when I will make a new covenant with the house of Israel and with the house of Judah.** At this point it is helpful to jump down to 8:13, **in that he saith, A new covenant, he hath made the first old.**

We need to be careful here not to write into the text. Many expositors teach that the New Covenant is fulfilled in the church or that we are living during a time of the fulfillment of the New Covenant now. This is not the place for a full treatment of this issue, but we need to carefully observe what the author says here about the New Covenant, and what he does not say. The larger argument he is making is for the superiority of Jesus to the old system, which includes the priesthood, the tabernacle, the sacrifices, the ministry and the covenant. In making this argument, he reminds his Jewish audience that in the Old Testament God said there would be another covenant. The Mosaic Covenant was always intended to be temporary, and never intended to make people right before God. The Mosaic Covenant was mediated between God and Israel through His servant Moses. That Covenant (or contract) came to an end when one party to it died, namely when Jesus died on the cross. (Colossians 2:14) But at the same time, Jesus' death inaugurated the New Covenant, a point the author will build on later. The contract is signed, as it were, but that does not mean that God will perform all of it at this time.

Here in chapter 8, his point is simply to argue that God said He would enter a New Covenant with Israel to replace the old. The author does not argue that the New Covenant is being fulfilled by the Church, or that it is being fulfilled presently. Instead, he quotes Jeremiah 31 to make his point that God foretold in the Old Testament that there would in the future be a New Covenant, and then argues, **in that** God **saith, A new covenant,** God **hath made the first** (i.e., the Mosaic Covenant) **old,** a term that means to be declared obsolete. Further, he speaks of **now,** at this point in time, **that which decayeth and waxeth old**—again, the Mosaic Covenant—**is ready to vanish away.** This point will be addressed further in chapter 10, but the reality is that the Mosaic Covenant was already disannulled (7:18) yet the Temple and Jewish religious practice continued. Shortly, the Roman General Titus will bring his troops into Israel, and to the Holy City, to quell the rebellion. And history tells the sad story of the destruction of Jerusalem and the Temple in A.D. 70, and it is this coming destruction that is the sense in which the old order is **ready to vanish away** completely.

Again, the author's sole point here in chapter 8 regarding the New Covenant was to establish that God said in the Old Testament that He would establish a New Covenant to replace the Mosaic Covenant. And this helps complete his argument that Jesus is a High Priest after the order of Melchisedec since the appointment of Jesus as High Priest in Psalm 110 *after* the establishment of the Levitical priesthood made it necessary that there would be another covenant. Unfortunately, there is sometimes confusion based on Hebrews 8 about the fulfillment of the New Covenant by the church and its present administration solely because the New Covenant passage from Jeremiah 31 is quoted. For this reason, a short excursus is beneficial here.

## Excursus on the New Covenant

We will not make a detailed exegesis of all the "New Covenant" passages, but it will be worthwhile to simply read the plain language from the Old Testament and draw some obvious conclusions. Keep in mind that the New Covenant is an expansion on the promised blessings to Abraham in what expositors refer to as the Abrahamic Covenant (see Genesis 12, 15, 17, 22).

> Jeremiah 31:31 Behold, the days come, saith the LORD, that I will make a new covenant with the house of Israel, and with the house of Judah: 32 Not according to the covenant that I made with their fathers in the day *that* I took them by the hand to bring them out of the land of Egypt; which my covenant they brake, although I was an husband unto them, saith the LORD: 33 But this *shall be* the covenant that I will make with the house of Israel; After those days, saith the LORD, I will put my law in their inward parts, and write it in their hearts; and will be their God, and they

shall be my people. 34 And they shall teach
no more every man his neighbour, and
every man his brother, saying, Know the
LORD: for they shall all know me, from
the least of them unto the greatest of
them, saith the LORD: for I will forgive
their iniquity, and I will remember their
sin no more.

This, of course, is the language quoted by the author of
Hebrews to prove the old was always temporary and God
promised something new and better. Importantly, note
that the New Covenant is to be made with "the house of
Israel, and with the house of Judah," in other words, with
the re-united nation and not with the church the Lord is
building at the present time. It is not part of the Mosaic
Covenant (Jeremiah 31:32) but entails promises "after
those days," pointing to the future after the nation is
reconstituted as a united nation. And look at what else
God promised as part of the New Covenant: to put the
Law on their hearts, that every Jewish person would
"know me," and that He will forgive their sin. These
things have not been fulfilled as most Jewish persons do
not accept Jesus as the Christ, the Son of God, and we do
a disservice to the text to "spiritualize" (apply arbitrary
meanings to the words to suit our theology) these words
rather than let their plain meaning speak.

Jeremiah 32:37 Behold, I will gather them
out of all countries, whither I have driven
them in mine anger, and in my fury, and in
great wrath; and I will bring them again
unto this place, and I will cause them to
dwell safely: 38 And they shall be my

people, and I will be their God: 39 And I will give them one heart, and one way, that they may fear me for ever, for the good of them, and of their children after them: 40 And I will make an everlasting covenant with them, that I will not turn away from them, to do them good; but I will put my fear in their hearts, that they shall not depart from me.

This passage adds an important point, that the New Covenant will not be fulfilled until national Israel is regathered to her land. While there is a narrow strip of land today called Israel that may be the seed of what God will do later, it is not all the land promised to Abraham (see Genesis 15:18) and certainly we do not see all Jewish people regathered to the land. Nor have we seen the sort of national revival in Israel this passage envisions, but instead, Israel is a completely secular nation.

Jeremiah 50:4 In those days, and in that time, saith the LORD, the children of Israel shall come, they and the children of Judah together, going and weeping: they shall go, and seek the LORD their God. 5 They shall ask the way to Zion with their faces thitherward, *saying*, Come, and let us join ourselves to the LORD in a perpetual covenant *that* shall not be forgotten.

Isaiah 55:3 Incline your ear, and come unto me: hear, and your soul shall live; and I will make an everlasting covenant with you, *even* the sure mercies of David.

> Isaiah 61:8 For I the LORD love judgment, I hate robbery for burnt offering; and I will direct their work in truth, and I will make an everlasting covenant with them. 9 And their seed shall be known among the Gentiles, and their offspring among the people: all that see them shall acknowledge them, that they *are* the seed *which* the LORD hath blessed.

Again, the Jeremiah passage speaks of a national revival of the Jewish people that has not happened. Isaiah makes clear that the New Covenant builds on the Abrahamic seed promises and looks to a time when the Gentiles acknowledge God's blessing of Israel, which is the opposite of what we see today.

> Ezekiel 37:21 And say unto them, Thus saith the Lord GOD; Behold, I will take the children of Israel from among the heathen, whither they be gone, and will gather them on every side, and bring them into their own land: 22 And I will make them one nation in the land upon the mountains of Israel; and one king shall be king to them all: and they shall be no more two nations, neither shall they be divided into two kingdoms any more at all: 23 Neither shall they defile themselves any more with their idols, nor with their detestable things, nor with any of their transgressions: but I will save them out of all their dwellingplaces, wherein they have sinned, and will cleanse them: so shall they

be my people, and I will be their God. 24 And David my servant *shall be* king over them; and they all shall have one shepherd: they shall also walk in my judgments, and observe my statutes, and do them. 25 And they shall dwell in the land that I have given unto Jacob my servant, wherein your fathers have dwelt; and they shall dwell therein, *even* they, and their children, and their children's children for ever: and my servant David *shall be* their prince for ever. 26 Moreover I will make a covenant of peace with them; it shall be an everlasting covenant with them: and I will place them, and multiply them, and will set my sanctuary in the midst of them for evermore. 27 My tabernacle also shall be with them: yea, I will be their God, and they shall be my people. 28 And the heathen shall know that I the LORD do sanctify Israel, when my sanctuary shall be in the midst of them for evermore.

The Ezekiel passage also prophecies a regathering of the Jewish people to the Promised Land, but adds more detail. When this occurs, God will place one king to rule over them, idolatry and rebellious deeds will be eliminated, and they will be purified and again be God's people. This envisions a future where Israel, that presently characteristically rejects Jesus Christ, will embrace him in faith. Indeed, Ezekiel prophecies that "David" will be their king, which is likely a reference to the Davidic king Jesus Christ, in fulfillment of 2 Samuel 7. Note further that at that time God will dwell with the Jewish people, his sanctuary or temple will be among them, and the Gentile nations will know that God sanctifies Israel. Once again, none of this has yet occurred, and if we let the text speak for itself, these things await future fulfillment when Christ returns. Only by allegorizing (applying our arbitrary presuppositions to) the text can we make these things find fulfillment in the first century or today. And nothing in the Hebrews text or anywhere else in the New Testament suggests such a thing.

A covenant is analogous to a contract. Contracts often provide for future performance, so that the parties may sign the contract today and provide for services or other promises to be performed at some future date. The New Covenant was inaugurated by Jesus' blood, which he offered in the heavenly Temple (Hebrews 9; see also Matthew 26:28; Mark 14:24; Luke 22:20). This was analogous to God signing the contract, but that does not mean that all the promises are now, or even that any of the promises are now. The promises are to Israel (not the church) and the promises, as seen above, have not occurred yet. Nothing in the New Testament says those promises are being fulfilled now, or that they are to the church instead of Israel. Rather, in Romans 11:26-27, Paul expressly teaches that the New Covenant blessings will be provided to Israel (not the church) when "the Deliverer" Jesus returns: "And so all Israel shall be saved: as it is written, There shall come out of Sion the Deliverer, and shall turn away ungodliness from Jacob: For this *is* my covenant unto them, when I shall take away their sins." The New Covenant is made with Israel, but the blood of that covenant made the historical parenthesis we live in possible (sometimes called the Church Age) because all people of all times are redeemed by that same blood. Thus, when we celebrate the Lord's Supper, we remember the "blood of the new testament, which is shed for man [i.e., Jew and Gentile] for the remission of sins," but this does not mean the New Covenant is being fulfilled by us, and we do so with a looking forward to the new age to come when all the promises will be fulfilled to Israel, a time of blessings for Christians as well as Hebrews repeatedly points out. In this way, the promised blessings to the nations in the Abrahamic Covenant are brought to pass by the New Covenant.

When Israel rejected the Kingdom Jesus offered, he turned to building his church, and as Paul teaches in Romans 9, Israel's disobedience in killing Messiah made salvation available to all peoples, but there will be a future time when Israel is grafted back in to the vine (Romans 10-11) that will coincide with the second advent. The book of Revelation pictures a revival in Israel during the tribulation immediately before Christ returns. Relating this to what we have already seen in Hebrews, Jesus presently is the High Priest at the right hand of the Majesty on high waiting for the Father to make his enemies his footstool, which finds fulfillment during the tribulation and with Jesus' return (see especially Revelation 19). Jesus will return to take what is his and institute his global kingdom, and at that time the promises of the already inaugurated New Covenant will be fulfilled as Jesus administers the New Covenant as the High Priest after the order of Melchisedec. Revelation 5:10 speaks of Christians being "made...unto our God kings and priests." As Jesus' partners or fellows (Gr. *metachoi*), we will serve as ministers or servants of the New Covenant with him. (2 Corinthians 3:6)

Just know that reasonable minds can disagree on the fine points and putting aside the view that the church is the fulfillment of the New Covenant, some premillennial dispensationalists would say there is another covenant in place now with the church, many say the church is the recipient of the "spiritual blessings" of the New Covenant, and others (my view) would argue that believers today are under the Lord Jesus' program of building his church and not a covenant. The better answer, in my view, seems to be that the nations will be blessed in the Kingdom when the New Covenant promises to Israel are fulfilled, thus bringing a complete fulfillment of the ancient promises to Abraham.

## Closing

Older is not always better, and newer is not always better. Within churches today, there is always a new fad, new movement, new book or new model for growth (e.g., purpose driven, simple, house church, etc.), and implicit in each is the idea that everything before, even what was new and hot 5 years ago, was off track. Many a young pastor today presumes most things that were done in churches not too long ago need to be discarded simply because those things are not new. At the same time, far too many churches are dying on the vine as the pastor and congregation grow old together, never changing in any way and never reaching the next generation so that the church would continue. These issues produce all kinds of conflict and everyone has an opinion. The Bible plainly teaches that we need to see what God is doing and go with His plan. Such was the case with the first century Jewish Christians to whom Hebrews is addressed. They faced the choice of the old and the new, but only one was what God was in. Yet we can imagine the allure of the old, sewn into their very culture, and how easy it may have seemed to go back. The author of Hebrews shows them that the Melchisedecan priesthood of Jesus and the New Covenant was always the plan, and now was the time so get on board with what God is doing no matter the cost.

## Application Points

- **MAIN PRINCIPLE:** Jesus is the High Priest of the New Covenant, which was foretold in the Old Testament, by which God will forgive Israel's sins and place His Law on their hearts.

- The Old Covenant or Mosaic Covenant ended when the New Covenant was inaugurated.

## Discussion Questions

1. According to Hebrews 8, who are the parties to the New Covenant?

2. What are the blessings God promises in the New Covenant and which of them (if any) have already been completely fulfilled?

3. What was the fault with the Mosaic Covenant?

# Chapter 10

# A Better Tabernacle and Sacrifice

Certain of the Psalms are called a "song of degrees" or "song of ascents" because the faithful worshippers sang these songs as they walked (ascending) up to Jerusalem. With great joy they would sing: "I will lift up mine eyes unto the hills, from whence cometh my help. My help cometh from the Lord, which made heaven and earth." (Psalm 121:1-2) They looked forward with great anticipation to arriving at the Holy City, and especially to the Temple: "I was glad when they said unto me, Let us go into the house of the LORD. Our feet shall stand within they gates, O Jerusalem...Whither the tribes go up...to give thanks unto the name of the LORD." (Psalm 122:1-4) For they understand that at that place they could experience the presence of God: "Unto thee lift I up mine eyes, O thou that dwellest in the heavens." (Psalm 123:1) And they could praise Him: "Our help is in the name of the LORD, who made heaven and earth." (Psalm 124:8) Yet we realize, these faithful worshipers faced limitations in their worship. Except for the priests, they could not enter the Temple, and except for the High Priest, none could enter the Holy of Holies, and the worship involved a continuity of animal sacrifices year in and year out, so that they left the Temple each time with the conscious realization that their sin remained. In our modern churches, we can easily allow ourselves to take worship lightly, perhaps in part because most of us do not have to walk for days to get to church with an animal in tow for the sacrifice. As we move into Hebrews 9, we need to discover how Jesus removed barriers and forever changed worship for the faithful believers, yet at the same time probe the question so often ignored today about the ancient principles of worship that remain.

## Scripture and Comments

In chapter 7, the author of Hebrews argued from the recorded meeting of Abraham and Melchisedec in Genesis 14 and from Psalm 110 that the priesthood of Melchisedec is superior to the priesthood of Aaron (or the Levitical priesthood). Then in chapter 8 he argued from the Old Testament that there is not only another priesthood, but a heavenly temple and a New Covenant. The author now continues to build on the notions of a better priesthood, better temple, and a New Covenant as he relates the old to the new.

> Hebrews 9:1 Then verily the first *covenant* had also ordinances of divine service, and a worldly sanctuary. 2 For there was a tabernacle made; the first, wherein *was* the candlestick, and the table, and the shewbread; which is called the sanctuary.

> 3 And after the second veil, the tabernacle which is called the Holiest of all; 4 Which had the golden censer, and the ark of the covenant overlaid round about with gold, wherein *was* the golden pot that had manna, and Aaron's rod that budded, and the tables of the covenant; 5 And over it the cherubims of glory shadowing the mercyseat; of which we cannot now speak particularly.

The author will use the basic layout of the Tabernacle to illustrate how under the old order there were so many barriers to God. There are some expositors who would assign a specific meaning to each facet of the Tabernacle (e.g., the color of the veil represents x, the candlestick represents y, etc.), but that certainly is not the author's intent here, for he says of the Tabernacle that **we cannot now speak particularly** or individually. He writes that **verily** or truly under **the first** or old **covenant** there were **ordinances of divine service and a worldly** or earthly **sanctuary**. Within the **first** room (the Holy Place) of the **tabernacle ... was the candlestick, and the table, and the shewbread**. The **candlestick** refers to the Menorah or lampstand, which was made of pure gold, had seven branches and was located in the **first** room or the Holy Place to always provide light there, as it were, leading the way to the Lord in the Holy of Holies. (Exodus 25:31-39, 37:17-24). The **table** was a wooden table overlaid in gold that was required to always have the **showbread** upon it. (Exodus 25:23-30, 37:10-16)

The author continues to "walk through" the Tabernacle, saying that **after** or beyond **the second veil** or curtain is the room called the **Holiest of all** (or the Holy of Holies). In other words, the **second veil** operates as a doorway or barrier between the first room (the Holy Place) and the second room (the Holy of Holies). He refers to the **veil** as the **second veil** because there is also a doorway or barrier, that is, a first veil, at the entry to the Holy Place from the Inner Court. Only the Levitical priests could enter through the first veil, and even then only at appointed times. The Temple would ultimately have the same basic interior layout and at the moment Jesus died on the cross it was the **second veil** that was "rent in twain from the top to the bottom; and the earth did quake...." (Matthew 27:51) In verses 4 and 5, he describes the contents of the **Holiest of all**. First, it **had the golden censer** or altar of incense, about which we read in the Old Testament:

> Exodus 30:6 And thou shalt put it before the vail that *is* by the ark of the testimony, before the mercy seat that *is* over the testimony, where I will meet with thee.

> Exodus 40:5 And thou shalt set the altar of gold for the incense before the ark of the testimony, and put the hanging of the door to the tabernacle.

Note that Moses wrote that the **censer** would be placed "before the vail" so that the **censer** was located in the Holy Place, not the Holy of Holies as one might understand from the language **the Holiest of all; which had the golden censer, and the ark of the covenant.** Rather, as the incense burned, the smoke would flow under the **second veil** into the Holy of Holies. Thus, as Arnold Fruchtenbaum points out in his commentary,

"He is not emphasizing the *place* where it stood but its *liturgical function*." [1]

Also within the **Holiest of all** is **the ark of the covenant overlaid round about with gold.** (Exodus 25:10-18, 26:33). Within the **ark is the golden pot that had manna** (Exodus 16:33-34), **and Aaron's rod that budded** (Numbers 17:8-11), **and the tables of the covenant** or ten commandments (Exodus 25:16-21, 40:20). On the top of the **ark** were statues of **the cherubims** (angelic beings) **of glory shadowing** or hanging over **the mercyseat** (the flat top of the ark, which was in basic form a rectangular wooden box overlaid with gold), guarding the presence of God, as it were, hearkening back to the cherubim God placed at the east of the garden of Eden after Adam and Eve were expelled from God's presence. (Genesis 3:24) And at this point, the author points out that his purpose in describing the Tabernacle is not to dwell on any individual aspect, but to focus on the bigger picture to make a point, which we will see below.

> <u>6</u> Now when these things were thus ordained, the priests went always into the first tabernacle, accomplishing the service *of God.* <u>7</u> But into the second *went* the high priest alone once every year, not without blood, which he offered for himself, and *for* the errors of the people: <u>8</u> The Holy Ghost this signifying, that the way into the holiest of all was not yet made manifest, while as the first tabernacle was yet standing: <u>9</u> Which *was* a figure for the

---

[1] Arnold G. Fruchtenbaum, *Ariel's Bible Commentary, The Messianic Jewish Epistles* (Tustin: Ariel Ministries 2005), 114.

> time then present, in which were offered both gifts and sacrifices, that could not make him that did the service perfect, as pertaining to the conscience; 10 *Which stood* only in meats and drinks, and divers washings, and carnal ordinances, imposed *on them* until the time of reformation. 11 But Christ being come an high priest of good things to come, by a greater and more perfect tabernacle, not made with hands, that is to say, not of this building; 12 Neither by the blood of goats and calves, but by his own blood he entered in once into the holy place, having obtained eternal redemption *for us.*

The writer now focuses on the priestly ministry within the Tabernacle. **Into the first tabernacle**, meaning the first room or the Holy Place, **the priests went always...accomplishing the service of God.** In contrast, **into the second** room, i.e., the Holy of Holies, **the high priest** went **alone once every year.** Again, there is a focus on barriers; only **priests** could enter the Holy Place but only the **high priest** could enter the Holy of Holies, and even then only **once every year.** And on that one time a year when the **high priest** could enter, he had to take **blood, which he offered for himself, and for the errors** or sins **of the people.** We see this procedure outlined in Leviticus 16, including that the high priest (Aaron at that time) had to offer a sacrifice for himself, as a sinful man, and a separate sacrifice for the people, and sprinkle the blood at the mercy seat. The **Holy Ghost** or Holy Spirit was **signifying** through this elaborate procedure in Leviticus 16 **that the way into the holiest of all** (or Holy of Holies) **was not yet made manifest** or revealed by God, **while as the first tabernacle was yet standing.**

Obviously, Leviticus 16 allowed a procedure for the High Priest to enter once a year, but as long as the **first tabernacle was yet standing**, and by implication the old covenant was in force, access to God was limited to the High Priest. Access by other worshipers **was not yet made manifest** or known. And all of this was **a figure** or **type for the time then present, in which were offered both gifts and sacrifices, that could not make him that did the service perfect, as pertaining to the conscience.** The old system and the tabernacle, in so limiting access to God, stood as an illustration to God's people insofar as even the High Priest offering the sacrifice did not have his sins removed and was not made **perfect** inwardly or **pertaining to the conscience.** After making the prescribed sacrifices that enabled the limited access to God, the priest completed his service, yet retaining a guilty **conscience** of his sin. The old system was not designed to purge the **conscience,** but stood as **a figure** or type or illustration for the nation Israel for what the Messiah would accomplish by his sacrifice of himself. This is not to suggest that they should necessarily have understood this at the time, but rather, when Messiah came and accomplished the task, they should be able to see the connection. What they should have seen at the time is that sin requires the shedding of blood, but the benefits of the shedding of animal blood obviously does not remove sin since it must be repeated.

That the old system could not purge the **conscience** is not surprising because it **stood only in meats and drinks, and diverse washings, and carnal** or fleshly (outward) ordinances, **imposed on them until the time of reformation**, in other words, only temporarily in place until the new order would be implemented (recall, the temporary nature of the old was the subject of chapter 8). The old system consisted of rituals and restrictions that affected outward matters and not the inner man, but the time of **reformation** has come. The word **reformation** (Greek *diorthosis*) is used only here in the New Testament and has the idea of reshaping something or restoration. With the inauguration of the New Covenant, the age of the **reformation** is here, even though the promises to Israel await future fulfillment. Thus he writes that Jesus **Christ being come an high priest of good things to come...by his own blood he entered in once into the holy place, having obtained eternal redemption for us.** As the author has often pointed out, Jesus is our **high priest** after the order of Melchisedec. He did not enter the earthly tabernacle (and particularly the Holy of Holies) with its earthly rituals on the one day a year that a Levitical high priest was permitted to enter (namely the Day of Atonement), but instead entered the **greater and more perfect** heavenly **tabernacle, not made with hands** of men but by the hand of God himself, **not** the earthly **building**. Indeed, Jesus entered the heavenly **holy place** just **once** to provide **his own blood** and not **the blood of goats and calves** so as to obtain for believers not a mere temporary outward cleansing to be repeated annually but **eternal redemption**, in one moment forever buying us away from sin and death.

Notice that Jesus is the **high priest of good things to come** even though his sacrifice and purchase of our **eternal redemption** was a past one-time occurrence. Like so much of the book, there is a future orientation in this statement that follows up on the notion of the New Covenant being a time of **reformation**. Jesus' sacrifice for us was a tremendous benefit of his being High Priest in that he purged our conscience of sin, but there is much more **to come**. As we get to verse 28 the author returns to the "more," saying that as "Christ was once offered to bear the sins of many; and unto them that look for him shall he appear the second time without sin unto salvation." The **good things to come** looks forward to the High Priest's return to provide the full orb of salvation to the "heirs of salvation" (1:14) who have received the **eternal redemption** and to perform the New Covenant promises to redeemed Israel. This points to the kingdom blessings of the future.

> 9:13 For if the blood of bulls and of goats, and the ashes of an heifer sprinkling the unclean, sanctifieth to the purifying of the flesh: 14 How much more shall the blood of Christ, who through the eternal Spirit offered himself without spot to God, purge your conscience from dead works to serve the living God? 15 And for this cause he is the mediator of the new testament, that by means of death, for the redemption of the transgressions *that were* under the first testament, they which are called might receive the promise of eternal inheritance. 16 For where a testament *is*, there must also of necessity be the death of the testator. 17 For a testament *is* of force after men are dead: otherwise it is of no strength at all while the testator liveth.

The author next points out the superiority of Jesus' blood to that of animals by making a comparison. He begins the comparison by focusing on the animals involved in the Day of Atonement feast: **For if the blood of bulls and of goats, and the ashes of an heifer sprinkling the unclean, sanctifieth to the purifying of the flesh.** He already pointed out that these sacrifices do not purge the conscience, and here states that their efficacy is merely to purify **the flesh**, in other words, to provide ritual purity (he noted earlier the fleshly limitations of the rituals). His point is that, though limited, if mere animal blood had such benefits, how much more so the Son's blood: **How much more shall the blood of Christ, who through the eternal Spirit offered himself without spot to God, purge your conscience.** The blood of animals that is part of the cursed universe is offered by mere men as part of fleshly rituals in the earthly tabernacle, but it does provide ritual purity. The Christ's sinless blood was offered in the heavenly tabernacle **through the eternal Spirit** and the much greater (more valuable) sacrifice provides the much greater result of inward cleansing of **your conscience from dead works to serve the living God.**

This last point is important—the redemption has an immediate purpose of bringing to an end **dead works,** which contextually points to the earthly rituals that only purified the flesh but were **dead** or useless in that they could never purge the conscience of sin. Now, with our conscience purged, we are able to set aside continuing the earthly rituals and instead engage in serving **the living God.** The verb **serve** is the Greek *latreuo*, which means priestly service or worship. The word was used in verse 9 in reference to priestly service. Paul used the noun form of this verb to make a similar point in Romans 12:1:

"I beseech you therefore, brethren, by the mercies of God, that ye present your bodies a living sacrifice, holy, acceptable unto God, which is your reasonable **service**." Since we no longer need to toil in repetitive ritualistic worship that does not cleanse the conscience, and since there is no need for any further sacrifice (Jesus dealt with that issue once for all), we are freed by our High Priest to provide priestly service to God.

The author, having explained that the new order is better than the old and released those redeemed from any further ritual obligations under the old, addresses the effect of the new on those who lived under the old covenant. Thus he says, **for this cause** or reason Jesus **is the mediator** (a "go between" as between God and humanity) **of the new testament** or covenant, **that by the means of** his death God provided **for the redemption of the transgressions that were under the first** or old **testament** (covenant). His point is that that while the old covenant rituals only cleansed outwardly, Jesus' sacrifice as the mediator under the New Covenant washes away the sins of those old testament believers, that **they which are called might receive the promise of eternal inheritance**. Everything the author has been saying about the limited efficacy of the animal sacrifices and the old covenant rituals naturally raises the question of where that leaves the Old Testament saints like Moses, and this passage answers that by saying that the promises to them were fulfilled in Christ. Because their **transgressions** have been redeemed or paid for by Jesus' sacrifice, they also will enjoy the fulfillment of the **good things to come** referenced earlier, which here is referenced as their **eternal inheritance** in Messiah's kingdom.

The author now, by way of illustration, likens the New Covenant to **a testament**, in the sense of a will (i.e., a last will and testament). This is a natural transition since he just mentioned their **eternal inheritance**, which by its nature points to permanent blessings received after death. The author notes that when you consider the effect of a will, **there must also of necessity be the death of the testator**, that is, the death of the person whose will or last testament is under consideration. Until a person dies, the rights under the will are subject to change. The **testament** or will becomes **of force** only **after men are dead** and at that point its terms are fixed. It is the death of the testator that fixes the rights of his heirs in his estate, thus making the will **of force** or binding legal effect. But until that death occurs (i.e., **while the testator liveth**), the will **is of no** legal **strength at all** since it is subject to change and the beneficiaries have not yet received what has been bequeathed to them. This provides an illustration of the New Covenant, which came **of force** upon the death of Jesus.

18 Whereupon neither the first *testament* was dedicated without blood. 19 For when Moses had spoken every precept to all the people according to the law, he took the blood of calves and of goats, with water, and scarlet wool, and hyssop, and sprinkled both the book, and all the people, :20 Saying, THIS *IS* THE BLOOD OF THE TESTAMENT WHICH GOD HATH ENJOINED UNTO YOU. 21 Moreover he sprinkled with blood both the tabernacle, and all the vessels of the ministry. 22 And almost all things are by the law purged with blood;

and without shedding of blood is no remission.

That the New Covenant required blood seems only natural since even the **first testament** did. **For when Moses had spoken every precept to all the people according to the law, he took the blood of calves and of goats, with water, and scarlet wool, and hyssop, and sprinkled both the book** of the Law, **and all the people.** The background for this passage is in the ratification of the Mosaic Covenant by the people of Israel, through Moses, as recorded in Exodus. After Moses tells the people the commandments in Exodus 20-23, we read a summary statement followed by the office ratification as a blood covenant:

> Exodus 24:3 And Moses came and told the people all the words of the LORD, and all the judgments: and all the people answered with one voice, and said, All the words which the LORD hath said will we do. 4 And Moses wrote all the words of the LORD, and rose up early in the morning, and builded an altar under the hill, and twelve pillars, according to the twelve tribes of Israel. 5 And he sent young men of the children of Israel, which offered burnt offerings, and sacrificed peace offerings of oxen unto the LORD. 6 And Moses took half of the blood, and put *it* in basons; and half of the blood he sprinkled on the altar. 7 And he took the book of the covenant, and read in the audience of the people: and they said, All that the LORD

hath said will we do, and be obedient. 8
And Moses took the blood, and sprinkled
*it* on the people, and said, Behold the
blood of the covenant, which the LORD
hath made with you concerning all these
words.

Prior to the ratification of the Mosaic Covenant, its
terms were not in effect. It was something like an
executory contract that was not yet signed on the dotted
line by the people. But once it was ratified, it was a
blood covenant ratified by animal blood whose terms
could not be changed or discarded so long as either party
to the covenant (namely Israel and God) lived. Thus, in
verse 20, we read Moses' words, **This is the blood of the
testament** or covenant **which God has enjoined unto you.**
By accepting the terms, they (Israel nationally) pledge
their lives. Moses then **sprinkled with blood both the
tabernacle, and all the vessels of the ministry.** This was
done both to cleanse these man-made articles and set
them apart for use in the administration of the Law
under this **testament.** The author draws the conclusion
that **almost all things are by the law purged with blood.**
He says **almost** because some items were only cleansed
with water and others not cleansed, but when it comes to
dealing with sin, there is always the use of blood: **without
shedding of blood is no remission** or forgiveness of sin.

23 *It was* therefore necessary that the
patterns of things in the heavens should be
purified with these; but the heavenly things
themselves with better sacrifices than
these. 24 For Christ is not entered into the
holy places made with hands, *which are* the

figures of the true; but into heaven itself, now to appear in the presence of God for us: 25 Nor yet that he should offer himself often, as the high priest entereth into the holy place every year with blood of others; 26 For then must he often have suffered since the foundation of the world: but now once in the end of the world hath he appeared to put away sin by the sacrifice of himself. 27 And as it is appointed unto men once to die, but after this the judgment: 28 So Christ was once offered to bear the sins of many; and unto them that look for him shall he appear the second time without sin unto salvation.

Since the shedding of blood is necessary for purification from sin, it was **necessary that the patterns of things in heavens** (i.e., the earthly sketch of the heavenly) **should be purified with these** animal sacrifices. By comparison of the lesser to the greater, he concludes that **the heavenly things** for which the earthly were only sketches must **themselves** also be cleansed, but **with better sacrifices** (blood) **than these** animal sacrifices. The better blood was provided by Jesus **Christ,** who had **not entered into the holy places made with hands** (i.e., in the earthly tabernacle). Recall that Jesus was not a Levitical priest and so could provide no priestly service in the earthly tabernacle nor could he even enter the Holy of Holies, but in any event, the earthly **holy places** were only **figures of the true** tabernacle in heaven. Jesus **entered...into heaven itself, now to appear in the presence of God for us.** In contrast to the Levitical high priest entering the Holy of Holies once per year and only in the presence of a manifestation of God at the ark of the covenant, Jesus entered the heavenly Holy of Holies and stood **in the** very **presence of God**. As our High Priest, Jesus once paid it all but he is still able to step before God the Father, as he will do in the future when the Father is ready to place everything under Jesus' feet. (Revelation 5) Note that what Jesus did in the heavenly tabernacle he did **for us** or on our behalf, for he himself was sinless and had no need to make a sacrifice on his own behalf.

The earthly was a sketch—not an exact representation— of the heavenly. In particular, whereas **the** earthly Aaronic **high priest entereth into the holy place every year with blood of others**, Jesus does not **offer himself often** but only once. If it were otherwise **then must** Jesus **often have suffered since the foundation of the world,** but instead, **now once** (key word is **once**) **in the end** or consummation **of the world** or ages **hath he appeared to put away sin by the sacrifice of himself.** What the Levitical high priest did was repeated each year because it did not **put away** sin, but what Jesus did in the heavenly tabernacle was a one-time climactic historical event that did **put away sin** permanently because it was not based on animal sacrifices but **the sacrifice of himself.** The reference to **the end of the world** or ages means that prior history was all working up to this point. All of human history has two pivot points—the first and second advents of Jesus—that all other events move to.

The priestly work of Jesus did not end with this offering of himself in the heavenly tabernacle. The author asserts the truism that **it is appointed unto men once to die, but after this the judgment.** The author is not concerned here with the exceptions (e.g., Enoch, Elijah). As a general proposition, everyone has one candle to burn, and when their life ends, the quality of their life is judged. We have a saying that the proof is in the pudding; God's judgment will lay it all bare. But what of Jesus? When Jesus **Christ** died, he was **once offered** as a sacrifice **to bear the sins of many**, and indeed to **put away sin.** And so we might ask about the judgment? The answer is that God fully vindicated Jesus. History witnessed this in his resurrection, of course, but history future will witness Jesus' vindication again when he returns. Here, as throughout Hebrews, we see references to the future return of Jesus to institute his kingdom. (e.g., Hebrews 10:13: "From henceforth expecting till his enemies be made his footstool.") We know that when Jesus returns, it will mean judgment for his adversaries, but **unto them that look for him shall he appear the second time without sin unto salvation.** When Jesus appeared the first time, he did so to die on a cross **to bear the sins of many**, but when he appears **the second time** his purpose will not be to bear sins but to bring **salvation** to the "heirs of salvation" as referenced in 1:14. The sin payment necessary for our justification is past; this future **salvation** is not justification but all the promised blessings that are ours in Christ and that await future fulfillment during his kingdom. We must throughout this book keep in mind that the author addresses an afflicted audience for whom this earthly life may never be easy, but who were assured that their perseverance would result in a future **salvation** or deliverance at the return of Christ and blessings against which the present tribulation could not compare. The author has repeatedly referred to this future **salvation.** (Hebrews 1:14; 2:3, 10; 5:9) The future **salvation** relates directly to Jesus' kingdom and our participation in that kingdom.

## Closing

Great songs often end with a crescendo. Hebrews 9 unveils what happened in heaven when the Son of God entered the heavenly tabernacle and offered his own blood, not for himself, but for us. When he did this, he inaugurated the New Covenant, perfected the conscience of God's worshipers, and brought down all the barriers to God inherent in the old tabernacle. But the crescendo of the chapter is in the very last verse: "So Christ was once offered to bear the sins of many; and unto them that look for him shall he appear the second time without sin unto salvation." The first century churches were consumed with anticipation of Jesus' return. How easy it is today to give lip service to expecting the Lord's return but not allow the anticipation to be so real and present that it is transformative. When Jesus returns, he will bring salvation, the final deliverance into eternal blessings as we dwell with Jesus as joint-heirs of salvation. It is this truth that should orient our lives and our perspective on the trials of this age, as well as the need to display God's grace in Christ Jesus to those around us with our works and our words as we relate how Jesus removed the barriers and ushered us into the very presence of God.


## Application Points

- **MAIN PRINCIPLE:** The tabernacle presented the ancient Jews a means of enjoying the blessing of God's presence but also presented many barriers (limitations) reminding us of our sin problem, but Jesus dealt finally with sin and death, removing the barriers to God for those who identify with the Son by faith.

- A future salvation—deliverance into the blessings of permanently dwelling with God—awaits Christians when Jesus returns.

## Discussion Questions

1. What is the significance of the curtains and the cherubim in the tabernacle?

2. How was Jesus' priestly service discussed in Hebrews 9 the same as / different than the priestly service of the Levitical High Priest during Yom Kippur?

3. What were the benefits to worshipers of the sacrifices the Levitical High Priest made once a year on Yom Kippur? What were the benefits of Jesus' one sacrifice to Christian worshippers?

4. What principles of Old Testament worship changed based on Jesus' sacrifice of himself? What old principles remain intact (if any)?

5. What is the salvation that believers will obtain when Jesus returns?

6. How would the return of Christ and a future salvation at that time be important to the audience of Hebrews?

# Chapter 11

# Cast Not Away Your Confidence

There is no such thing as Christian living without a Biblical theological foundation, and by the same token, the theology rings hollow if it is not reflected in our lives so that others may see it. Jesus captured this in the Sermon on the Mount:

> Matthew 7:24 Therefore whosoever heareth these sayings of mine, and doeth them, I will liken him unto a wise man, which built his house upon a rock:25 And the rain descended, and the floods came, and the winds blew, and beat upon that house; and it fell not: for it was founded upon a rock.26 And every one that heareth these sayings of mine, and doeth them not, shall be likened unto a foolish man, which built his house upon the sand:27 And the rain descended, and the floods came, and the winds blew, and beat upon that house;

and it fell: and great was the fall of it.

The book of Hebrews is doctrinally heavy, with the author laying a solid theological foundation, often employing very technical arguments, from the beginning of the book through 10:18, at which point he transitions to the "so what" of the matter. All of the arguments about how Jesus is better are intended to be transformative. Hebrews has been rightly called the greatest Christological treatise ever written, but the book is no ivory tower piece. It is an urgent call to action based on having our lives reoriented to God's Son. The author puts the Son, his priestly ministry, his sacrifice, and his return to establish his kingdom on display, reminding us of the benefits and privilege of all that the Son has done for us, all that he does now, and the future blessings that are ours when he returns. And critically, he reminds us that we are not in this alone and urges us to be a faithful part of a local church and to minister into the lives of those around, taking on a responsibility for the spiritual well-being of fellow believers. The warning to his audience is that they lack endurance, and the message to them and to us is, in light of all that we know and understand about the Son, hold fast to your confidence in God and His word.

## Scripture and Comments

The chapter break between chapters 9 and 10 does not signal a change of topic. The author's argument concerning Jesus' better sacrifice continues over from chapter 9, reminding us that the priestly work of Jesus was better than that of Aaron because of a better tabernacle, better priesthood, better covenant, and better sacrifice.

> <u>Hebrews 10:1</u> For the law having a shadow of good things to come, *and* not the very image of the things, can never with those sacrifices which they offered year by year continually make the comers thereunto perfect. 2 For then would they not have ceased to be offered? because that the worshippers once purged should have had no more conscience of sins. 3 But in those *sacrifices there is* a remembrance again *made* of sins every year. 4 For *it is* not possible that the blood of bulls and of goats should take away sins.

The author stated in 7:19 that "the law made nothing perfect" and in 9:9 that the old order "was a figure for the time then present, in which were offered both gifts and sacrifices, that could not make him that did the service perfect, as pertaining to the conscience." The Levitical offerings provided an outward cleansing that allowed people limited access to God, but could not permanently cleanse the inward man. Moreover, the old order served "unto the example and shadow of heavenly things" (8:5), that is, of the ministry in the heavenly tabernacle. Expanding this idea, the author now states that **the law** was **a shadow of good things to come, and not the very image of the things**. The Word **image** is the Greek *eikon*, meaning a statue or profile. As a mere **shadow**, the Law **can never with those** animal **sacrifices which** the Levitical priests **offered year by year continually make the comers thereunto perfect**. It could not make a person right with God, or in the author's terms, cleanse a person's conscience. We know that the animal sacrifices were incapable of making anyone **perfect**, for otherwise those sacrifices **would...have ceased to be offered.** Inherent in the argument is that once you are made **perfect** (purged of sins), it need never be repeated, but since the sacrifices were repeated, then necessarily they were not efficacious to remove sin. The author phrases this point as a rhetorical question, but the point is that **the worshipers once purged** (made perfect in their conscience) **should have had no more conscience of sins** and thus no more need for sacrifices. That the sacrifices were done **year by year continually** proves their ineffectiveness for making anyone **perfect.**

Indeed, **in those** Levitical **sacrifices there is a remembrance again made of sins every year.** In other words, every year the Feast Day of Atonement or Yom Kippur is repeated, and in so doing, people are reminded that their sins remained. The annual sacrifices cover but do not remove the guilt of the sin or consciousness of the sin. Indeed, **it is not possible that the blood of bulls and of goats should take away sins.** This is why John the Baptizer's statement in John 1:29 is so profound, "Behold the Lamb of God, which taketh away the sin of the world." He did not say the Lamb of God that covers sins temporarily, but takes them away, the implication being that he does so permanently. Animal blood cannot do that.

> 5 Wherefore when he cometh into the world, he saith, SACRIFICE AND OFFERING THOU WOULDEST NOT, BUT A BODY HAST THOU PREPARED ME: 6 IN BURNT OFFERINGS AND *SACRIFICES* FOR SIN THOU

HAST HAD NO PLEASURE. 7 THEN SAID I, LO, I COME (IN THE VOLUME OF THE BOOK IT IS WRITTEN OF ME,) TO DO THY WILL, O GOD. 8 Above when he said, SACRIFICE AND OFFERING AND BURNT OFFERINGS AND *OFFERING* FOR SIN THOU WOULDEST NOT, NEITHER HADST PLEASURE *THEREIN*; which are offered by the law; 9 Then said he, LO, I COME TO DO THY WILL, O GOD. He taketh away the first, that he may establish the second. 10 By the which will we are sanctified through the offering of the body of Jesus Christ once *for all*.

In contrast to mere animal blood, the author will explain, God became flesh so that He could shed His own blood. The author quotes David's words from Psalm 40:6-8, set forth below:

> Psalm 40:6 Sacrifice and offering thou didst not desire; mine ears hast thou opened: burnt offering and sin offering hast thou not required. 7 Then said I, Lo, I come: in the volume of the book *it is* written of me, 8 I delight to do thy will, O my God...

If we compare the quote in Hebrews 10:5-7 with Psalm 40:6-8 we see differences. In particular, Psalm 40:6 has the phrase "mine ears has thou opened," which are replaced in Hebrews 10:5 with **but a body hast thou prepared me** taken from the Greek Septuagint. The point of Psalm 40:6 is that God is more interested in a heart of willing obedience (a living sacrifice) than an animal (dead) sacrifice. The Septuagint gave an interpretive paraphrase and extended the notion of God's preparing David's ears to listen to the idea of preparing his entire body a living sacrifice in the sense of providing service to God. In Psalm 40:7-8, David proclaims that he is prepared to do God's will, as it is written of him in the **volume of the book.** This gives the passage a prophetic sense, and the author understands the reference to the greater Son of David, Jesus, in his incarnation, who was the exemplary model of willing obedience to God, even to the point of offering his body on a Roman cross. As Paul wrote in Philippians 2:6-8 of Jesus: "Who, being in the form of God, thought it not robbery to be equal with God: But made himself of no reputation and took upon him the form of a servant, and was made in the likeness of men: And being found in fashion as a man, he humbled himself, and become obedient unto death, even the death of the cross."

The author adds commentary in 10:8-9 explaining that the **sacrifices and offering and burnt offerings** that God finds no pleasure in are the Levitical sacrifices **offered by the law,** whereas the psalmist offering prophetically the Words of Jesus willingly offered himself to do the Father's will, **Lo, I come to do thy will, O God.** And the point is that God **taketh away the first,** that is the animal sacrifices (and by implication the Mosaic Covenant) **that** God **may establish the second,** that is, the New Covenant inaugurated by Jesus' willing sacrifice of himself. Thus, by God's decision to replace the **first** with the **second, we are sanctified through the offering of the body of Jesus Christ once for all.** The term **sanctified** refers to believers being positionally separated and made holy by the sacrifice of Jesus. The KJV adds **for all** (in italics in some printings) to emphasize the point that **Jesus Christ** died **once for all** time. Unlike the repetitive animal sacrifices, Jesus was willingly offered once and no more sacrifice for sin will ever be necessary again.

> 11 And every priest standeth daily ministering and offering oftentimes the same sacrifices, which can never take away sins: 12 But this man, after he had offered one sacrifice for sins for ever, sat down on the right hand of God; 13 From henceforth expecting till his enemies be made his footstool. 14 For by one offering he hath perfected for ever them that are sanctified. 15 *Whereof* the Holy Ghost also is a witness to us: for after that he had said before, 16 THIS *IS* THE COVENANT THAT I WILL MAKE WITH THEM AFTER THOSE DAYS, SAITH THE LORD, I WILL PUT MY LAWS INTO THEIR HEARTS, AND IN THEIR MINDS WILL I WRITE THEM; 17 AND THEIR SINS AND INIQUITIES WILL I REMEMBER NO MORE. 18 Now where remission of these *is, there is* no more offering for sin.

This verse confirms that the Temple was still standing since the Levitical priesthood was still operational there, which is another indication that the book was written prior to the destruction of the Temple in A.D. 70. At the time the book was written, **every** Levitical **priest standeth daily ministering and offering oftentimes the same sacrifices**. There were many priests with duties at the Temple, day after day seemingly without end, and the point of their offering **the same sacrifices** is that no animal sacrifice ever provided for a permanent solution to our sin problem because such **sacrifices...can never take away sins.** (see Hebrews 9:12) In contrast, **after Jesus had offered one sacrifice for sins for ever,** namely of himself, Jesus did not remain standing in a continual ministry of making sacrifices and offerings but instead ceased forever from that aspect (i.e., making a sacrifice) of his priesthood and **sat down on the right hand of the father, from henceforth expecting** or waiting **till his enemies be made his footstool** in fulfillment of Psalm 110:1 ("The LORD said unto my Lord, Sit thou at my right hand until I make thine enemies thy footstool."). That fulfillment will occur in the future as God gathers the enemies for destruction and Jesus returns with an immediate victory over them. (Revelation 19:11 ff.) This means we are living in the period of Jesus' **expecting** or waiting and looking forward to when the waiting ends and he returns.

Again, in contrast to the repeated animal sacrifices, **by one offering** of his own body, **he hath perfected for ever them that are sanctified** or made holy. It is inexplicable that some commentators argue from Hebrews that believers can lose, forfeit, or throw away their eternal salvation. We have seen thus far in this study that none of the so-called "warning passages" provide any support for this idea. What's more is that in this passage we have the writer explaining that those who **are sanctified** by Jesus' sacrifice are also **perfected forever.** The term **sanctified** means set apart or made holy and as believers in Christ we are positionally sanctified, a truth he already confirmed in Hebrews 10:10 (also, e.g., 1 Corinthians 1:2: "Unto the church of God which is at Corinth, to them that are sanctified in Christ Jesus, called to be saints...."). In our Christian walks, our position should become more and more the reality of our experience, a point our author will focus on in chapter 12. But the point here is that those "sanctified through the offering of the body of Jesus Christ once for all" (10:10) are also **perfected**. The term means completed or matured depending on the context and looks forward to the completion of all aspects of our salvation in Christ, yet our author speaks here in the past tense. There may be no stronger apologetic for the fact that a person who is placed in Christ can never fall out of Christ by any means thereafter than the fact that from God's perspective our completion, while experientially future for us, is already a past completed action. We see this reflected in other places where, for example, believers are in the past tense "glorified" (Romans 8:30) and "raised up together...in Christ Jesus" (Ephesians 2:6). If we can cast away our eternal security in Christ then it must be that we are able to change the past.

The reality of the permanent efficacy of Jesus' sacrifice is affirmed by the Words of **the Holy Ghost** who **after that he had** promised the New Covenant in Jeremiah 31:33 explained in Jeremiah 31:34 (**This is the covenant that I will make with them after those days...**) that the result would be that **their sins and iniquities will I remember no more**. The conclusion is inescapable. The Old Covenant involved a daily ministration of sacrifices and offerings, but Jesus inaugurated the New Covenant in his blood and his once for all time sacrifice permanently and forever dealt with our sin problem. When we say that the efficacy of that sacrifice may fade away by our own conduct, we belittle the sacrifice and doubt God's assurance that our sins He **will remember no more**. Because Jesus' sacrifice provided for **remission** or forgiveness (compare the use of the same term in Ephesians 1:7 and Colossians 1:14) forever and God **will remember** the sin **no more, there is no more offering for sin.** This means that Jesus will never need to make another sacrifice and the ongoing Levitical sacrifices at the time Hebrews was written no longer had any utility before God. Those sacrifices were once the appropriate **offering for sin** that looked forward to the Messiah, but now were hollow rituals. For this reason, those recipients of Hebrews that are flirting with a potential return to Judaism in the face of their afflictions are misguided; there is nothing left to go back to except obsolete rituals.

> 19 Having therefore, brethren, boldness to enter into the holiest by the blood of Jesus, 20 By a new and living way, which he hath consecrated for us, through the veil, that is to say, his flesh; 21 And *having* an high priest over the house of God; 22 Let us draw near with a true heart in full assurance of faith, having our hearts sprinkled from an evil conscience, and our bodies washed with pure water. 23 Let us hold fast the profession of *our* faith without wavering; (for he *is* faithful that promised;) 24 And let us consider one another to provoke unto love and to good works: 25 Not forsaking the assembling of ourselves together, as the manner of some *is*; but exhorting *one another:* and so much the more, as ye see the day approaching.

The **therefore** in 10:19 is a critical "therefore" because it marks the conclusion of the theological foundation portion of the epistle. To this point the author made various arguments for the superiority of Jesus to the old order, and now he will turn to the practical outworking of that in their lives. In chapter II he will give numerous examples of past saints who serve as examples of lives of obedience and steadfast endurance, and then in chapter 12 he will bring it to a head with the concepts of the Father's training program for us and our living in view of the heavenly city.

So he says, **having therefore, brethren**, yet another reminder that their eternal destiny is never called into doubt in this book. **Having...boldness to enter into the holiest by the blood of Jesus**. In chapter 9, he explained that Jesus entered into the Holy of Holies in the heavenly temple to offer his own blood. In contrast to the old order that only permitted the High Priest once a year to enter, the **blood of Jesus** made a way for us to boldly enter **by a new and living way, which he hath consecrated for us, through the veil, that is to say, his flesh**. The Temple had a veil separating the Holy Place from the Holy of Holies, a veil that kept out all but the High Priest, who could only enter on Yom Kippur with animal blood. When Jesus offered himself, that physical veil was "was rent in twain from the top to the bottom" (Matthew 27:51; also Mark 15:38; Luke 23:45). The true veil was **his flesh**, and in that moment of his sacrifice the old order ended and access to God was no longer through that old order, but **by a new and living way**. The term **new** is the Greek *prosphatos,* is used only here in the entire New Testament, and means according to Strong's, "previously (recently) slain (fresh)." Thus, we have a sort of contrast of words with a "freshly slain" and "living way" that Jesus **consecrated** or inaugurated **for us** by his sacrifice. The point is that we no longer have access to God on the basis of continual animal sacrifices that never remove sin, but forever on the basis of the "freshly slain" Jesus. This way to access God is living because no more physical sacrifices will ever be needed and because the one who made the ultimate sacrifice lives with resurrection life. (see Romans 5:10) We approach God on the basis of what Jesus completed once for all and on the basis of his continuing life, now seated at the right hand of the Father. No matter how much time passes, his sacrifice is fresh, it retains its continuing vitality and efficacy forever.

We have in Jesus **an high priest** after the order of Melchisedec **over the house of God**, that is, over the heavenly tabernacle. In view of the replacement of the old order of continual dead sacrifices that provided only limited access to God, by this **new and living way** and thus far superior way we are urged to **draw near** to God **with a true heart in full assurance of faith** in what Jesus did for us and where Jesus is presently seated, **having our hearts sprinkled from an evil conscience, and our bodies washed with pure water**. In contrast to the animal sacrifices that did not remove sin and only provided for a sort of ritual cleansing, Jesus' sacrifice accomplished the inner cleaning of our conscience that the author alluded to in prior verses:

> 9:9 Which *was* a figure for the time then present, in which were offered both gifts and sacrifices, that could not make him that did the service perfect, as pertaining to the **conscience**;

9:14 How much more shall the blood of Christ, who through the eternal Spirit offered himself without spot to God, purge your **conscience** from dead works to serve the living God?

10:2 For then would they not have ceased to be offered? because that the worshippers once purged should have had no more **conscience** of sins.

In the Old Testament the sprinkling of blood was used in rituals to symbolize cleansing, but Jesus' blood accomplished an inner / conscience cleansing. Jesus also accomplished for us the washing of our **bodies...with pure water**. This is reminiscent of Ezekiel 36:25 that speaks of the New Covenant blessings: "Then will I sprinkle clean water upon you, and ye shall be clean: from all your filthiness, and from all your idols, will I cleanse you." Jesus addressed our sin with finality, and in view of the superiority of what we have in Jesus in contrast to the old order, the exhortation is to **hold fast the profession of our faith without wavering; (for he is faithful that promised)**. The Hebrews were getting off track because of the trials they faced. We must look at our own circumstances and ask, what will we allow to get us off track? What failing of personal relationships, loss of possessions or change of circumstances would cause us to abandon living out our faith with endurance? Some healthy introspection is warranted, but we need to be careful not to look down our nose at others. The writer reminds us here of our responsibility to our brethren to help them in their spiritual growth. Thus he writes, **let us consider one another to provoke unto love and to**

**good works.** There are, in fact numerous "one another" verses in the New Testament, a few of which are outlined here: honor one another (Romans 12:10), love one another (Romans 13:8; Galatians 5:14; Ephesians 4:2; 1 Thessalonians 4:9; 1 Peter 1:22), do not place stumblingblocks before one another (Romans 14:13), bear with one another's weaknesses and build people up (Romans 15:1-6), instruct one another (Romans 14:14), serve one another (Galatians 5:13), do not devour one another (Galatians 5:15), bear one another's burdens (Galatians 6:2), be kind, compassionate and forgiving to one another (Ephesians 4:32), teach and exhort one another (Colossians 3:16), encourage and build up one another (1 Thessalonians 5:11; Hebrews 10:25), exhort others to endure (Hebrews 3:13), and provoke to love and good works (Hebrews 10:24).

Now the point is this—you cannot do all these things for one another unless you are around one another, i.e., an active part of a local church. There are no "lone ranger" Christians (at least, those who would be are NOT within God's will). Our American sense of independence and self-sufficiency may say to others, "stay out of my business," but that is completely unbiblical. As shown above, we have obligations to one another that require us to get into each other's lives. We have to move beyond the senseless nonsense of shallow conversation with our brethren about weather and sports and deal with the real issues of life. In my view, largely because of the shallowness of most of our "at church" relationships, when the trials come (and they will) people as a first response bolt from church. The author writes here, **not forsaking the assembling of ourselves together, as the manner of some is.** In the face of the Hebrews' present trial of persecution, some of them had already bolted from church. Now consider this—if persecution for your faith is not an excuse to skip church, how is it that many of us skip church because...

- the weather is bad

- the weather is good

- my kids have a ball game / practice this morning

- we overslept / we were up so late Saturday

- it is so hard to get kids ready in the morning

- the preacher may go over 20 minutes with his sermon

- "I am just not being fed"

- we had family in from out-of-town

- we just wanted to have family time

You can make your own list but there is not one of these pathetic excuses you would dream of telling your boss as an excuse for missing an important meeting or deadline, so do not say these silly things to God. Somewhere along the way a great many Christians decided church participation and attendance were optional, or that they need only go on Mother's Day or Easter to be sure God is still around. I do not want to be legalistic here and realize there are times when our missing church is legitimate (e.g., you have the flu), but these should be few and far between for most of us. In general, if it would not keep you from going to work, it should not keep you from going to church. And we need to look out for those that appear to be drifting away, not to judge but **exhorting another** to endurance. Life is tough and we need our church family to function as a family, **so much the more, as ye see the day approaching**. The author understood that judgment was pronounced on that generation of Israel that rejected Jesus and the rebellion in Israel was stirring up several years before the destruction of Jerusalem in A.D. 70. The Romans began gathering the troops and moving toward Jerusalem in about A.D. 66. Hebrews was likely written at or about this time so that the author and his audience could look around at present events and see that the temporal judgment that Jesus himself announced for that generation was on the horizon. The concern and the reason why he tells them to exhort those who are drifting away is because if they re-identify with the generation under judgment, when the hammer falls, they may find themselves standing under it. They run the risk of temporal judgment for disobedience (not loss of salvation) just like that generation in the wilderness used as the example in Hebrews 3 suffered temporal judgment even though God forgave them.

> <u>26</u> For if we sin wilfully after that we have received the knowledge of the truth, there remaineth no more sacrifice for sins, <u>27</u> But a certain fearful looking for of judgment and fiery indignation, which shall devour the adversaries. <u>28</u> He that despised Moses' law died without mercy under two or three witnesses: <u>29</u> Of how much sorer punishment, suppose ye, shall he be thought worthy, who hath trodden under foot the Son of God, and hath counted the

blood of the covenant, wherewith he was sanctified, an unholy thing, and hath done despite unto the Spirit of grace? 30 For we know him that hath said, VENGEANCE *BELONGETH* UNTO ME, I WILL RECOMPENSE, saith the Lord. And again, THE LORD SHALL JUDGE HIS PEOPLE. 31 *It is* a fearful thing to fall into the hands of the living God.

With verse 26 we find one of the most misunderstood of all New Testament passages, used by some to teach that when you willfully sin you lose your salvation (meaning your justification), and by others to teach that willfully sinning proves you were never saved to begin with (you are a professor and not a possessor). Both camps read verse 26 out of its context and ignore the plain import of the words. The issue throughout the book, and indeed even in the previous verse, is giving up in the face of adversity and returning to the empty Pharisaic Judaism of their day. The author both encourages and warns, and certainly his audience has **received the knowledge of the truth**, that is, the knowledge of the inauguration of the New Covenant in the blood of Jesus Christ and all the benefits that brought to believers, including a purged conscience by Jesus' once for all time sacrifice. A return to Judaism is a return to non-efficacious sacrifices that have no value because the Mosaic Covenant and Aaronic priesthood are no longer recognized by God. Thus, the warning to them is that in the obsolete Levitical system, **there remaineth no more sacrifice for sins**.

At this point, a short excursus concerning the temporal judgment on the generation of Israel that characteristically rejected Jesus is in order. In Matthew 3, the prophet

John the Baptizer is plainly aware of a coming judgment on Israel when the unbelieving Pharisees and Sadducees come to him: "O generation of vipers, who hath warned you to flee from the wrath to come?...And now also the axe is laid unto the root of the tree...." (Matthew 3:7, 10) In Matthew 12, Jesus heals a demon-possessed man (Matthew 12:22) and is accused by the Pharisees of having done this miracle through demonic means (Matthew 12:24). This becomes a fundamental turning point in Jesus' earthly ministry in which his offer of the Messianic kingdom to that generation of Israel is revoked (the generation that does turn to Jesus will see the fulfillment of the kingdom blessings promised in the Old Testament). Jesus said, "All manner of sin and blasphemy shall be forgiven unto men: but the blasphemy against the Holy Ghost shall not be forgiven unto men...whosoever speaketh against the Holy Ghost, it shall not be forgiven him, neither in this world, neither in the world to come." (Matthew 12:31-32) Those Jews that witness Jesus' miracles and ascribe his power to Satan are confirmed to be judged both temporally ("neither in this world") and eternally ("neither in the world to come"), and unfortunately this was true of most of the Jewish leaders (we see an exception, for example, in Nicodemus) and a substantial portion of the populace.

Jesus refers to that generation in Israel as a "generation of vipers" and tell them that "by thy words thou shalt be condemned." (Matthew 12:34, 37) At this point some of the scribes and Pharisees demand a sign, to which Jesus condemns them as "an evil and adulterous generation." The term adulterous here means they turned away from God. The only sign they will be shown is the sign of Jonah, i.e., Jesus' resurrection after they crucify him.

(Matthew 12:40) Indeed, "the men of Nineveh shall rise in judgment with this generation, and shall condemn it" and similarly "the queen of the south shall rise up in the judgment with this generation, and condemn it." (Matthew 12:41-42) The judgment begins in Matthew 13 as Jesus starts teaching in parables, the interpretation of which is hidden to the Jews who have no faith in God. (Matthew 13:11-16) The focus going forward is the building of the church, and while more Jewish people will come to have saving faith in Jesus, the judgment on that generation stands, including the impending destruction of the Temple. (see Matthew 23:38-39; 24:2)

When Peter preaches on Pentecost in Acts 2, Jews and proselytes from Israel and abroad are present, and Peter directs his convicting sermon to "ye men of Israel" (Acts 2:22) that crucified Messiah. Peter says to them of Jesus that "ye have taken, and by wicked hands have crucified and slain." (Acts 2:23) Yet God raised him up, "therefore let all the house of Israel know assuredly, that God hath made that same Jesus, whom ye have crucified, both Lord and Christ." (Acts 2:32, 36) Peter's moving sermon convicts them ("they were pricked in their heart") and they ask him what they should do. (Acts 2:37) Peter's response to those he accuses of crucifying Jesus is: "Repent, and be baptized every one of you in the name of Jesus Christ for the remission of sins, and ye shall receive the gift of the Holy Ghost." (Acts 2:38) He then extends the promise to everyone else at Pentecost (Acts 2:39), and exhorted the audience, "Save yourselves from this untoward generation." (Acts 2:40) Peter is not just preaching eternal life in Jesus, but how the Jewish people in his audience could be delivered from the coming temporal judgment on that "untoward generation."

With this background in mind, as we turn back to the text in Hebrews, we see that not only is the old system replaced by the New Covenant (e.g., Hebrews 7:12), but the hammer is about to fall on the rebellious generation of Israel in fulfillment of prophecy (e.g., Matthew 23:36-38, 24:1-2). The stern warning here to the believers receiving the epistle is that if they **sin willfully** by returning to Judaism and re-identifying with the generation of Israel that is under judgment (if they identify with those that said give us Barabbas), then they only have **a certain fearful** or terrifying **looking for** or expectation **of judgment and fiery indignation, which shall devour the adversaries.** These words point to temporal judgment, which they will look forward to in fear because it was prophesied by Jesus himself. This is not about going to hell or the lake of fire, for that will be the permanent abode of non-believers. Rather, the judgment that falls will **devour**, i.e., consume (the word often is translated eat), which is used here as an expression that simply means they will die. But who will die? It is the **adversaries** or enemies of Jesus. In other words, if you re-identify with the generation that rejected Jesus and demanded his crucifixion, thus identifying with his enemies, you may die under the judgment coming upon them. We know this occurred in A.D. 70 when Titus took the city and the beautiful Temple where the adversaries tried to stone Jesus (John 8:59) was destroyed. Once again, as shown in prior chapters, the author is concerned about both temporal and eschatological consequences because they both stem from the same disobedience. In the passage at hand, it is the possibility of physical death that is at issue.

The verses that follow build the argument that a return to Judaism will result in temporal punishment. The author points out that **he that despised Moses' law died without mercy under two or three witnesses.** First, note that what he is saying parallels the warning passage of 2:2-3: "For if the word spoken by angels [i.e., the Law] was steadfast, and every transgression and disobedience received a just recompence of reward; How shall we escape, if we neglect so great salvation; which at the first began to be spoken by the Lord, and was confirmed unto us by them that heard him." Under the Law, for certain violations the death penalty was prescribed if the violation was established by at least two witnesses. (e.g., Deuteronomy 17:6, 19:15) Given that violations of the Law might be met with temporal punishment, **of how much sorer** or more severe a **punishment, suppose ye, shall he be thought worthy, who hath trodden under foot the Son of God, and hath counted the blood of the covenant, wherewith he was sanctified, an unholy thing, and hath done despite unto the Spirit of grace?** To return to Judaism is to trod **under foot the Son of God** because it is turning away from the once for all time sacrifice of the Son on the cross, the very **blood of the** new **covenant**, in favor of the animal blood of the Levitical system, thus counting Jesus' blood **an unholy thing.** What our author is saying is that since the New Covenant is superior to the Old Covenant, disregarding the New Covenant will be met with temporal judgment just as disregarding the Old Covenant resulted in temporal judgment. The Jews that rejected Jesus viewed his crucifixion as just recompense for his being a blasphemer; they did not see his blood as the holy blood of the sinless Son of God, but that of a sinner rightly judged by God. For his audience to re-identify with that group of people was to re-identify with what they stand for, regardless of whether they actually share the belief. Remember that the cursed generation of Israel blasphemed the Holy Spirit (Matthew 12), and some in his audience are considering a return to Judaism and re-identification with that generation, thus rendering an insult **(done despite)** to the Holy Spirit **(the Spirit of grace)**, which Jesus taught was unforgivable.

Our author further supports his warning of temporal judgment by quoting from Deuteronomy 32:35 **(Vengeance belongeth unto me, I will recompense)** and 32:36 **(The Lord shall judge his people)**, both of which were warnings to Israel of the consequence of continued disobedience to the Law of Moses. In forceful and frightening words, he summarizes the warning of what will happen if they return to Judaism and re-identify with Jesus' adversaries: **It is a fearful thing to fall into the hands of the living God.** They are considering a return to Judaism because of persecution by mere men, and they need to understand that it is far better to be at odds with the world and at peace with God than the other way around. How many today will conform to the world to fit in or be thought "cool" as if God is winking at their heart attitude?

> <u>32</u> But call to remembrance the former days, in which, after ye were illuminated, ye endured a great fight of afflictions; <u>33</u> Partly, whilst ye were made a gazingstock both by reproaches and afflictions; and partly, whilst ye became companions of them that were so used. <u>34</u> For ye had

compassion of me in my bonds, and took joyfully the spoiling of your goods, knowing in yourselves that ye have in heaven a better and an enduring substance.

Having sounded again the warning of the temporal consequences of a return to Judaism, he once more provides words of encouragement based on their history of faithfulness to the Lord. He asks them to **call to remembrance the former days, in which, after ye were illuminated, ye endured a great fight of afflictions.** In other words, he says, remember how it was shortly after you came to know Jesus (**after ye were illuminated** or enlightened; cf. Hebrews 6:4) when you endured persecution. He describes that experience to include being personally **made a gazingstock** (publicly exposed) to **reproaches** (or taunts or mocking) **and afflictions,** and at other times **companions of them that were so used.** They endured through the persecution while maintaining **compassion** on the author who was at that time **in bonds** (jail). When their Jewish persecutors stole their material goods, they took it **joyfully.** How could they do this without responding in violence or getting angry at God? The reason is they were **knowing in** themselves that they had **in heaven a better and an enduring substance.** What they believed they had in God was better than anything they owned in this world. Jesus taught in the Sermon on the Mount: "Lay not up for yourselves treasures upon earth, where moth and rust doth corrupt, and where thieves break through and steal: But lay up for yourselves treasures in heaven, where neither moth nor rust doth corrupt, and where thieves do not break through nor steal." (Matthew 6:19-20) Enduring persecution and staying true to the Lord will not result in material blessings but it will build an account in heaven. In other words, our life of endurance now will translate into eternity in the form of eternal blessings there. The author calls his audience to remember how they endured in the past with such a great appreciation for this truth that they could endure the theft of their material goods with joy because of their focus on God's promised future blessings in heaven, rightly understanding that they were only losing that which they could not keep to gain that which they could not lose.

> 35 Cast not away therefore your confidence, which hath great recompence of reward. 36 For ye have need of patience, that, after ye have done the will of God, ye might receive the promise. 37 For YET A LITTLE WHILE, and HE THAT SHALL COME WILL COME, AND WILL NOT TARRY. 38 NOW THE JUST SHALL LIVE BY FAITH: BUT IF *ANY MAN* DRAW BACK, MY SOUL SHALL HAVE NO PLEASURE IN HIM. 39 But we are not of them who draw back unto perdition; but of them that believe to the saving of the soul.

Having issued a stern warning and called to their remembrance their past faithfulness, he comes to another **therefore** application, namely that they would **cast not away** their **confidence, which hath great recompense of reward.** The word **confidence** is the Greek *parrhesia*, which Strong's defines as "outspokenness, i.e., frankness, bluntness, publicity; by implication, assurance...." The term is often used of speaking openly and boldly. (e.g., Mark 8:32; John 7:13,

26, 18:20; Acts 2:29, 4:13) It is the same term translated "boldly" in Hebrews 4:16 and "boldness" in Hebrews 10:19. The author is encouraging them not to return to Judaism but to stay the course with great boldness, knowing that such faithfulness to God will result in a **great** (Greek *mega*) **recompense of reward**. The phrase **recompense of reward** translates a single Greek term, *misthapodosia*, which can mean a positive or negative reward (as in Hebrews 2:2). The term derives from the verb *apodidomi*, which means "to give away" or "recompense, render, requite, restore, reward, sell, yield." The verb form is the word Jesus uses in Matthew 16:27: "and then he [Jesus] shall **reward** every man according to his works." The point here is that for believers, steadfast endurance in the face of affliction (or persecution) results in future rewards from God. This is a consistent theme for the entire book. God never promises the Christian life will be easy, or that the faithful will have material wealth, but he does promise that a life of faith will be rewarded in heaven, so that Jesus would tell us to lay up our treasure there. Those who do not steadfastly endure face the prospect of forfeiting rewards and possibly temporal judgment.

In verse 36, the author points out the root problem his audience has, which is the root issue the whole book is written to address. They **have need of patience**, that is, of endurance. All of the theological framework, the warning passages, and even what will follow in chapters 11 and 12, is to address this core issue of endurance, with the author hoping to encourage them to endure in the face of affliction, knowing **that, after ye have done the will of God, ye might receive the promise**. Their continued endurance is **the will of God** for their lives, and their lifetime of endurance will result in receiving **the promise**. By receiving **the promise** is not meant that in heaven a promise will be made to them. Rather, it is that which has already been promised them that will be received after a lifetime of endurance, which is how the term **promise** was consistently used earlier in the book (e.g., 4:1, 6:12, 6:17, 8:6, 9:15). The **promise** in view is the "promise" of "entering into his rest" (4:1), the "better promises" of the New Covenant (8:6), "the promise of eternal inheritance" under the New Covenant (9:15), and "the promises" to be fulfilled after their lifetimes (11:13, 39). The **promise** refers to the blessings in the eternal Kingdom (the "world to come" of 2:5) that Jesus will implement at the Second Coming.

Thus, the author says of Jesus' return, **for yet a little while, and he that shall come will come, and will not tarry**. The New Testament always emphasizes the imminence of the return of Jesus Christ. Those who would endure affliction now in view of receiving the promise later need to catch hold of the fact that from God's perspective, the Son is returning soon **and will not tarry**. In saying these words, the author quotes Isaiah 26:20 (a passage concerning the future day of the Lord) when he says **for yet a little while** and Habakkuk 2:3 (a passage concerning the coming temporal judgment God is bringing on Judah through the Babylonians) which he applies to Jesus and says **he that shall come will come, and will not tarry**. The author then quotes from Habakkuk 2:4: **Now the just shall live by faith**. This same passage is also quoted in Romans 1:17 and Galatians 3:11. While they wait patiently for the Lord's return, they are to **live** out their lives **by faith**, that is, on the basis of the Word of God, with His promised future blessings in view. Indeed, those who fail to endure (**if any man draw back**) have this warning from God: **my soul shall have no pleasure in him.** Resist the urge to make expressions like this always about heaven and hell. Our heavenly Father takes great pleasure in our living a life of faithful endurance, but no pleasure in our lack of endurance, or in the case of the Hebrews, if they fall back into Judaism, which the author warned will have temporal consequences (judgment). This is in the same way that we as parents take no pleasure in our children's disobedience; it has nothing to do with terminating the relationship.

The encouragement that follows is that **we are not of them who draw back unto perdition** or destruction, but rather, **them that believe to the saving of the soul.** The term soul here is the Greek *psuche* that means life and only rarely has the sense of one's immaterial spirit. The point here has nothing to do with whether they will be "saved" in the sense of justification, but whether their Christian life will end in destruction or temporal judgment as he has warned, or instead a life of endurance (living by faith, living what they believe) so that they are spared the coming judgment. We should note that it is possible that a further meaning is intended here. Jesus used the same words in Matthew 16 speaking to his already saved / justified (except Judas Iscariot) apostles about discipleship:

> Matthew 16:25 For whosoever will save his **life** shall lose it: and whosoever will lose his **life** for my sake shall find it. 26 For what is a man profited, if he shall gain the whole world, and lose his own **soul?** or what shall

a man give in exchange for his **soul**? 27 For the Son of man shall come in the glory of his Father with his angels; and then he shall reward every man according to his works.

The Greek term *psuche* is translated "life" in Matthew 16:25 and "soul" in 16:26, but plainly has the same meaning in both places since Jesus has not changed subjects. To his apostles Jesus taught that following your own will in this lifetime will result in a loss of that life; in other words, all that you accomplish will have only temporary significance and will end when this life is over. In contrast, living out God's will for your soul/life requires you to lose your soul/life (your agenda) now for a soul/life that you can keep or save because it will have eternal significance when the Son of man returns to "reward every man according to his works." Putting this all together, the author says, "Don't fail to endure and return to Judaism, which may result in your destruction, but stay the course living by faith, avoiding the coming judgment and your lives of faith/works will translate into rewards when Jesus returns."

## Closing

The most famous of all traitors was General Benedict Arnold of the American Continental Army. He became the commander of the fort at West Point, New York, but decided to surrender it to the British. He had distinguished himself in many ways, but was passed by for promotion, others took credit for some of his accomplishments and there were allegations of misconduct. These and other factors influenced him to change sides, for which he was commissioned as a general in the British army. In due time, and to this day, his very name carries the brand of a traitor. James wrote that "friendship of the world is enmity with God." (James 4:4) Christians can become spiritual Benedict Arnold's when they change sides, but the reality is that most people will not see that they have changed sides. The deception is believing that you can have a vibrant relationship with God and a teaspoon of the world at the same time, but James says embracing the world makes you a spiritual Benedict Arnold. The Hebrews were considering defecting because of affliction and it is likely they had no idea that they were on the verge of being spiritual Benedict Arnold's, which is why the author told them they lacked endurance. What will it take for you to stop enduring in obedience and change sides? And in this day, what does changing sides look like? Will the desire to fit in or not be ridiculed as old fashioned or unenlightened cause you to cross the line? Will lust for the world's entertainment or philosophy be enough?

## Application Points

- **MAIN PRINCIPLE:** Jesus' high priestly ministry, and in particular his sacrifice of his own blood, removed the veil and granted us access to God so that we can now grow in our relationship to God as we endure in obedience to His Word.

- A believer who continues in sin may face temporal judgment and lose out on the rewards promised to those who endure in the life of faith.

## Discussion Questions

1. What are the "good things to come" in verse 1?

2. What was the problem (or limitation) of the animal sacrifices under the Law of Moses?

3. If God does not take pleasure in animal sacrifices, what is it, according to Hebrews 10, that He does take pleasure in?

4. Is the Mosaic Covenant still in force today?

5. How can we provoke one another to good works?

6. In a local church, do you bear some responsibility for the spiritual health of your brethren? If so, what should you be doing about it?

7. What are acceptable reasons for forsaking assembling together?

8. In verse 35, he tells them to "cast not away therefore your confidence." Who makes the decision to cast confidence away? And why?

9. What does it mean to live by faith?

# Chapter 12

# The Hall of Fame of Faith

It comes to a surprise to some people that the Bible is not about achieving the American dream, climbing the career ladder, realizing financial independence, or achieving a position of great affluence. We do well to ask, what is success? For those who do not know Jesus Christ, and sometimes even for Christians, success is manipulating the three Ps—people, possessions and personal circumstances—to achieve a sense of happiness. But the Bible defines success when it says of Noah that he "walked with God." (Genesis 6:9) What greater thing could be said of a mortal than he / she "walked with God"? We should do all that we do with a spirit of excellence, and if doing so results in God's provision of material blessings, then praise Him for that. However, our purpose is not to achieve the world's counterfeit success, but to live out lives of faith so that God could say of us, he / she "walked with God." As we dive in to the most famous chapter of Hebrews, we are immersed in that great cloud of witnesses whose lives were lives of faith. They were not perfect people, for no one ever is.

God is not looking for perfect people. He is in the business of doing the extraordinary with very ordinary people, of hitting home runs with crooked sticks. Their example of faith, despite their shortcomings, should motivate and encourage us to live out our lives in faith as examples to everyone in our sphere of influence of the power of God's grace in our lives.

## Scripture and Comments

Now we come to the most well known chapter of Hebrews, often referred to as the "Hall of Faith" or the "Hall of Fame of Faith," and so it is. Unfortunately, it is often misread as a chapter about what justifying faith looks like, but as we have seen over and again to this point, the author assumes his audience is composed of believers and speaks to them only as believers. The issue is whether, in light of their present affliction, they will continue the *life of faith* that all believers are called to, that is, whether they will continue in obedience to God's Word. It is that sort of faith-response to God's Word that is at issue throughout the book and that is illustrated here in Chapter 11 by examples pulled from the Old Testament of believers in the past who exemplified lives of faith. The chapter cannot be properly understood apart from its moorings. Chapter 10 ends with a prescription from the doctor—they need endurance so that they will receive the inheritance God promised them:

> Hebrews 10:35 Cast not away therefore your confidence, which hath great recompence of reward. 36 For ye have need

of patience, that, after ye have done the will of God, ye might receive the promise. 37 For yet a little while, and he that shall come will come, and will not tarry. 38 Now the just shall live by faith: but if *any man* draw back, my soul shall have no pleasure in him. 39 But we are not of them who draw back unto perdition; but of them that believe to the saving of the soul.

The other bookend of chapter 11 is Hebrews 12:1, another exhortation to endurance like that displayed by the real-life examples from Chapter 11: "Wherefore, seeing we also are compassed about with so great a cloud of witnesses, let us lay aside every weight, and the sin which doth so easily beset us, and let us run with patience the race that is set before us." Between the bookends we find a description of what faith looks like in the life of a believer followed by several examples, and all of this is offered to his audience as an encouragement to endure in the marathon race of life.

Hebrews 11:1 Now faith is the substance of things hoped for, the evidence of things not seen. 2 For by it the elders obtained a good report. 3 Through faith we understand that the worlds were framed by the word of God, so that things which are seen were not made of things which do appear.

This first verse is not so much a definition of **faith** as a description of what it looks like, from the perspective of a life of faith under observation. We see this in his statement that **by it**, that is, by faith, **the elders** (past believers) **obtained a good report**, as recorded in the Old Testament. In other words, while **faith** is itself not visibly seen, faith responses are seen, and what was seen in the lives of **the elders** evidenced that they were people who believed what God said and acted on it. Thus, the author describes **faith** as **the substance of things hoped for** and **the evidence of things not seen.**

Since Genesis 1, God revealed himself to humanity in various ways. Recall how Hebrews opens: "God, who at sundry times and in divers manners spake in time past unto the fathers by the prophets, hath in these last days spoken unto us by his Son...." (Hebrews 1:1-2) Throughout history, people had the opportunity to respond to the light given them, and God's revelation is often in terms of promised future blessings. The person that responds faithfully in the "now" does not yet have the blessings, yet so intense is their conviction of the truth of God's Word that the future blessing has a present tangible sense to it and their lives are reoriented in view of the promises, and this is the life of **faith** that is the exhortation of Hebrews. For them, what they believe is a present possession, real to them and observable to others who see how the reality of God's Word changes their lives. Thus, their **faith** is in every sense **the substance** or present outward reality **of things hoped for,** indeed, the observable **evidence of things not seen.**

From the beginning, faith is bound up in what God says. You cannot separate the concepts of faith from God's Word, for faith—believing and trusting—must have content, and as concerning the person of God, the content of faith is the Word of God. Indeed, our answer to all that is around us is an answer of faith. For it is through faith that we understand that the worlds (the universe, cf. Hebrews 1:2) were framed by the word of God, so that things which are seen were not made of things which do appear. In Genesis 1, God by His Word created (i.e., "let there be..."). He did not begin with "stuff", atoms, matter or even sub-atomic particles; He, by His Word, commanded everything into existence, which our verse here in Hebrews confirms. Many people today reject the Genesis account of creation, including many who profess to be Christians. By implication from Hebrews 11:3, they lack faith in this foundational portion of God's Word. To believe what is written about creation in Genesis serves as the prototypical example of taking God at his Word because God is the only witness to what occurred and our best science cannot provide a provable answer to the question. The flipside of this example of faith in what occurred in the distant past is to have faith in what is future, because again, the believer has only God's Word to trust. Faith in promised future blessings is analogous to faith in the creation account because in both instances we must rely solely on God's Word. The One who **framed** the universe by His Word is able to keep His promises, and believers throughout history have endured on the basis of God's Word.

> 4 By faith Abel offered unto God a more excellent sacrifice than Cain, by which he obtained witness that he was righteous, God testifying of his gifts: and by it he being dead yet speaketh.

The author begins his many examples of lives of faith with **Abel**, who **by** or on the basis of **faith...offered unto God a more excellent sacrifice than Cain**. The relevant portion of the background is found in Genesis 4:

<u>Genesis 4:3</u> And in process of time it came to pass, that Cain brought of the fruit of the ground an offering unto the LORD. 4 And Abel, he also brought of the firstlings of his flock and of the fat thereof. And the LORD had respect unto Abel and to his offering: 5 But unto Cain and to his offering he had not respect. And Cain was very wroth, and his countenance fell. 6 And the LORD said unto Cain, Why art thou wroth? and why is thy countenance fallen? 7 If thou doest well, shalt thou not be accepted? and if thou doest not well, sin lieth at the door. And unto thee *shall be* his desire, and thou shalt rule over him. 8 And Cain talked with Abel his brother: and it came to pass, when they were in the field, that Cain rose up against Abel his brother, and slew him.

The two sons of Adam and Eve brought sacrifices to God. There is no indication that these were "sin sacrifices" and no indication in the text that God required animal sacrifices as opposed to grain sacrifices. Both brothers brought sacrifices from their material substance; that one was a farmer and the other a herdsman is irrelevant. But throughout the Bible, as here, worship must come from a proper attitude and an obedient heart. We are not expressly told the purpose of these sacrifices, but that they were brought at the same time suggest these are essentially thank offerings or first-fruits offerings intended to recognize and give thanks to God for His abundant provision. To make such a sacrifice is, inherently, to express outwardly the belief that everything you have issues from the creator-sustainer God's good hand. In this way, the sacrifice is a fitting outward indication of faith.

Abel's sacrifice was **by faith**, and that is what made it **more excellent** to God than what **Cain** offered. Abel's sacrifice genuinely reflected his inward **faith** in God as the creator-sustainer who had provided him the very abundance from which the sacrifice came. By contrast, Cain had a sin issue, meaning that he was being disobedient to God while at the same time purporting to sacrifice to Him as Lord over his life: "If thou doest well, shalt thou not be accepted?" (Genesis 4:7) Jesus referred to Abel as "righteous Abel" (Matthew 23:35), but John referred to Cain as "evil": "Not as Cain, who was of that wicked one, and slew his brother. And wherefore slew he him? Because his own works were evil, and his brother's righteous." (1 John 3:12) Cain was characteristically wicked, and so his purported "worship" was empty, which rings through the ages a fearful warning to churchgoers today being misled by the "come as you are" teaching concerning worship. As Solomon wrote: "The sacrifice of the wicked is an abomination to the LORD: but the prayer of the upright is his delight." (Proverbs 15:8)

Abel's **more excellent sacrifice** was approved by God because it flowed from his life of **faith**. We must remember that at the time Abel lived, he had no Bible, and was primarily limited in his knowledge of God to what his parents taught him and any direct revelation from God, but the point is that whatever light of God he had, he believed it and lived accordingly, and his parents surely taught him that God was the creator-sustainer. We are not told how Abel came to understand that sacrifices would please God, but he did and so he sacrificed out of proper motivations. Cain went through the motions of worship without embracing the knowledge of God available to him. By Abel's **sacrifice...he obtained witness that he was righteous, God testifying of his gifts.** The text in Genesis, quoted above, says, "And the LORD had respect unto Abel and to his offering." In other words, God affirmed both Abel's character and his gifts (his worship). And though Abel died, his exemplary example of worship issuing from a life of faith **yet speaketh** to us these centuries later through the written record in Genesis.

> 5 By faith Enoch was translated that he should not see death; and WAS NOT FOUND, BECAUSE GOD HAD TRANSLATED HIM: for before his translation he had this testimony, that he pleased God. 6 But without faith *it is* impossible to please *him*: for he that cometh to God must believe that he is, and *that* he is a rewarder of them that diligently seek him.

As the author moves forward chronologically, his next example is **Enoch**, who **by faith... was translated that he should not see death.** The Old Testament witness to Enoch is quite limited. In Genesis 4 we read the sad tale of Abel and Cain, then Genesis 5 opens with a reminder that God made man in His image, but because of sin, their (Adam and Eve's) children are born in Adam's image. Genesis 5 then recounts the lineage of Adam and Eve through their son Seth, who begat Enos (5:6), who begat Cainan (5:10), who begat Mahalaleel (5:12), who begat Jared (5:15), and finally Jared begat Enoch at the age of 162 years old (5:18). We read of Enoch:

> Genesis 5:19 And Jared lived after he begat
> Enoch eight hundred years, and begat sons
> and daughters: 20 And all the days of Jared
> were nine hundred sixty and two years: and
> he died. 21 And Enoch lived sixty and five
> years, and begat Methuselah: 22 And
> Enoch walked with God after he begat
> Methuselah three hundred years, and begat
> sons and daughters: 23 And all the days of
> Enoch were three hundred sixty and five
> years: 24 And Enoch walked with God: and
> he *was* not; for God took him.

After this brief passage in Genesis 5, Enoch is not mentioned again until the genealogy of Luke 3 (see Luke 3:37), and then our present reference in Hebrews 11:5 and a short reference in Jude 14. What we are told is that "Enoch walked with God," which in the LXX is paraphrased as "Enoch pleased God," which is relied upon by the author of Hebrews when he says that Enoch **had this testimony, that he pleased God.** The account in Genesis says of Enoch, after his 365 years, that "he was not; for God took him." The Septuagint records that "he was not found, because God translated him," which again appears to be our author's source for his statement that **God had translated him.** The point is that Enoch exemplified a life of faith for over three centuries and his righteousness was vindicated in the fact that God took him without his ever experiencing death.

The author adds the commentary to his opening illustrations of Abel and Enoch that **without faith it is impossible to please** God. Each of these men pleased God because of their life of faith, and had they not lived by faith, they could not have been pleasing to God. The same is true for us today. We are blessed to have God's completed cannon, and in the United States, we are especially blessed to have access without persecution to the Holy Bible translated into English. But having the Word is not enough, and indeed, even knowing it is not enough. The life of faith is what pleases God, and that presupposes knowing the Word and rests on whether we live on the firm conviction that what God says to us is true. Thus, the one **that cometh** or draws near **to God must believe that** God **is, and that he is a rewarder of them that diligently seek him.** In this short statement, the author boils down the essentials of the requisite faith Abel and Enoch exemplified. It is not merely being a theist, but believing in the existence of the God of the Bible, which entails accepting as true what God has revealed of Himself (for us today, the Bible) "at sundry times and in divers manners [] in time past unto the fathers by the prophets, [but] hath in these last days spoken unto us by his Son." (Hebrews 1:1-2) This faith that is pleasing to God, in addition to believing in Him as He has revealed Himself, also recognizes that God rewards **them that diligently seek him.** When we think of Abel, Enoch, or even an example like Job, we are talking about men of faith that had no Bible, but they were men that diligently sought God by responding to the light of truth they had, and in response to that, God rewarded them with a good testimony and drawing near to them. The Bible says that God draws near to those who draw near to Him. (e.g., John 14:21, James 4:8)

> 7 By faith Noah, being warned of God of things not seen as yet, moved with fear, prepared an ark to the saving of his house;

by the which he condemned the world, and became heir of the righteousness which is by faith.

The next example of faith is **Noah**, who like the prior examples, is introduced with the phrase **by faith**. In Genesis 6:9, we read this testimony of Noah: "These are the generations of Noah: Noah was a just man and perfect in his generations, and Noah walked with God." Recall that Enoch also had the testimony that he "walked with God" (Genesis 5:22, 24), which the author took as indicating that his life pleased God. Noah was **warned** by **God of things not seen as yet**, which reflects the account of Genesis 6:

> Genesis 6:11 The earth also was corrupt before God, and the earth was filled with violence. 12 And God looked upon the earth, and, behold, it was corrupt; for all flesh had corrupted his way upon the earth. 13 And God said unto Noah, The end of all flesh is come before me; for the earth is filled with violence through them; and, behold, I will destroy them with the earth...17 And, behold, I, even I, do bring a flood of waters upon the earth, to destroy all flesh, wherein *is* the breath of life, from under heaven; *and* every thing that *is* in the earth shall die. 18 But with thee will I establish my covenant; and thou shalt come into the ark, thou, and thy sons, and thy wife, and thy sons' wives with thee...22 Thus did Noah; according to all that God commanded him, so did he.

The Bible strongly implies that before the Flood it never rained, but instead water misted from the ground, and so it is possible that the people of Noah's generation had never even seen rain, much less a deluge. (Genesis 2:5-6) In any event, they certainly had not seen anything like the judgment God warned Noah about in Genesis 6:13, 17, but Noah heeded God's warning of a future judgment. The author of Hebrews says Noah was **moved with fear** and thus obeyed God's directive by preparing **an ark to the saving of his house** (his family). As we reflect on the Flood narrative, we must ask why God had Noah build the ark rather than just making it for him. We read in Genesis that Noah survived 350 years after the Flood (Genesis 9:28) and died at the age of 950 years (Genesis 9:29). Noah was 500 years old when he begat Shem, Ham and Japheth (Genesis 5:32) and the flow of the text suggests that he began the ark shortly thereafter, and thus this construction project took decades. For all of that time, it stood as a picture of God's grace to the world, that in the midst of the much deserved coming judgment God also provided a way out to any who by faith would enter the ark. But as it turns out, none would enter except Noah and his family. Noah's building of this magnificent ark over the course of decades was at the same time a powerful testimony to God's grace and Noah's faith, but the Flood that followed just as God said it would made the ark Noah built serve also as a picture of condemnation of **the world** outside the ark as the waters rose and they perished. By his faith response to God's warning, Noah **became an heir of the righteousness that comes by faith.**

8 By faith Abraham, when he was called to go out into a place which he should after

receive for an inheritance, obeyed; and he went out, not knowing whither he went. 9 By faith he sojourned in the land of promise, as *in* a strange country, dwelling in tabernacles with Isaac and Jacob, the heirs with him of the same promise: 10 For he looked for a city which hath foundations, whose builder and maker *is* God.

Abraham also lived **by faith,** which we see first in his life as recorded in Genesis **when he was called to go out into a place which he should after receive for an inheritance, obeyed; and he went out, not knowing whither he went.** When we think of Abraham as a man of faith, what often first comes to mind is Genesis 15:6: "And he believed in the Lord; and he counted it to him for righteousness." But Abraham's first recorded act of faith was in Genesis 12 when God said "Go" and he went:

Genesis 12:1 Now the LORD had said unto Abram, Get thee out of thy country, and from thy kindred, and from thy father's house, unto a land that I will shew thee: 2 And I will make of thee a great nation, and I will bless thee, and make thy name great; and thou shalt be a blessing: 3 And I will bless them that bless thee, and curse him that curseth thee: and in thee shall all families of the earth be blessed. 4 So Abram departed, as the LORD had spoken unto him; and Lot went with him: and Abram *was* seventy and five years old when he departed out of Haran. 5 And Abram

took Sarai his wife, and Lot his brother's
son, and all their substance that they had
gathered, and the souls that they had
gotten in Haran; and they went forth to go
into the land of Canaan; and into the land
of Canaan they came.

As we read the account, God said, "Get thee out of thy
country...unto a land that I will shew thee." We may
think of faith in terms of God calling us to a specific
place or task and our responding, but what we often see
is God calling us in a general direction without telling us
where He is leading. When my children were young and
we were driving somewhere, they would always ask
where, and sometimes my response was, "you are on a
need to know basis and you don't need to know." God
asks us to trust Him while He drives (leads us) and we
will learn what we need to know in His timing. That is
what happened in the life of Abraham. Way back in
Genesis 12, God called Abraham (then Abram) to another
land and promised him blessings, and the text says, "so
Abram departed." The author of Hebrews comments, **he
went out, not knowing whither he went.** Abraham lived
out his faith by leaving on the basis of God's promise of
the land and blessings.

Abraham also acted **by faith** when **he sojourned in the
land of promise, as in a strange country, dwelling in
tabernacles with Isaac and Jacob, the heirs with him of
the same promise.** The point is that Abraham went to
and remained in the land even though the land would not
be his during his lifetime, but instead the promise would
be confirmed again to Isaac and Jacob, but the land
promise would not be fulfilled until centuries later when

God led Israel out of Egypt to the Promised Land. In Stephen's sermon in Acts, he explained this:

> Acts 7:1 Then said the high priest, Are these things so? 2 And he said, Men, brethren, and fathers, hearken; The God of glory appeared unto our father Abraham, when he was in Mesopotamia, before he dwelt in Charran, 3 And said unto him, Get thee out of thy country, and from thy kindred, and come into the land which I shall shew thee. 4 Then came he out of the land of the Chaldaeans, and dwelt in Charran: and from thence, when his father was dead, **he removed him into this land, wherein ye now dwell.** 5 **And he gave him none inheritance in it, no, not** *so much as* **to set his foot on: yet he promised that he would give it to him for a possession, and to his seed after him, when** *as yet* **he had no child.**

Note Stephen's explanation that I have bolded. Abraham reoriented his entire life on the basis of God's promises, most of which (like the land promise) he would never see in his lifetime. This exemplifies living in the now on the basis of God's promised future blessings, and that is what the author is encouraging his audience to do.

The author offers commentary not recorded in Genesis, namely that Abraham **looked for a city which hath foundations, whose builder and maker is God.** He will again reference the city in 11:16, 12:22 and 13:14; in 12:22 the city is called "the heavenly Jerusalem," and in Revelation 3:12, 21:2 and 21:10 it is called the "new

Jerusalem" and "the holy Jerusalem." More notes on the city are provided in the notes to 12:22. It is important to note here that just as Abraham lived out his time on earth in view of and obedience to God's Word, his focus was not on a permanent earthly destiny in the Promised Land, but a heavenly destiny. The same is true for all Christians: "For here have we no continuing city, but we seek one to come." (Hebrews 13:14)

> 11 Through faith also Sara herself received strength to conceive seed, and was delivered of a child when she was past age, because she judged him faithful who had promised. 12 Therefore sprang there even of one, and him as good as dead, *so many* as the stars of the sky in multitude, and as the sand which is by the sea shore innumerable.

Next up is Abraham's wife, who **through faith... received strength to conceive seed, and was delivered of a child when she was past age, because she judged him faithful who had promised.** This testimony is not reflected in Sarah's response that we read in Genesis:

> Genesis 18:11 Now Abraham and Sarah *were* old *and* well stricken in age; *and* it ceased to be with Sarah after the manner of women. 12 Therefore Sarah laughed within herself, saying, After I am waxed old shall I have pleasure, my lord being old also? 13 And the LORD said unto Abraham, Wherefore did Sarah laugh, saying, Shall I of a surety bear a child, which am old? 14 Is any thing too hard for

the LORD? At the time appointed I will return unto thee, according to the time of life, and Sarah shall have a son. 15 Then Sarah denied, saying, I laughed not; for she was afraid. And he said, Nay; but thou didst laugh.

We must assume the author is made aware of a subsequent change of heart that is not recorded in Genesis, a repentance (change of mind) to faith (belief) in God's promise that she would bear Abraham a son. The apostle Paul's testimony of Abraham is thus: "He staggered not at the promise of God through unbelief; but was strong in faith, giving glory to God; and being fully persuaded that, what he had promised, he was able also to perform." (Romans 4:20-21) We may suppose that in due time, Sarah's initial disbelief dissipated and she followed the example of her husband. When she believed, God honored her faith and she bore the child of promise, Isaac.

Building on the example of Sarah's faith, the author returns his focus to Abraham, commenting that **therefore sprang there even of one** man, namely Abraham, **and him as good as dead, so many as the stars of the sky in multitude, and as the sand which is by the sea shore innumerable**. The references to the stars of the sky and the sand on the seashore are references to the promises of Genesis 15:5 and 22:17. In his old age, after living many years believing God's promise of a child, Abraham fathered Isaac, and through the centuries the nation Israel **sprang** into existence with a great population.

13 These all died in faith, not having received the promises, but having seen

them afar off, and were persuaded of *them*, and embraced *them*, and confessed that they were strangers and pilgrims on the earth. 14 For they that say such things declare plainly that they seek a country. 15 And truly, if they had been mindful of that *country* from whence they came out, they might have had opportunity to have returned. 16 But now they desire a better *country*, that is, an heavenly: wherefore God is not ashamed to be called their God: for he hath prepared for them a city.

The author will continue the example of Abraham in verse 17, with these verses providing a parenthetical commentary. He says in reference to Abraham, Sarah, Isaac and Jacob, **these all died in faith, not having received the promises.** They lived their lives **in faith**, believing God's promised future blessings (e.g., Genesis 15, 17) but never receiving during their lifetimes what God promised, thus passing away **in faith.** They lived with one foot in heaven's door, **having seen** what God promised **afar off, and were persuaded of them, and embraced them.** They understood that the blessings were in the distant future, but were of such a mighty conviction of the veracity of God's promises that they oriented their lives around those promised future blessings, and while they lived in the "now," they **confessed that they were strangers and pilgrims on the earth.** When we read of their lives in Genesis, we realize they were not "aloof" or "too heavenly minded to be any earthly good." They lived productive lives but their focus was always oriented first on God's promises, and in particular, they were focused on their future heavenly destiny. They are ambassadors of heaven living on earth but not setting roots in the sense that they fully realize the temporariness of their time on earth measured against the eternity of their destiny in the heavenly city. The author writes, **For they that say such things**, that is, those who **confess** that they are only pilgrims on this planet, **declare plainly that they seek a country**, namely the heavenly city.

The patriarchs did not think of Abraham's original home in Ur of the Chaldees as home. For **if they were thinking about where they came from, they would have had an opportunity to return.** When the "going got rough" (e.g., when famine hit), they might have returned to Ur if they considered Ur their true home, but they did not. Living by faith in God's promises, **now they desire a better country, that is, an heavenly** dwelling place. These were certainly not people without failings, but they were people who maintained their conviction of God's promises and grew in their faith, and for this reason **God is not ashamed to be called their God.** Further, God **hath prepared for them a city**, the New Jerusalem. Surely the audience of Hebrews, amidst the persecution and the warning of a coming judgment on Israel, must feel like people without a home. These verses remind them they are only pilgrims and encourage them to live with their eyes on the heavenly city God has prepared.

> 17 By faith Abraham, when he was tried, offered up Isaac: and he that had received the promises offered up his only begotten *son*, 18 Of whom it was said, THAT IN ISAAC SHALL THY SEED BE CALLED: 19 Accounting that God *was* able to raise *him*

up, even from the dead; from whence also he received him in a figure.

The author now returns to the faith of the patriarchs, referencing the events of Genesis 22, when he was commanded by God to sacrifice Isaac:

<u>Genesis 22:3</u> And Abraham rose up early in the morning, and saddled his ass, and took two of his young men with him, and Isaac his son, and clave the wood for the burnt offering, and rose up, and went unto the place of which God had told him. 4 Then on the third day Abraham lifted up his eyes, and saw the place afar off. 5 And Abraham said unto his young men, Abide ye here with the ass; and I and the lad will go yonder and worship, and come again to you. 6 And Abraham took the wood of the burnt offering, and laid *it* upon Isaac his son; and he took the fire in his hand, and a knife; and they went both of them together. 7 And Isaac spake unto Abraham his father, and said, My father: and he said, Here *am* I, my son. And he said, Behold the fire and the wood: but where *is* the lamb for a burnt offering? 8 And Abraham said, My son, God will provide himself a lamb for a burnt offering: so they went both of them together. 9 And they came to the place which God had told him of; and Abraham built an altar there, and laid the wood in order, and bound Isaac his son, and laid him on the altar upon the wood.

<u>10</u> And Abraham stretched forth his hand, and took the knife to slay his son. <u>11</u> And the angel of the LORD called unto him out of heaven, and said, Abraham, Abraham: and he said, Here *am* I. <u>12</u> And he said, Lay not thine hand upon the lad, neither do thou any thing unto him: for now I know that thou fearest God, seeing thou hast not withheld thy son, thine only *son* from me. <u>13</u> And Abraham lifted up his eyes, and looked, and behold behind *him* a ram caught in a thicket by his horns: and Abraham went and took the ram, and offered him up for a burnt offering in the stead of his son. <u>14</u> And Abraham called the name of that place Jehovahjireh: as it is said *to* this day, In the mount of the LORD it shall be seen.

As we see, Abraham took Isaac to sacrifice him in obedience to God, but was so convinced of God's promise that Isaac was the promised child through whom a nation would be raised that he told those with him: "Abide ye here with the ass; and I and the lad will go yonder and worship, and come again to you." The author says that **by faith Abraham, when he was tried** or tested, **offered up Isaac: and he that had received the promises** of an innumerable lineage **offered up his only begotten son.** Of course, we know that through the angel of the Lord, Abraham was stopped after he demonstrated his faithful obedience, but the fact remains that Abraham here showed perhaps the greatest faith recorded in all the Bible. He responded to God's command in the moment based on God's promised future blessings **that in Isaac**

**shall thy seed be called** (a reference to Genesis 21:12), demonstrating the belief the author hopes to see in his audience. When Abraham took his son up the mountain to worship, he was **accounting that God was able to raise him up, even from the dead.** The author adds that **when also** Abraham **received** Isaac back alive, it was **in a figure** or as an illustration or type, by implication, of the resurrection of Jesus.

> <u>20</u> By faith Isaac blessed Jacob and Esau concerning things to come.

The next patriarchal example of faith is Isaac, who **by faith...blessed Jacob and Esau concerning things to come.** When Abraham died, not having seen the promises all fulfilled in his lifetime, God confirmed the promises to Abraham's son Isaac. (Genesis 26:1-5) Isaac's wife Rebekah was barren and he petitioned God: "Isaac intreated the LORD for his wife, because she was barren: and the LORD was intreated of him, and Rebekah his wife conceived." (Genesis 25:21) Importantly, God told Rebekah, who was pregnant with twins: "Two nations are in thy womb, and two manner of people shall be separated from thy bowels; and the one people shall be stronger than the other people; and the elder shall serve the younger." (Genesis 25:23) The first child born was named Esau "and after that came his brother out, and his hand took hold on Esau's heel; and his name was called Jacob." (Genesis 25:25-26) Culturally, Esau had the "birthright" as the eldest to the better blessing from their father Isaac, but when they were adults, Jacob purchased that birthright from Esau in return for a bowl of soup and some bread. (Genesis 25:32-34) The story reflects that Rebekah favored Jacob and Isaac favored Esau, especially because Esau was a hunter and he loved Esau's venison. (Genesis 25:28) It may be that Isaac would have tried to pass the birthright to Esau, which would have ran counter to what God had already announced to Rebekah.

When Isaac was old he asked Esau to "make me savoury meat, such as I love, and bring it to me, that I may eat; that my soul may bless thee before I die." (Genesis 27:4) Rebekah conspired with Jacob to prepare Isaac the food and trick him into believing that Jacob was Esau so that Isaac would give Jacob the blessing before Esau returned. The ruse worked and Isaac granted Jacob the greater blessing regarding the future: "Therefore God give thee of the dew of heaven, and the fatness of the earth, and plenty of corn and wine: Let people serve thee, and nations bow down to thee: be lord over they brethren, and let thy mother's sons bow down to thee: cursed be every one that curseth thee, and blessed be he that blesseth thee." (Genesis 27:28-29) But importantly, Isaac also blessed Esau regarding future things. (Genesis 27:39-40) Despite the conspiracy, the blessings Isaac pronounced were based on his firm conviction of the truth of what God said to Abraham and then later confirmed to him, and in this way, **by faith Isaac blessed Jacob and Esau concerning things to come.** The last few words here are important—**concerning things to come.** As the author proceeds in this chapter, we will see that those original promises to Abraham concerning future blessings will be handed down through the generations and continue to prompt and guide the faithful, and in this way Isaac and others after him provide moving examples to the audience of Hebrews about living now on the basis of God's Word about future blessings.

The epilogue further underscores Isaac's faith. Although Esau earlier sold his birthright for a bowl of soup, he apparently later regretted his foolishness and then purposed in his heart to kill Jacob, and when Rebekah found out she had Jacob flee to Haran. (Genesis 27:43-45) Although Isaac knew he had been tricked by Jacob, he again blessed him and sent him away for his own safety: "And God almighty bless thee, and make thee fruitful, and multiple thee, that thou mayest be a multitude of people; and give thee the blessing of Abraham, to thee, and to thy seed with thee; that thou mayest inherit the land wherein thou art a stranger, which God gave unto Abraham." (Genesis 28:3-4) Isaac no doubt knew that God had said the elder would serve the younger, and now Isaac accepted that by God's providence the greater blessing went to Jacob. We also note that God subsequently confirmed the Abrahamic blessings to Jacob as He had previously done to Isaac. (Genesis 28:12-15)

> <u>21</u> By faith Jacob, when he was a dying, blessed both the sons of Joseph; AND WORSHIPPED, *LEANING* UPON THE TOP OF HIS STAFF.

The next patriarchal example of the life of faith is **Jacob, who by faith...when he was dying, blessed both the sons of Joseph.** We must remember that Jacob ultimately would die in Egypt, obviously not receiving the land first promised to Abraham or seeing the lineage of Abraham become a nation, yet as he was nearing death he was still firmly convinced of the veracity of the promises: "...and Israel strengthened himself, and sat upon the bed. And Jacob said unto Joseph, God Almighty appeared unto me at Luz in the land of Canaan, and blessed me, and said unto me, Behold, I will make thee fruitful, and multiply thee, and I will make of thee a multitude of people; and will give this land to thy seed after thee for an everlasting possession." (Genesis 48:2-4) As the text continues, we read how Jacob took Joseph's two sons and blessed them, and in particular, as to Ephraim, said, "his seed shall become a multitude of nations." (Genesis 48:19) Jacob also assured Joseph that "God shall be with you, and bring you again unto the land of your fathers." (Genesis 48:21) After this, Jacob blessed his other sons, telling them "that which shall befall you in the last days." Thus again, we see the prophetic nature of the blessing, just as it was with Isaac's blessing of Jacob. The author then says that Joseph **worshipped** God, **leaning upon the top of his staff**, which emphasizes his faith in the midst of his weakened state as his passing drew near. Genesis 47:31 reads: "And Israel bowed himself upon the bed's head." In the LXX, on which our author relies, the text says **staff** instead of "bed's head."

> <u>22</u> By faith Joseph, when he died, made mention of the departing of the children of Israel; and gave commandment concerning his bones.

The next patriarchal example of faith is **Joseph, who by faith...when he died, made mention of the departing of the children of Israel; and gave commandment concerning his bones.** As he neared death and realized he would die in Egypt, yet believing God's Word that He would give them a land and build them into a nation, Joseph made arrangements to be reinterred in the Promised Land at such future time as God would bring them to the Land. The text in Genesis records the following:

> Genesis 50:24 And Joseph said unto his brethren, I die: and God will surely visit you, and bring you out of this land unto the land which he sware to Abraham, to Isaac, and to Jacob. 25 And Joseph took an oath of the children of Israel, saying, God will surely visit you, and ye shall carry up my bones from hence. 26 So Joseph died, *being* an hundred and ten years old: and they embalmed him, and he was put in a coffin in Egypt.

Note that when Moses led the people out of Egypt centuries later, they followed Joseph's instructions, which confirms for us how these patriarchal words and God's promises were passed down orally: "And Moses took the bones of Joseph with him: for he had straitly sworn the children of Israel, saying, God will surely visit you; and ye shall carry up my bones away hence with you." (Exodus 13:19) And in Joshua 24:32, as they finally entered the Promised Land, we find: "And the bones of Joseph, which the children of Israel brought up out of Egypt, buried they in Shechem, in a parcel of ground which Jacob bought...and it became the inheritance of the children of Joseph."

> 23 By faith Moses, when he was born, was hid three months of his parents, because they saw *he was* a proper child; and they were not afraid of the king's commandment. 24 By faith Moses, when he was come to years, refused to be called

the son of Pharaoh's daughter; 25 Choosing rather to suffer affliction with the people of God, than to enjoy the pleasures of sin for a season; 26 Esteeming the reproach of Christ greater riches than the treasures in Egypt: for he had respect unto the recompence of the reward. 27 By faith he forsook Egypt, not fearing the wrath of the king: for he endured, as seeing him who is invisible. 28 Through faith he kept the passover, and the sprinkling of blood, lest he that destroyed the firstborn should touch them.

The author now fast-forwards hundreds of years to the events preceding the Exodus and the **faith** life of Moses' **parents**, who **when he was born...hid** him **three months**. The background for Moses' parents hiding him is in Exodus:

Exodus 1:8 Now there arose up a new king over Egypt, which knew not Joseph. 9 And he said unto his people, Behold, the people of the children of Israel *are* more and mightier than we: 10 Come on, let us deal wisely with them; lest they multiply, and it come to pass, that, when there falleth out any war, they join also unto our enemies, and fight against us, and *so* get them up out of the land. 11 Therefore they did set over them taskmasters to afflict them with their burdens. And they built for Pharaoh treasure cities, Pithom and Raamses. 12 But the more they afflicted them, the more they multiplied and grew. And they were grieved because of the children of Israel.... 15 And the king of Egypt spake to the Hebrew midwives, of which the name of the one *was* Shiphrah, and the name of the other Puah: 16 And he said, When ye do the office of a midwife to the Hebrew women, and see *them* upon the stools; if it *be* a son, then ye shall kill him: but if it *be* a daughter, then she shall live. 17 But the midwives feared God, and did not as the king of Egypt commanded them, but saved the men children alive...20 Therefore God dealt well with the midwives: and the people multiplied, and waxed very mighty... 22 And Pharaoh charged all his people, saying, Every son that is born ye shall cast into the river, and every daughter ye shall save alive.

We see in Exodus 1:22 that Pharaoh pronounced a death sentence on all baby boys, but Moses' **parents...saw he was a proper child; and they were not afraid of the king's commandment**. The Greek term *asteios* is translated **proper**, and is only used here and in Acts 7:20: "In which time Moses was born, and was exceeding fair [*asteiso*]..." According to BDAG, the term "denotes good breeding, refinement." As we have already seen, the oral tradition was being passed down, and it is not improbable that Moses' parents knew what God told Abraham about the people being in Egypt for 400 years, then God judging Egypt and delivering the people from Egypt "with great substance." (Genesis 15:13-14) They started to put two and two together, much as Daniel did in seeing the coming end of the 70 years of Babylonian captivity as recorded in Daniel 9. In some way, Moses looked exceptional and his parents likely related this to the promises to Abraham, and thus defied Pharaoh's **commandment** and **hid** him **three months.** In Exodus 2:2, we read the clear connection between his being "goodly" and his mother hiding him: "And the woman conceived, and bare a son: and when she saw him that he was a goodly child, she hid him three months." Of course, any parent would look at their infant and see them as good, but more was going on here. Moses' parents were holding on to the promises given the patriarchs and saw in the infant Moses something that set them to thinking he might stand against the Pharaoh and be a deliverer. When Moses' mother placed him in the river she exercised tremendous faith.

Moses also **by faith...when he was come to years, refused to be called the son of Pharaoh's daughter.** Moses exercised **faith** in the same promises as the patriarchs and his parents, and he must have examined how his life had worked out. All Jewish people at that time, except one, served as slaves in Egypt, and many young baby boys had been murdered, yet Moses not only survived, but was raised and educated as a prince. He did not consider this mere good luck, but saw God's providential hand in it. Thus, he chose to identify with the Jewish people, **to suffer affliction with the people of God** instead of enjoying **the pleasures of sin for a season.** Moses believed he would be their deliverer and he accepted that; the **sin for a season** would have been turning his face from God's calling so that he could continue in the lap of luxury as the son of Pharaoh's daughter temporarily, yet forfeiting the permanent blessings available doing God's will.

Moses was motivated in his decision in that he esteemed **the reproach of Christ greater riches than the treasures of Egypt.** While Moses realized God would use him as a deliverer, he also realized God's Hand was on the nation Israel from whom would come the ultimate deliverer, and to identify with the coming deliverer / Messiah was more valuable than any earthly **treasures.** Moses was not so much focused on present circumstances, but instead was looking down the road to all God had for His people. Moses **had respect unto the recompense of the reward,** that is, his eyes were focused on the greater rewards available to those in Christ. And this is exactly what the author of Hebrews is encouraging his audience to see, the much more valuable rewards that Christ will give to those that endure. (Matthew 16:27)

Moses had correct insight into what was happening in his life and in the life of the nation Israel, but his methodology was incorrect, much as was Abraham's when he thought he would help God along in His promises by fathering a child through Hagar. The backdrop for what the author says next is the following from Exodus 2:

> Exodus 2:11 And it came to pass in those days, when Moses was grown, that he went out unto his brethren, and looked on their burdens: and he spied an Egyptian smiting an Hebrew, one of his brethren. 12 And he looked this way and that way, and when he saw that *there was* no man, he slew the Egyptian, and hid him in the sand. 13 And when he went out the second day, behold, two men of the Hebrews strove together:

and he said to him that did the wrong,
Wherefore smitest thou thy fellow? 14 And
he said, Who made thee a prince and a
judge over us? intendest thou to kill me, as
thou killedst the Egyptian? And Moses
feared, and said, Surely this thing is known.
15 Now when Pharaoh heard this thing, he
sought to slay Moses. But Moses fled from
the face of Pharaoh, and dwelt in the land
of Midian: and he sat down by a well.

In this scene, Moses delivers a Jewish man from an
Egyptian who is "smiting" him by killing the Egyptian,
then hiding the body. The next day he sees two Jewish
men fighting and asks them why, to which one of them
responds by referring to the prior day's murder and
saying, "Who made thee a prince and a judge over us?"
Moses then realized his secret was out, but we also see in
this response that there is not an attitude of acceptance
of Moses as their leader. Pharaoh then issued a warrant
for Moses' arrest and he fled the jurisdiction. In his
sermon in Acts 7, Stephen gives us a little more insight
into Moses' misunderstanding about how God would use
him as a deliverer:

> Acts 7:22 And Moses was learned in all the
> wisdom of the Egyptians, and was mighty
> in words and in deeds. 23 And when he was
> full forty years old, it came into his heart to
> visit his brethren the children of Israel. 24
> And seeing one *of them* suffer wrong, he
> defended *him*, and avenged him that was
> oppressed, and smote the Egyptian: 25 For
> he supposed his brethren would have

understood how that God by his hand would deliver them: but they understood not. 26 And the next day he shewed himself unto them as they strove, and would have set them at one again, saying, Sirs, ye are brethren; why do ye wrong one to another? 27 But he that did his neighbour wrong thrust him away, saying, Who made thee a ruler and a judge over us? 28 Wilt thou kill me, as thou diddest the Egyptian yesterday? 29 Then fled Moses at this saying, and was a stranger in the land of Madian, where he begat two sons.

We need to understand that Moses did not flee out of fear of Pharaoh, but because of the rejection of him by his own people. Yet in in fleeing, our author tells us, it was **by faith** that Moses **forsook Egypt, not fearing the wrath of the king** or Pharaoh, **for he endured, as seeing him who is invisible.** Moses no doubt realized that any notion of the people of Israel throwing their arms around him as their deliverer at that time was misplaced, but he retained the conviction that God would use him as their deliverer and his fleeing the jurisdiction was in pursuit of the will of the **invisible** God. He did not allow the rejection to remove his focus from God, and that is what the life of faith is about. We must keep our focus on God and the assurance of His Word, not on our circumstances. After Moses' preparation in Midian, he returned to Egypt and was accepted as Israel's deliverer. After Pharaoh continued to resist despite the plagues, God brought the final plague on the first born (Exodus 12:29-30), and by **faith** Moses **kept the passover, and the sprinkling of blood, lest he that destroyed the firstborn**

**should touch them** (Exodus 12:28). Moses trusted God's Word concerning the keeping of the first Passover, and leading the rest of the people to do the same, so as to escape the effect of the plague. This fundamental obedience again identifies a life of faith.

> 29 By faith they passed through the Red sea as by dry *land*: which the Egyptians assaying to do were drowned.

This next example of faith is tremendously important to seeing that a prominent view of the book is obviously incorrect. Many expositors take the overall message of the book as a warning to unsaved Jewish persons within the early church who were "professors" and not "possessors." This view is difficult to understand in light of the repeated affirmations that the author is speaking to a believing audience, and here we find the proverbial last nail on the coffin. Recall that in Chapter 3 the author uses as an example the generation of Israel that died in the wilderness and did not enter the Promised Land because they believed the spies who said the land could not be taken instead of the Word of God. I suggested in the notes for Chapter 3 that this ancient generation of Israel did not lose their salvation in the sense of their justification, but lost the physical blessing of entering the Promised Land, which serves as an example and warning to us that if we fail to endure in our Christian walk, we run the risk of losing out on rewards at the bema. But for the "professor not possessor" viewpoint presented by many expositors, that ancient generation proved by their lack of works—their refusal to enter the land because of the negative report from the spies—that they were never saved (justified) to begin with. They had made an empty profession of faith, and nothing more. Yet now we find ourselves past the middle of the hall of fame of faith, and who do we find in the framed picture on the wall? We find none other than the generation who died in the wilderness. They were believers who started well but did not finish well, and for the faith they demonstrated at the beginning, we find them here in the hall of fame, for **by faith they passed through the Red sea as by dry land** as they followed the lead of God's man Moses out of Egypt. The author reminds us of their faith in resisting the army of Pharaoh fast on their trail as **they passed through the Red Sea, which the Egyptians assaying to do were drowned.**

This generation who exercised such extraordinary faith as they fled Egypt would later face the prospect of entering the Promised Land and fail, for which reason they lost out on the blessed rest of the Promised Land. But they were believers, and like them, genuine Christians can start strong and somewhere along the way, perhaps in the face of affliction, fail to endure. The audience of Hebrews was facing this challenge, and so also are many Christians today. Will rough waters push you away from the Savior or draw you tighter in his arms?

> 30 By faith the walls of Jericho fell down, after they were compassed about seven days. 31 By faith the harlot Rahab perished not with them that believed not, when she had received the spies with peace.

The generation that entered the Promised Land had to take **Jericho**, a heavily fortified city with great **walls** (two walls surrounded the city and Rahab lived between the walls). Reasoning from man's perspective, we would expect to take the city with a larger army and better weapons, but listen to God's plan:

> Joshua 6:1 Now Jericho was straitly shut up because of the children of Israel: none went out, and none came in. 2 And the LORD said unto Joshua, See, I have given into thine hand Jericho, and the king thereof, *and* the mighty men of valour. 3 And ye shall compass the city, all *ye* men of war, *and* go round about the city once. Thus shalt thou do six days. 4 And seven priests shall bear before the ark seven trumpets of rams' horns: and the seventh day ye shall compass the city seven times, and the priests shall blow with the trumpets. 5 And it shall come to pass, that when they make a long *blast* with the ram's horn, *and* when ye hear the sound of the trumpet, all the people shall shout with a great shout; and the wall of the city shall fall down flat, and the people shall ascend up every man straight before him.

People living by sight would never risk their lives with this plan, but people trusting God, living **by faith**, do what God says and leave the results to Him. God honored their obedience and **the walls of Jericho fell down, after they were compassed about seven days.** In Joshua 2, we read how a Gentile woman named Rahab responded to the light she had from God (primarily what she heard that God did for Israel in taking them out of Egypt) and saved the spies, only asking that they would spare the life of her and her family:

<u>Joshua 2:8</u> And before they were laid down, she came up unto them upon the roof; 9 And she said unto the men, I know that the LORD hath given you the land, and that your terror is fallen upon us, and that all the inhabitants of the land faint because of you. 10 For we have heard how the LORD dried up the water of the Red sea for you, when ye came out of Egypt; and what ye did unto the two kings of the Amorites, that *were* on the other side Jordan, Sihon and Og, whom ye utterly destroyed. 11 And as soon as we had heard *these things*, our hearts did melt, neither did there remain any more courage in any man, because of you: for the LORD your God, he *is* God in heaven above, and in earth beneath. 12 Now therefore, I pray you, swear unto me by the LORD, since I have shewed you kindness, that ye will also shew kindness unto my father's house, and give me a true token: 13 And *that* ye will save alive my father, and my mother, and my brethren, and my sisters, and all that they have, and deliver our lives from death. 14 And the men answered her, Our life for yours, if ye utter not this our business. And it shall be, when the LORD hath given us the land, that we will deal kindly and truly with thee.

We read in Joshua 6 how the army spared her life. (Joshua 6:17, 22, 25) The author's commentary on this event is that **by faith the harlot Rahab perished not with**

**them that believed not**, that is, the rest of the inhabitants of Jericho who had the same light she had yet failed to believe; but she demonstrated the faith in her heart when **she had received the spies with peace.**

> 32 And what shall I more say? for the time would fail me to tell of Gedeon, and *of* Barak, and *of* Samson, and *of* Jephthae; *of* David also, and Samuel, and *of* the prophets: 33 Who through faith subdued kingdoms, wrought righteousness, obtained promises, stopped the mouths of lions, 34 Quenched the violence of fire, escaped the edge of the sword, out of weakness were made strong, waxed valiant in fight, turned to flight the armies of the aliens. 35 Women received their dead raised to life again: and others were tortured, not accepting deliverance; that they might obtain a better resurrection: 36 And others had trial of *cruel* mockings and scourgings, yea, moreover of bonds and imprisonment: 37 They were stoned, they were sawn asunder, were tempted, were slain with the sword: they wandered about in sheepskins and goatskins; being destitute, afflicted, tormented; 38 (Of whom the world was not worthy:) they wandered in deserts, and *in* mountains, and *in* dens and caves of the earth.

At this point the author basically says, "I can do this all day." That is, the Bible is full of examples of imperfect people who lived the life of faith, even in the face of adversity. We read, **and what shall I more say? For the time would fail me to tell of....** Of course, he will mention in a cursory manner more examples by name, and others by their trials. He would have his audience know both that they have a rich heritage of believers before them that endured and that many of them endured much more severe circumstances than the present trial of persecution (but not unto death) from nonbelieving Jews. There were the judges (the term connotes a deliverer and not a judge in modern sense) such as **Gedeon, Barak, Samson, and Jephthae,** who despite their faults exercised courage as deliverers from Israel's enemies based on their faith in God's Word to them. He also mentions King **David** and **Samuel** and **the prophets.** All of these men **through faith subdued kingdoms** (e.g., the Judges and David), **wrought righteousness** (e.g., David and Samuel), **obtained promises** of God (e.g., Gedeon, Barak, David), **stopped the mouths of lions** (e.g., prophet Daniel, Samson, David), **quenched the violence of fire** (e.g., Daniel's friends Hananiah, Mishael and Azariah), **escaped the edge of the sword** (e.g., Moses, Elijah, Elishah, Jephthah, David), **out of weakness were made strong** (e.g., Gedeon, Samson, David), **waxed valiant in fight** (e.g., Barak), and **turned to flight the arms of the aliens** (e.g., David). Of course, he is not saying that each of these men did all of these things, but collectively **through faith** they accomplished these things.

Moreover, faithful **women received their dead raised to life again.** We see this in the examples of the Widow of Zarephath (Elijah raised her son in 1 Kings 17), the Shunammite woman (Elisha raised her son in 2 Kings 4), and the Widow of Nain (Jesus raised her son in Luke

7:11-15), Mary and Martha (Jesus raised their brother in John 11). Yet **others were tortured, not accepting deliverance; that they might obtain a better resurrection.** We think, for example, of the record of Stephen in the book of Acts, who was stoned for preaching the Word of God, and in particular, the gospel of Jesus Christ, but the word **tortured** is the Greek verb *tumpanizo*, which Strong's says means "to stretch on an instrument of torture resembling a drum, and thus beat to death." Such was the death meted out to Eleazar and others in the Maccabaean times as recorded in 2 Maccabees. While God delivered some from death, others were not delivered but were willing martyrs who reckoned that the **better resurrection** in the future "world to come" or the heavenly Jerusalem was more valuable than life today. In other words, the future life of blessing for the one who endures for God is more valuable than the life available now that requires denying God. Still **others had trial of cruel mockings and scourgings, yea, moreover of bonds and imprisonment,** such as the prophet Jeremiah (see Jeremiah 20, 37-38), and John the Baptizer (see Matthew 14). Indeed, looking back on those who came before us, **they were stoned** (e.g., Zechariah in 2 Chronicles 24:21, Stephen in Acts 7, Paul in Acts 14), **they were sawn asunder** (e.g., Isaiah), **were slain with the sword** (e.g., prophets referenced in 1 Kings 19:10), **they wandered about in sheepskins and goatskins** (e.g., Elijah), **being destitute, afflicted, tormented...they wandered in deserts, and in mountains, and in dens and caves of the earth.** He notes parenthetically of these great people of faith that **the world was not worthy of them,** but we must remember while we are in the world we are to display the grace (not justice) of God to those around us.

39 And these all, having obtained a good report through faith, received not the promise: 40 God having provided some better thing for us, that they without us should not be made perfect.

The author focused significant attention on these examples from the hall of fame of faith, and the message speaks as loudly today as it did in the first century. We all face trials, although most of us in the United States, for the moment, are not persecuted like the audience of Hebrews, and certainly not tortured or martyred like those before them. The exhortation is to endure in obedience to God's Word in view of his promises. And the critical "punchline" that the author would have us understand about those before us is that they **obtained a good report through** living out lives of **faith**, yet **received not the** fulfillment of **the promise.** To be sure, some were given promises they saw fulfilled, but **the promise** in view was being a part of the world to come, dwelling in the heavenly city with God. They did not receive the fulfillment but lived their lives with their eyes on it, fully convinced that God would bring the fulfillment even if not during their earthly lives. That is what he calls on his audience to do in the first century—endure in the face of trials with your eyes on Jesus and the glorious future salvation when he returns.

Now, if all of the promises were already fulfilled, then first century Christians, and Christians today, have nothing to look forward to. As it turns out, **God...provided some better thing for us, that they** (the examples of the past) **without us should not be made perfect.** The **better thing** is the New Covenant that was the subject of prior chapters, inaugurated by Jesus Christ, the Son of God and High Priest after the order of Melchisedec. Those under the old covenant and **us**, namely the audience of Hebrews and by application the believers on this side of the cross, will share in the blessings of the New Covenant together when Christ returns and performs the promises to redeemed Israel. In his outstanding commentary on Hebrews, F.F. Bruce writes: "They and we together now enjoy unrestricted access to God through Christ, as fellow-citizens of the heavenly Jerusalem. The 'better plan' which God made embraces the better hope, the better promises, the better covenant, the better sacrifices, the better and abiding possession, and the better resurrection which is their heritage, and ours." [1]

## Closing

The apostle Paul wrote in 2 Corinthians 5:7 that "we walk by faith, not by sight." This captures the essence of what motivated the lives of faith that are extolled in Hebrews 11. To walk by sight is to walk based on the circumstances of life. A person who walks by sight has their sense of well-being determined by their circumstances, and so is motivated to manipulate their circumstances to try to achieve a sense of happiness or affluence. They cannot see beyond the circumstances, and therefore, are subject to them. The person who walks by faith makes decisions on the basis of their faith—their firm conviction of the veracity of God's Word—with an understanding of the

---

[1] F.F. Bruce, *The Epistle to the Hebrews Revised* (Grand Rapids: William B. Eerdman's Publishing Company 1990), 330.

reality around them through God's eyes and not how the world system seeks by deception to delineate what is reality. In this way, they live presently on the basis of God's truth and they live with a perspective that is not trapped within the present but instead looks beyond now to the world to come. Their decisions are made within this broader scope of understanding and their sense of well-being is not tethered to present circumstances but their eternal perspective. Even in trials, they live by the conviction that Jesus is better than anything the world has to offer because the world is passing away but the heavenly country they aspire to is forever.

## Application Points

- **MAIN PRINCIPLE:** Follow the examples of the lives of faith recorded in the Bible whose convictions about the promises of God were so intense that they reoriented their lives around God's Word, who lived productive lives in the present but always with a focus on His promises and the future heavenly city as their place of citizenship.

- Put your afflictions and trials in perspective by reflecting on those examples of lives of faith in the Bible who were tortured or violently killed for their faith.

## Discussion Questions

1. Articulate what faith is, or what it looks like, in your own words?

2. Based on verse 3, what ingredients or elements did God use to create the universe? Why does the author discuss creation in the context of the Hall of Faith?

3. Why did God reject Cain's sacrifice?

4. According to verse 10, Abraham looked for the heavenly city? How did he know about it?

5. What does it mean in verse 13 that they "died in faith, not having received the promises, but having seen them afar off, and were persuaded of them, and embraced them"?

6. Can you think of some lives of faith in the Bible that are not mentioned specifically in Hebrews 11? What did they do that demonstrated their faith?

7. Can you think of some of some lives of faith in persons you know today?

# Chapter 13

# God's Training Program

A marathon is a running event where the participants who have trained intensely run 42.195 kilometers or a little over 26 miles. For those who do not know Christ, life is a series of short sprints as one bounces from circumstance to circumstance, hoping the next is better than the last. For those who know Christ, our present time on earth takes on an entirely new dimension and we see that our lives are not a series of sprints but a marathon with the goal of finishing the race well. Most anyone can run short sprints, but it takes real endurance to finish a 26-mile race. The most difficult part of a long race is rough terrain or running on an incline, but those are the parts that improve our endurance. The Christian life will present trials where we may be tempted to stop running. And just as those who train for marathons are so highly motivated to finish the race, so also the Christian must run with the finish line ever in view, gripped by the reality of God's Word, discerning that the present world is temporary and the heavenly city lies beyond the finish line. The long-distance run is the life of endurance we are called to, and the race is a time of learning and growing, especially in the difficult parts of the race (the rough terrain), so that we arrive at the finish line as mature believers prepared to serve in the world to come. We must take life as serious business and run to win. (1 Corinthians 9:24)

## Scripture and Comments

Chapters 12 looks back at the theological foundation of the first ten chapters of Hebrews and the examples of lives of faith from the Hall of Fame of Faith in chapter 11 and then pulls it all together into the core teaching of the book of Hebrews, a critical area for all Christians. We need to catch hold of the fact that our lives now, among other things, are a time of training for the world to come. God is about the business of maturing us, especially through trials of life. In the context of how God uses such trials for our good, President Ronald Reagan wrote in a personal letter, "It takes a lot of fire and heat to make a piece of steel." It is imperative in developing a Biblical worldview that we come to understand why God permits His children to face affliction and trials of various sorts rather than giving all of us lives of ease and material comfort.

> 12:1 Wherefore seeing we also are compassed about with so great a cloud of witnesses, let us lay aside every weight, and the sin which doth so easily beset *us*, and let us run with patience the race that is set before us, 2 Looking unto Jesus the author and finisher of *our* faith; who for the joy

that was set before him endured the cross, despising the shame, and is set down at the right hand of the throne of God. 3 For consider him that endured such contradiction of sinners against himself, lest ye be wearied and faint in your minds.

These opening verses of chapter 12 make application of chapter 11 and bridge us to what the author has to say about our participation in God's training program. He begins with **wherefore** (or therefore), signaling a conclusion drawn from the preceding material. Then he continues, **seeing we also are compassed about with so great a cloud of witnesses**. He paints the picture of present believers as participants in a race and the spectators are those saints of the past that he reviewed in chapter 11. Of course, when he says his audience is **compassed about** with those heroes of chapter 11, he means they are in the considered deliberation of the minds of his audience. Those heroes of the faith are **witnesses** that the race before them can be won through obedience and steadfast endurance. Of course, in most games, the spectators watch the participants, but here the author draws the participants' attention to the spectators as examples of how to run to win. He further calls upon them to **lay aside every weight, and the sin which doth so easily beset us**. These two phrases do not mean the same thing but they are related. Obviously, a runner would never want to take on extra weight, and so he instructs them generally to **lay aside every weight**, which would include anything that distracts them from running to win and may negatively affect their endurance. These are the issues of life, and often the attractions of the world, that get our attention focused away from the

finish line and the world to come so that we slow down
or even stop running. But he also says to **lay aside...the
sin**, not just any sin, but **the sin which doth so easily
beset us.** Here he is not speaking generally, but of the
specific sin of being a quitter, failing to press forward
with steadfast endurance. For his audience in their
unique context, quitting meant a return to Judaism,
whereas for us today quitting the race may look very
different, but the negative results of quitting will still
follow (refer to all the warnings earlier in the book about
lost blessings).

Putting this together, the warning here is to be vigilant in
our lives about not taking on extra weight (distractions)
that might cause us to falter and to volitionally reject the
temptation to quit, which temptation will naturally be
more intense if we allow ourselves to take on unnecessary
weight. Thus he urges his readers, **let us run with
patience** or endurance **the race that is set before us.**
Note that the word **race** is the Greek *agon* from which
we get the English term agony. As suggested in the
introduction, the author has in mind a marathon, not a
50-yard sprint.

Having drawn his audience's attention to the examples of
faith from chapter 11, he now draws their attention to the
ultimate example of obedience and steadfast endurance,
Jesus. They are to run **looking unto Jesus the author and
finisher of our faith.** Jesus is the **author**, meaning chief or
leader of their **faith** (and ours), as well as the **finisher** or
perfecter or completer of their **faith**. In other words,
Jesus is the one who begins their **faith** and carries it
through to the end of the race. He is our example
throughout our faith life, **who for the joy that was set**

before him finished the race in obedience to the Father and endured the cross. May I say that joy is different than happiness. While happiness is an emotion associated with present circumstances, joy is rooted in our relationship to the Father, a delight in Him and in glorifying Him that supersedes temporal circumstances. We are to look to Jesus as the example, and Jesus looked beyond the cross to the joy that was set before him, namely to accomplish His will in completing the redemptive work as the greater High Priest, and then to sit at the right hand of the Father. With his eye on the prize, Jesus endured the cross, thus modeling endurance to us. To die on the cross was a humiliation, but Jesus endured...despising the shame or humiliation that the cross brought him because of the joy before him, and finished the race and is set down at the right hand of the throne of God, having completed the once for all sacrifice he made as our High Priest after the order of Melchisedec, as the author explained in chapter 9.

We are to consider or contemplate (the Greek is *analogizomai* from which we get the English "analogize") Jesus who endured such contradiction or hostility or adversity of sinners against himself. The ultimate example of obedience and endurance in Jesus should resonate with his audience. The nonbelieving Jews cried out "crucify him" (Mark 15:13). His audience is facing persecution (not yet to death) from non-believing Jews analogous to what Jesus faced. Remember that Jesus offered himself a willing sacrifice: "Thinkest thou that I cannot now pray to my Father, and he shall presently give me more than twelve legions of angels?" (Matthew 26:53). Jesus could have stopped it—he could have quit the race—but instead endured, and the author calls on his audience to follow the greatest example against the backdrop of the great **witnesses** of the past and keep their focus **unto Jesus, lest ye be wearied and faint in your minds.** The term **wearied** captures the sense of fatigued, but **faint in your minds** is not mere physical faintness. The word **minds** is the Greek *psuche*, usually rendered soul or life, and the warning is about being faint of life. In other words, he says, stay properly oriented so you do not become fatigued and depressed.

> 4 Ye have not yet resisted unto blood, striving against sin. 5 And ye have forgotten the exhortation which speaketh unto you as unto children, MY SON, DESPISE NOT THOU THE CHASTENING OF THE LORD, NOR FAINT WHEN THOU ART REBUKED OF HIM: <u>6</u> FOR WHOM THE LORD LOVETH HE CHASTENETH, AND SCOURGETH EVERY SON WHOM HE RECEIVETH.

Unlike Jesus, they had **not yet resisted unto blood** or death in their **striving against sin.** We know there were martyrs in the early church in Jerusalem like Stephen (Acts 7:59) and this suggests the churches who our author is writing to are in and around Judea but outside Jerusalem. The word translated **striving against** is the Greek *antagonizomai* (from which we get "antagonize") and one of its roots is *agon,* translated "race" in 12:1; here it means to strive or struggle against. Verses 5 and 6 get to the root of their problem. Remember, this audience had pressed forward with endurance for some time, ministering to one another and growing to relative maturity (see Hebrews 10:32-36), and then as many began faltering they had regressed back to being spiritual infants again (Hebrews 5:12-14). They had **forgotten** (disregarded or paid little attention to) **the exhortation** captured in the words of Proverbs 3:11-12 applied **unto you as unto children.** We read in Proverbs 3:11-12:

> Proverbs 3:11 My son, despise not the chastening of the LORD; neither be weary of his correction: 12 For whom the LORD loveth he correcteth; even as a father the son *in whom* he delighteth.

Note that "even as a father the son in whom he delighteth" from Proverbs 3:12 reads **and scourgeth every son whom he receiveth** taken from the Septuagint, as the author so often does in quoting the Old Testament.

Applying the wisdom of Solomon to his audience, the tone is set with **my son.** This passage is applied to God's children, and they are told to **despise not the chastening of the Lord.** The word **chastening** is the Greek *paideia* and is the key term throughout the passage. The translation as **chastening** (and in newer translations often as "discipline") is usually taken by modern readers solely in a negative or punitive sense, but the Greek term is broader. According to the lexicon BDAG, the primary meaning is "the act of providing guidance for responsible living, upbringing, training, instruction." Strong's defines the term as "tutorage, i.e. education or training; by implication, disciplinary correction." The term often has the sense of training a child and is related to the Greek noun *paidion* (used, for example, in Luke 2:21 and Hebrews 11:23), which means according to BDAG "a child, normally below the age of puberty." Outside our passage in Hebrews 12, the term is used only two other places in the New Testament, but both are very informative of the fuller sense of this critical word:

> Ephesians 6:4 And, ye fathers, provoke not your children to wrath: but bring them up in the **nurture** and admonition of the Lord.

> 2 Timothy 3:16 All scripture *is* given by inspiration of God, and *is* profitable for doctrine, for reproof, for correction, for **instruction** in righteousness.

We see that in Ephesians 6:4 the term translated "chastise" (or discipline in many newer translation) in Hebrews 12 is translated "nurture," and in 2 Timothy 3:16 it is translated "instruction" (and in some newer translations, "training"). There has been no indication from the context of Hebrews up to this point that his audience is under divine discipline in the sense of punitive discipline yet. They have been warned of the dangers of falling back into Judaism, but the author nowhere says God is presently punishing them, or specifically using non-believing Jewish persecutors as tools of judgment. It is imperative that Hebrews 12 not be pulled from its moorings. And to properly exegete the verses that follow, it is important to read the term as "discipline" (the full orb of discipline in the sense of molding a child's behavior and not mere negative consequences although that is included) or "training" or "training program." As we will see, the primary emphasis of the training here in Hebrews, consistent with their present experience, is training through affliction or trials. This is not to say that God does not negatively discipline believers, but simply that the term *paideia* and the context of everything in the book up to this point requires a broader understanding of "chastisement" or "discipline" than simply being taken to the woodshed.

Turning back to the text at hand, the author says, applying the words of Solomon to the Hebrews as God's children (and by application to us), **My son, despise not thou the** training program **of the Lord, nor faint when thou are rebuked** (convicted of a fault) **of him.** Part of God's training program for His children includes being rebuked or convicted of faults, and no one enjoys a rebuke even if it is for their own good, so he warns his audience not to **despise** God's training. Continuing from Proverbs 3, he says, **for whom he loveth he** trains, **and scourgeth every son whom he receiveth.** The term **scourgeth** is the Greek *mastigoo,* which according to BDAG means "to beat with a whip or lash," or when used figuratively, "to punish with discipline in mind." This captures the side of discipline or training that entails negative consequences, and the point is that God trains those **whom he loveth,** i.e., His children, and when necessary takes them to the woodshed. Sometimes there is no other way to get through to us.

Keeping in mind the context of the book, the author wants his audience to understand that their present affliction brought about by their Jewish persecutors is used of God as part of their training. God is not punishing them, but He is using this period of affliction as part of His discipline or training of them as children to mold who they are. People often ask why bad things happen to good people. God is sovereign, meaning that nothing comes to pass that is not either caused by or permitted by God. While we cannot always know why God permits a particular event or circumstance to arise, we know that God uses the trials of life to train His children. That is what good parents do; they do not create a fairy tale existence for their children so that they never face any challenges, but instead they permit their children at the right time to learn and grow through facing the sorts of challenges life brings. Bad things happen to believers and non-believers because we live in a fallen world, but as God's children, all of our lives are a training ground for the "world to come" of which the author referenced earlier, and it seems that times of running through the rough terrain, or running uphill, are especially used by God to train us in endurance (not quitting). It helps to see how James teaches this same principle of training through trials:

> James 1:2 My brethren, count it all joy when ye fall into divers temptations; 3 Knowing *this*, that the trying of your faith worketh patience. 4 But let patience have *her* perfect work, that ye may be perfect and entire, wanting nothing.

The reason James tells his readers to "count it all joy" when they face trials is because of how God uses their trials to grow them. Note the similarities to what the author of Hebrews teaches throughout the book. James wrote, "knowing...that the trying" or testing "of your faith worketh patience" or endurance. James does not mean that the trial itself grows us, but that a proper response to a trial grows us by producing steadfast endurance, which is the same trait the author of Hebrews is addressing throughout the book. James would continue and explain God's provision of wisdom for the trials (James 1:5), the importance of laying aside sin and living out the Word (James 1:21-22), and the result of endurance, the crown of life (James 1:12). Note as well how the apostle Paul taught the same principle in Romans:

> Romans 5:1 Therefore being justified by faith, we have peace with God through our Lord Jesus Christ: 2 By whom also we have access by faith into this grace wherein we stand, and rejoice in hope of the glory of God. 3 And not only *so*, but we glory in tribulations also: knowing that tribulation worketh patience; 4 And patience, experience; and experience, hope: 5 And hope maketh not ashamed; because the love of God is shed abroad in our hearts by the Holy Ghost which is given unto us.

A proper response to trials in God's training program produces a life that reflects endurance, and endurance is what leads to being "perfect and entire, wanting nothing," that is, to completion or maturity. Or in Paul's words, a proper response to tribulation develops in us "patience" or endurance, which develops in us "experience" (or proven character), which then produces "hope". When we relate this process to what the author of Hebrews described in Hebrews 5:11-14 about how the spiritual maturing process involves learning to skillfully apply the meat of God's Word to life, we see that God allows us to experience trials as part of our training, and our response to the training is to be based on a skillful use of the Word of God to discern good and evil.

> 7 If ye endure chastening, God dealeth with you as with sons; for what son is he

whom the father chasteneth not? <u>8</u> But if ye be without chastisement, whereof all are partakers, then are ye bastards, and not sons. <u>9</u> Furthermore we have had fathers of our flesh which corrected *us*, and we gave *them* reverence: shall we not much rather be in subjection unto the Father of spirits, and live? <u>10</u> For they verily for a few days chastened *us* after their own pleasure; but he for *our* profit, that *we* might be partakers of his holiness. <u>11</u> Now no chastening for the present seemeth to be joyous, but grievous: nevertheless afterward it yieldeth the peaceable fruit of righteousness unto them which are exercised thereby.

Now, the author will explain the purpose of God's training program, but first he assures them that their being in the training program, even if it gets tough, is a good thing because it assures them they are children. He says, **if ye endure** training, **God dealeth with you as with sons**, meaning as with those who have a place of privilege and inheritance. He then asks rhetorically, **for what son is he whom the father** trains **not?** Relating to how our earthly fathers discipline or train us, everyone understands that if there is no training at all, that would generally suggests there is no father / child relationship. The author now casts the issue as a hypothetical by saying **if ye be without** training, but before finishing the hypothetical he pauses to ensure them it is a hypothetical because they **are all partakers** of God's training and by implication are all God's children, i.e., believers. The hypothetical is **if ye be without** training, **then ye are**

**bastards, and not sons.** In other words, if you are not in God's training program, then you are not His children with all the rights and privileges thereto, but illegitimate children with no rights, privilege or inheritance, and in short, unsaved. So again, affliction in the life of a believer is not a bad thing from the standpoint of God's growth program for us. Those who teach a so-called "prosperity gospel" where faith leads to material and physical blessings and an absence of trials are describing a Christian life that the Bible describes as the lives of **bastards, and not sons.**

Recognizing that as God's children we are in His training program, and that trials are a central part of the program, our response to the trials, according to James, should be "joy" because God is working in our lives to grow us up. We need to have a perspective on trials that recognizes what God is doing, is grateful to God for His work in our lives, and we need to press forward in endurance. The author relates the program to how earthly fathers train children, for **we have had** earthly **fathers that corrected us, and we gave them reverence**, and for this reason God is entitled to more. He asks rhetorically, **shall we not much rather be in subjection unto the Father of spirits, and live?** Earthly parents train their physical offspring, but the **Father of spirits**—the God who made us His spiritual children (or spirits) through the sacrifice of the Son—deserves not just **reverence** but our **subjection** to His training. Earthly fathers for **a few days** (a short time) train their children **after their own pleasure**, but in contrast, God trains us **for our profit, that we might be partakers of his holiness.** The goal of God's training is holiness. (see also Romans 12:1; 2 Corinthians 3:18; Ephesians 2:21; Colossians 1:22; 1 Peter 1:16) There are a lot of other things some would insert in the place of holiness, but it does not say that the goal is happiness, health, wealth, affluence, etc., but holiness, that very attribute of God wherein He is a cut above and beyond all that is earthly. The goal of the race is that we would finish looking like Him, not the person we were at the start of the race.

Obviously, when the training is through affliction, it is tough. So he says **now... for the present**, that is, during the training, the **discipline** or training is not **joyous... but grievous** or painful. Yet **afterward**, after enduring through the training, **it yieldeth the peaceable fruit of righteousness unto them which are exercised thereby.** The author indicated before that God uses the training so that we can partake in His holiness. This will be reflected outwardly in **the peaceable fruit of righteousness.** We see many examples of this in the Scripture. Job, for instance, was called by God "perfect and upright," which in functional terms looked like fearing God and eschewing evil. (Job 1:1) The notion of fearing God is more than reverential awe, but carries the idea of a person who recognizes God's authority over them, their obligations to God, and a healthy understanding of the consequences of disobedience. God referred to Noah as "righteous" (Genesis 7:1), a man who "found grace in the eyes of the Lord" (Genesis 6:8) and "a just man and perfect in his generations...Noah walked with God." (Genesis 6:9).

The training program uses affliction to make us holy and righteous, but merely facing trials is not enough, for we must be **exercised** by those trials. The term **exercised** is the Greek *gumnazo* from which we get the English "gymnasium" and that we saw in Hebrews 5:14: "But strong meat belongeth to them that are of full age, even those who by reason of use have their senses **exercised** to discern both good and evil." The term *gumnazo* means vigorous exercise, which here fits the race metaphor in the background of the present passage. In Hebrews 5:10 ff, the author encourages his audience to press forward from spiritual infancy to spiritual maturity, which involves leaving behind a diet of milk and moving to a diet on the meat of the Word and so training their senses by skillful use of the Word as to properly interpret (use their senses) life, and this pictures a growth process that God expects every believer to be engaged in. Here in Hebrews 12, the same growth process is under consideration, and the author calls it "discipline" or "training", with a primary focus of training through affliction, and he says that if they are **exercised** by the program it will produce the **peaceable fruit of righteousness** in their lives, i.e., the proven character Paul spoke of in Romans 5:4. It is those who are engaged in the program, applying the Word skillfully, obediently, and pressing forward in steadfast endurance, who grow toward maturity, holiness, and bear the fruit of righteousness.

> 12 Wherefore lift up the hands which hang down, and the feeble knees; 13 And make straight paths for your feet, lest that which is lame be turned out of the way; but let it rather be healed. 14 Follow peace with all *men*, and holiness, without which no man shall see the Lord: 15 Looking diligently lest any man fail of the grace of God; lest any root of bitterness springing up trouble

*you*, and thereby many be defiled; <u>16</u> Lest there *be* any fornicator, or profane person, as Esau, who for one morsel of meat sold his birthright. <u>17</u> For ye know how that afterward, when he would have inherited the blessing, he was rejected: for he found no place of repentance, though he sought it carefully with tears.

The author begins with **wherefore** or therefore to introduce the application points to be drawn for his audience's participation in the training program with one another. We must remember that Christians are not islands unto themselves. Americans pride themselves on independence and self-sufficiency, but God wants believers to form a community and look to each other's spiritual well-being and growth. They must help one another, and especially help those that are weaker or struggling. Thus, continuing the race metaphor, he says they should **lift up the hands which hang down** (strengthen the hands), **and the feeble knees** (reinvigorate the knees), **and make straight paths for your feet** (so they can move forward), **lest that which is lame be turned out of the way** (not let the feet get out of joint); **but let it rather be healed.** We need to help each other along in the race. Further, they (and we) should **follow peace with all men.**

In addition to our obligations to one another, we should **follow...holiness** or sanctification. The pursuit of personal **holiness** is necessary for a person to **see the Lord.** But what is it to **see the Lord?** After Job conversed with God, he said, "I have heard of thee by the hearing of the ear" (a reference to the oral traditions passed down to him), but "now mine eye seeth thee." (Job 42:5) While Job did see a theophany as God spoke to him "out of the whirlwind" (Job 39:1), his point was not the visual sight of the theophany but his increased understanding and perception of who God is after God interrogated him. Thus he added, "Wherefore I abhor myself, and repent in dust and ashes." (Job 42:6) Job's greater understanding of God, described in terms of seeing Him, brought a greater realization of his own sinfulness. The same thought seems to be in view in Matthew 5:8 when Jesus said, "Blessed are the pure in heart: for they shall see God", and again in John 14:21, when Jesus said, "He that hath my commandments, and keepeth them, he it is that loveth me: and he that loveth me shall be loved of my Father, and I will love him, and will manifest myself to him." In 1 John 3:6, we read that "whoever sinneth hath not seen him..." Truly, as we draw near to God, He draws near to us. Thus we may say that running to win results in a life characterized by righteousness and coming to see God—to know Him better. I would note here that an alternative understanding of this clause that still fits the context is that he is referencing others seeing God in our lives as they see **peace** and **holiness** in us.

Paul wrote to the Corinthians that "there hath no temptation taken you but such as is common to man: but God is faithful, who will not suffer you to be tempted above that ye are able; but will with the temptation also make a way to escape, that ye may be able to bear it." (1 Corinthians 10:13) And the author of Hebrews earlier stated, "Let us therefore come boldly unto the throne of grace, that we may obtain mercy, and find grace to help in time of need." (Hebrews 4:16) God is not going to place on us more than we can bear, but by His grace enablement, we can bear a great deal more than we know, but we must seek His grace and endure. The author implores his audience to look **diligently lest any man fail of the grace of God**. He is not talking about a loss of salvation, but of someone quitting the race rather than laying hold of the available grace enablement for the moment. All of us engaged in the race need to look around us and make sure our brothers and sisters are not getting beat down to the point of quitting and in that sense falling short **of the grace of** God. The author also implores them to watch **diligently...lest any root of bitterness springing up trouble you, and thereby many be defiled**. A poisonous root produces a poisonous fruit, and just as quitting will take us out of the race, the fruit of **bitterness** has the ability to **defile** those that partake of it, which is just the sort of heavy weight to overburden them and take them out of the race. It takes time and a negative sort of care (watering) for **bitterness** to grow, bear fruit, and defile others. Bitter people spew their poison on others, causing others to be angry, division and strife. More than anything this will come out in words. As James tells us, the tongue is like that small spark that burns down the whole forest.

The author also warns them to be **looking diligently...lest there be any fornicator or profane person**. The term **fornicator** is the Greek *pornos* from which we get the English term porn, and according to lexicon BDAG the word means "one who practices sexual immorality." This broad concept would include all sexual activity outside of God's boundary for physical intimacy, which is exclusively within a marriage between a man and a woman. This is mentioned here because it is such a consuming sin that draws entirely on the flesh and distracts us from spiritual matters as a sort of snare, and in particular, cuts us out of the race. But the author also warns about the **profane** or immoral **person** and uses **Esau** as the example, **who for one morsel of meat sold his birthright.** It will be helpful to read the sad report directly from Genesis 25:

> Genesis 25:29 And Jacob sod pottage: and Esau came from the field, and he *was* faint: 30 And Esau said to Jacob, Feed me, I pray thee, with that same red *pottage*; for I *am* faint: therefore was his name called Edom. 31 And Jacob said, Sell me this day thy birthright. 32 And Esau said, Behold, I *am* at the point to die: and what profit shall this birthright do to me? 33 And Jacob said, Swear to me this day; and he sware unto him: and he sold his birthright unto Jacob. 34 Then Jacob gave Esau bread and pottage of lentiles; and he did eat and drink, and rose up, and went his way: thus Esau despised *his* birthright.

As the elder brother, Esau culturally had the birthright, although God had said the line of blessing would pass through Jacob. Esau came in hungry one day and traded the birthright to Jacob for a bowl of soup, reasoning, "Behold, I am at the point to die," a clear hyperbole, and thus "what profit shall this birthright do unto me?" This was as lame an excuse for his conduct as we can imagine. What Esau gave up was the promised blessings of God, and he did so for immediate fleshly gratification, a mere bowl of soup. Could Esau not have made his own soup? Of course, but the birthright meant nothing to him in that moment, "thus Esau despised his birthright." Of course, he regretted the decision later yet **found no place of repentance**. Remember that repentance means a change of thinking or change of mind, and the point is that Esau was unable to get his father Isaac to change his mind and give him the blessing after Jacob tricked Isaac, even **though** Esau **sought it** (sought to get Isaac to change his mind) **carefully with tears**. Sin always promises so much and in the end delivers so little, and eventually there is a time of regret when the sinner realizes the larger import of what he gave up in return for immediate gratification. But our decisions have consequences despite the tears, as did Esau's poor choice.

While we tend to think of immoral people in terms of sexual sins, the Bible says immoral or profane people are those who forfeit God's blessings in favor of immediate physical gratification. The heart attitude of an immoral person (and this group includes fornicators) cares nothing for running the race with steadfast endurance in view of God's promises of future blessings, but instead will readily fall out of the race to get gratification now. In God's training program, he uses the horizontal where we live to train us. Some people look to manipulate the horizontal as they seek satisfaction and completion in persons, possessions, and present circumstances (the three P's). They live their lives oriented to the flesh in their heart attitude, and thus the expression of their thinking is a life lived after the flesh, and their experience is death (no sense of seeing God or having an intimate relationship with God):

> Romans 8:4 That the righteousness of the
> law might be fulfilled in us, who walk not
> after the flesh, but after the Spirit. 5 For
> they that are after the flesh do mind the
> things of the flesh; but they that are after
> the Spirit the things of the Spirit. 6 For to
> be carnally minded *is* death; but to be
> spiritually minded *is* life and peace.

In contrast to these profane persons, those engaged in
the race are those Paul describes as walking after the
Spirit, those whose minds (renewed minds per Romans
12:2) are focused on the things of God rather than fleshly
matters, and thus whose lives reflect living after the Spirit
and whose experience is described as "life and peace."
Thus, while the training program utilizes the horizontal,
the growing up is in the vertical in our relationship with
God, and those around us in the horizontal should see it
in our changed lives.

### Closing

In an April 21, 2014 story, the Washington Post reported
that a marathon runner fell just short of the 26-mile
mark. First one, and then two other runners, stopped to
help him finish, propping his arms on their shoulders.
Then two more stopped to help and the four runners
carried him to the finish line to the loud cheers of the
crowd. May I say that while the Christian life is a
marathon, it is not a competitive event. We run
alongside our fellow Christian brethren and we need to
minister to one another along the way. We are not in
this training program alone, and our eyes are on the

finish line not for ourselves only but those around us. Sometimes helping someone along is as simple as a note of encouragement or a willingness to listen. It almost always involves prayer for their spiritual well-being and growth. There may be a time when you need to carry someone or be carried. But there will never be a time when you need to trip another runner or trample a fallen runner.

## Application Points

- **MAIN PRINCIPLE:** The present life serves as God's training program for our experience in the world to come, and our response to trials, big and small, are a primary means of God teaching us endurance and growing us to maturity so that we will reflect His holiness.

- While you cannot make someone else grow, you can make it your business to be concerned for the growth and well-being of those within your sphere of influence and do what you can by way of prayer, encouragement, love, bearing burdens, etc., to help them along.

## Discussion Questions

1. What is the meaning the word translated in Hebrews 12 as chastisement or discipline?

2. How is it that God uses the trials of life to grow us?

3. What should be our perspective on trials and how as a believer should we deal with trials? In other words, what does endurance really look like?

4. Is endurance just a matter of being a "stronger" person?

5. Does the fact that a person encounters great difficulties in life guarantee that they will grow to maturity?

6. What are some examples of how we can help others not to "fail of the grace of God" (12:15)?

# Chapter 14

# Living Between the Bookends

When you are in a shopping mall looking for a particular store, the mall map invariably has a triangle that says, "you are here." The Bible is not just the revelation of who God is, but of who we are, and speaks to believers and non-believers and says, "this is who you are and this is where you are." Believers sojourn here, but our sphere of existence is "in Christ," and in the world to come our position in Christ will be our eternal experience.

For Paul, "in Christ" is the sphere in which God is working to reconcile the world to Himself: "To wit, that God was in Christ, reconciling the world unto himself, not imputing their trespasses unto them..." (2 Corinthians 5:19) The Father's goal is "that in the dispensation of the fullness of times he might gather together in one all things in Christ, both which are in heaven, and which are on earth; even in him." (Ephesians 1:10) Paul confirms that "salvation ... is in Christ Jesus" (2 Timothy 2:10), for it is in this sphere that we find "grace" (2 Timothy 2:1) and the "love of God" (Romans 8:39). For it is "in him" that Paul says we "walk," are "rooted and built up," and made "complete." (Colossians 2:6-10) As Paul preaches in his Mars Hill sermon, "For in him we live, and move, and have our being...." (Acts 17:28) In Ephesians 1 and 2, Paul emphasizes the spiritual benefits to those "in Christ." Paul says there that the Father "blessed us with all spiritual blessings in heavenly places in Christ." Paul recognizes that Christ is presently before the Father in heaven: "Which he wrought in Christ, when he raised him from the dead, and set him at his own right hand in the heavenly places." (Ephesians 1:20) And from Paul's perspective, we are before the Father and have all spiritual blessings at this moment if we are in Christ: "And hath raised us up together, and made us sit together in heavenly places in Christ Jesus." (Ephesians 2:6) These spiritual blessings are often referred to as positional truths or positional blessings because they are ascribed to us by virtue of our position in Christ. The author of Hebrews takes it one step further and puts our *you are here 'triangle'* just before the heavenly Jerusalem and he says, as one who fears the Lord, grasp hold of where you are and obey God's Word.

## Scripture and Comments

Having set down the theological foundation of the first ten chapters of the book and the real-life examples of lives of faith from chapter 11 and put their present experience in the context of God's training program, our author now connects the horizontal and the vertical. He shows us how God uses our time here to train us but even now our location is in Jesus Christ and that places us in heaven and not on earth. Knowing where we are should affect how we live.

> 12:18 For ye are not come unto the mount that might be touched, and that burned with fire, nor unto blackness, and darkness, and tempest, 19 And the sound of a trumpet, and the voice of words; which *voice* they that heard intreated that the word should not be spoken to them any more: 20 (For they could not endure that which was commanded, AND IF SO MUCH AS A BEAST TOUCH THE MOUNTAIN, IT SHALL BE STONED, OR THRUST THROUGH WITH A DART: 21 And so terrible was the sight, *that* Moses said, I EXCEEDINGLY FEAR AND QUAKE:)

Now, a comparison is made between the old order and the new by way of the imagery associated with the old order and the new heavenly Jerusalem. He means by this to encourage endurance and divert them from a return to Judaism, much as the apostle Paul did in 2 Corinthians 3:2-18 where the old order was characterized as a ministry of condemnation. He begins by describing where they are not, **for ye are not come unto the mount that might be touched, and that burned with fire, nor unto blackness, and darkness, and tempest.** What is in view is Israel's experience at Mount Sinai, which they were forbidden to touch. We find this background material in Exodus 19:12-25:

> Exodus 19:12 And thou shalt set bounds unto the people round about, saying, Take heed to yourselves, *that ye* go *not* up into

284

the mount, or touch the border of it: whosoever toucheth the mount shall be surely put to death: 13 There shall not an hand touch it, but he shall surely be stoned, or shot through; whether *it be* beast or man, it shall not live: when the trumpet soundeth long, they shall come up to the mount. 14 And Moses went down from the mount unto the people, and sanctified the people; and they washed their clothes. 15 And he said unto the people, Be ready against the third day: come not at *your* wives. 16 And it came to pass on the third day in the morning, that there were thunders and lightnings, and a thick cloud upon the mount, and the voice of the trumpet exceeding loud; so that all the people that *was* in the camp trembled. 17 And Moses brought forth the people out of the camp to meet with God; and they stood at the nether part of the mount. 18 And mount Sinai was altogether on a smoke, because the LORD descended upon it in fire: and the smoke thereof ascended as the smoke of a furnace, and the whole mount quaked greatly. 19 And when the voice of the trumpet sounded long, and waxed louder and louder, Moses spake, and God answered him by a voice. 20 And the LORD came down upon mount Sinai, on the top of the mount: and the LORD called Moses *up* to the top of the mount; and Moses went up. 21 And the

> LORD said unto Moses, Go down, charge the people, lest they break through unto the LORD to gaze, and many of them perish. 22 And let the priests also, which come near to the LORD, sanctify themselves, lest the LORD break forth upon them. 23 And Moses said unto the LORD, The people cannot come up to mount Sinai: for thou chargedst us, saying, Set bounds about the mount, and sanctify it. 24 And the LORD said unto him, Away, get thee down, and thou shalt come up, thou, and Aaron with thee: but let not the priests and the people break through to come up unto the LORD, lest he break forth upon them. 25 So Moses went down unto the people, and spake unto them.

In view of this background, it is apparent that the **mount that might be touched** is Mount Sinai. As Exodus 19 makes clear, to touch it would result in death, and the focus here is on the physical reality on this earth of Mount Sinai, and back then in Exodus 19, it **burned with fire** (Exodus 19:18 "the LORD descended upon it in fire"), was a place of **blackness** under the cloud (Exodus 19:16-18), and **tempest** or storm (Exodus 19:16 "there were thunders and lightnings"). The physical imagery combined with the threat of death for touching the mountain paints a frightening picture.

He continues the description of the historical experience at Mount Sinai that *is not* his audience's experience. There, Israel heard **the sound of a trumpet** (Exodus 19:16, 19 and 20:18) and **the voice of** the **words** of God (Exodus

19:19; also Deuteronomy 4:12). So frightening was the experience that **they that heard entreated that the word should not be spoken to them any more.** They begged that God would *not* speak to them because of the sheer terror of the experience (recall that Job did not have much to say when God spoke to him in the closing chapters of the book). They preferred that God speak to them only through Moses: "And they said unto Moses, Speak thou with us, and we will hear; but let not God speak with us, lest we die." (Exodus 20:19) The author says, in reference to the warning that any living thing that touched the mountain would die, **they could not endure that which was commanded.** This fear makes sense in view of the warning taken from Exodus 19:12-13: **And if so much as a beast touch the mountain, it shall be stoned, or thrust through with a dart.** Indeed, so fearful was the experience that even **Moses said,** as recorded in Deuteronomy 9:19, **I exceedingly fear and quake.**

> 22 But ye are come unto mount Sion, and unto the city of the living God, the heavenly Jerusalem, and to an innumerable company of angels, 23 To the general assembly and church of the firstborn, which are written in heaven, and to God the Judge of all, and to the spirits of just men made perfect, 24 And to Jesus the mediator of the new covenant, and to the blood of sprinkling, that speaketh better things than *that of* Abel.

Having described where his audience *is not* (**for ye are not**), he now describes where *they are* (**but ye are**), namely the heavenly Jerusalem. Again, he is speaking in terms of positional truth, which will in the future be experienced truth. The reality of this hope allows us to live with one foot in heaven's door. As addressed in the notes for chapter 10, Hebrews has become a stronghold for arguments that Christians can lose or throw away their justification, but the book is actually a stronghold for the orthodox position that Christians can do nothing to lose, forfeit or discard their justification, and the passage at hand is another proof text for this. In chapter 10, the author spoke of their final "perfection" (the completion of all of their salvation) in the past tense. (Hebrews 10:14) Thus, positionally, our perfection is past completed action, and in the passage at hand, our future eternal destiny in the heavenly city is positionally a present reality. Since the future is both past and now, we are guaranteed to experience it, which leaves no room for the notion of losing salvation in the now and never making it to the heavenly Jerusalem in the future since we are already positionally there.

Our author writes that in contrast to the Israel of old that came to Mount Sinai, where the old order was inaugurated in a frightening display of God's power (to teach them of His holiness), **ye are come unto mount Sion, and unto the city of the living God, the heavenly Jerusalem**. First note that we have **ye are come**, i.e., in the present tense. The Greek is actually in the perfect tense, which means past completed action with continuing consequences. Modern translation will generally translate this as "you have come." His audience (past tense) came **unto Mount Sion** with the continuing consequence of being there (present tense) positionally at the moment.

There is a real Mount Sion in Jerusalem, and often in the Bible **Sion** or Zion is used figuratively for the entire city of Jerusalem (e.g., 1 Kings 8:1, Psalm 102:21), but here **mount Sion** is used figuratively of the **heavenly Jerusalem.** He speaks of the city Abraham (11:10) looked for: "For he looked for a city which hath foundations, whose builder and maker is God." Indeed, many of the saints of old lived (11:16) with this city in view: "But now they desire a better country, that is, an heavenly: wherefore God is not ashamed to be called their God: for he hath prepared for them a city." The heavenly city is the future destiny of Christians as Jesus said in John 14:2-3: "In my Father's house are many mansions: if it were not so, I would have told you. I go to prepare a place for you. And if I go and prepare a place for you, I will come again, and receive you unto myself; that where I am, there you may be also." The term *mansions* is transliterated from the Latin translation of the New Testament, but the Greek term simply means dwelling places. Borrowing from the imagery of Jewish weddings, Jesus as the groom promised to go to his father's home and prepare dwelling places for his bride (the Church). After he completes the construction of the dwellings places and when it is time for the wedding ceremony, he will return to get his bride and take her to the dwelling places. Jesus will return to get his bride in the event often referred to as the Rapture. The ceremony is recorded in Revelation 19, and the heavenly city is described in detail in Revelation 21-22. Our author will say later to his audience and by application to us, "For here we have no continuing city, but we seek one to come." (Hebrews 13:14) Much could be said about the city, but that goes beyond the immediate subject matter here. I would, however, encourage the reader to review Revelation 19-22 and compare the features of the city to the features in the Garden of Genesis 1-3, for these are the bookends of the Bible.

The author now focuses on who is in the heavenly city. First, there is **an innumerable company of angels.** Second, there is **the general assembly and church of the firstborn.** Jesus is referred to by Paul as "the firstborn among many brethren" (Romans 8:29), the "firstborn of every creature" (Colossians 1:15), and "the firstborn from the dead" (Colossians 1:18). The point here is that in addition to the angels, the church Jesus promised to build and promised in John 14:2-3 would have a place in the New Jerusalem, will in fact be there. He confirms that they **are written** or enrolled **in heaven.** Third, there will be **God the Judge of all.** Fourth, there will be **the spirits of just men made perfect.** This is a reference to the Old Testament saints. The author previously made the point (9:15) that Jesus' sacrifice provided redemption for those under the old covenant or Mosaic Covenant. The reference here at least includes those, but the generality of the language more likely includes all saints prior to the **church of the firstborn.** Fourth, there will be **Jesus the mediator of the new covenant.** One may ask, who is not in the city? The description in Revelation 21-22 says that after the first 1,000 years of Jesus' kingdom, the new heavens and new earth are created. The heavenly city is suspended in the sky above the new earth and serves as the sole light source for the new earth. Revelation 21:24 says: "And the nations of them which are saved shall walk in the light of it: and the kings of the earth do bring their glory and honour into it." These are apparently references to the nations during the first 1,000 years (sometimes called the Millennial Kingdom) who do not join in Satan's final rebellion near the end of that 1,000 years, but instead are delivered through the final judgment.

The New Covenant was inaugurated by Jesus' sacrifice, and he provided his own blood on the mercy seat in the heavenly tabernacle. The reference to **the blood of sprinkling, that speaketh better things than that of Abel** is to Jesus' blood. Abel was the first human to offer an animal blood sacrifice, but Jesus' blood was better because it alone could sufficiently pay our sin penalty. The point here is simply that the blood remains on the mercy seat as a permanent feature of what is to come.

> <u>25</u> See that ye refuse not him that speaketh. For if they escaped not who refused him that spake on earth, much more *shall not* we *escape*, if we turn away from him that *speaketh* from heaven: <u>26</u> Whose voice then shook the earth: but now he hath promised, saying, YET ONCE MORE I SHAKE NOT THE EARTH ONLY, BUT ALSO HEAVEN. <u>27</u> And this *word,* Yet once more, signifieth the removing of those things that are shaken, as of things that are made, that those things which cannot be shaken may remain. <u>28</u> Wherefore we receiving a kingdom which cannot be moved, let us have grace, whereby we may serve God acceptably with reverence and godly fear: <u>29</u> For our God *is* a consuming fire.

In view of who is in the heavenly city and the redemption made available by Jesus' blood, his audience would be insane to want to re-identify with Judaism. So he makes application, **see that ye refuse not** God **that speaketh.** The comparison is between the consequences of refusing God's word at Mount Sinai with refusing God's Word at Mount Sion. **For if they** who associated with the Word of God spoken at Mount Sinai **escaped not who refused** God **that spake on earth** (from the physical Mount Sinai), **much more shall not we escape, if we turn away from** God **that speaketh from heaven** (i.e., the heavenly city). But escape from what? When God spoke back on Mount Sinai, his **voice then shook the earth** (see Exodus 19:18), **but now** God **hath promised** in Haggai 2:6: **Yet once more I shake not the earth only, but also heaven.** Whereas in Exodus 19 God shook the mountain on earth, according to Haggai 2:6, in the future the entire earth will be shaken, a reference to the future judgments of the Day of the Lord that will precede the implementation of the Kingdom.

At the point when he introduces Haggai 2:6, he says **now** God **hath promised.** The word **now** is the Greek *nun* and means "at this present time." Thus, we need to understand that our author is taking a verse that looks in the future to the final shaking but is making a present time (present to the moment his immediate audience would receive the message) application of **this word** through Haggai. He argues that the phrase **yet once more** points to the **removing of those things that are shaken, as of things that are made, that those things which cannot be shaken may remain.** As the author previously explained, the old order was always meant to be temporary and to be replaced with the New Covenant, to which the heavenly Jerusalem and heavenly tabernacle are associated. The former is temporary but the latter permanent. More generally, what is shakable is temporary and what is unshakable is permanent. Since Mount Sinai was shakable, the Mount and the Law associated with it are temporary, and the final shaking away of the old order is on the horizon. We are again reminded that the book was written in the A.D. 60s and the author could see the revolts beginning in Judah that would bring the Roman troops there to quash the rebellion. He was warning them of the near term shaking when God would use the Romans to completely remove the old order by destroying the Temple, which occurred in A.D. 70. Once that is complete, no vestige of the old would remain, but only the New Covenant, associated with the heavenly city and tabernacle, and those things in heaven, which **cannot be shaken**. Since God is about to shake away the last vestige of the old order, their focus should be solely to the new and the promised future blessings associated with the fulfillment of the New Covenant. Thus he says, **wherefore we receiving a kingdom which cannot be moved, let us have grace**.

When we see the phrase **let us have grace**, that may seem to come out of left field, but it crowns his argument. Recall what he wrote earlier about how to endure in the face of affliction: "Let us therefore come boldly unto the throne of grace, that we may obtain mercy, and find grace to help in time of need." (Hebrews 4:16) The concept of grace here is divine enablement and provision. His audience must volitionally choose to endure and not return to Judaism, but the means to endurance are available from God—from the throne of grace. They must choose to appropriate God's grace for the moment, and thus he says, **let us have** or appropriate **grace** for the moment. To paraphrase: "The old order was temporary, is now obsolete, and almost gone completely. Endure in view of the New Covenant, which is based on Jesus' blood, and is eternal. Endurance is not always easy and you cannot do it in your own strength, so seek God's grace for the moment."

The grace God provides will enable endurance so that they **may serve God acceptably with reverence and godly fear**. The verb "serve" is the Greek *latreuo*, which means religious service or worship and is typically used in connection with priestly service at the Temple. Paul uses the noun form of this term when he says in Romans 12:1: "I beseech you therefore, brethren, by the mercies of God, that ye present your bodies a living sacrifice, holy, acceptable unto God, which is your reasonable service." Our grace-enabled lives of faith are our reasonable or fitting worship. His audience needs **grace** to endure so they **may serve God** worshipfully and with **reverence** or awe, as well as with **godly fear**. The phrase **godly fear** is more than awe or respect, and instead has to do with recognition of obligations to God and consequences for shunning those obligations. The possibility of consequences leads the author to add from Deuteronomy 4:24, **For our God is a consuming fire**. He is a God of grace who provides divine enablement for endurance, but at the same time, He is also a God of judgment that will not allow them without consequence to shun His Word and return to Judaism. We err when we distort God so that He is no longer a person but a one-dimensional caricature wholly characterized by one attribute (e.g., love). Far better to face affliction or even death for living out grace-enabled lives of faith than conforming to the age and shunning God's Word as if the **God** that **is a consuming fire** just winks at our sin.

## Closing

The Bible begins and ends with God and humanity dwelling together. In the Garden back in Genesis, Adam and Eve dwelled with God. The Fall in Genesis 3 reflects humanity's expulsion from God's presence, but in Revelation 21-22, we find the curse lifted, sin is done away with, and we inhabit the new heavens and new earth with God. The Bible brings God's story, and ours, full circle, with the "garden", the dwelling of God together with His people, at both bookends. Today, we live between the bookends, gaining understanding and examples of the life of faith from looking back, strength and perspective from looking forward to the heavenly country that awaits, and grace enablement from God for the moment.

## Application Points

- **MAIN PRINCIPLE:** How we live out our lives, and especially how we respond to God's Word, needs to be determined from a proper perspective that while we experience the horizontal during our short sojourn on earth our position in Christ places us before the heavenly city, which is ever in our view and will in the future be experienced.

## Discussion Questions

1. What is positional truth?

2. What are some things God says are true of believers because of their position in Christ?

3. What is the point of the comparison between Mount Sinai on earth as it shook long ago and Mount Sion before the heavenly Jerusalem?

4. What are the implications of a believer standing before the heavenly Jerusalem and preferring the earthly Sinai?

# Chapter 15

# Final Exhortations

Every movie has credits at the end. Sometimes we wait through the credits hoping some "teaser" appears at the end, but most of the time the moment the credits hit, we quickly exit the theater. Sometimes the last parts of epistles like Hebrews are treated like the closing credits of a movie, as if they somehow deserve less attention. But we need to view these final exhortations of Hebrews not as closing credits but as the place where the author pulls all the theology down to the ground level and puts it, as J. Vernon McGee always said, where the rubber hits the road. This is where you plug the theology into the electric socket and light up the room.

## Scripture and Comments

The author now rounds third base and brings it home. He argued on many levels that Jesus is Better, he exhorted his audience to endure in steadfast obedience, provided examples of past saints who exemplified lives of faith, explaining how their present trials fit into God's training program, and showed his audience (and us) that in Christ they (and us) presently stand before the heavenly city. In day-to-day living these truths should change who we are and what we do.

> Hebrews 13:1 Let brotherly love continue. 2
> Be not forgetful to entertain strangers: for
> thereby some have entertained angels
> unawares. 3 Remember them that are in
> bonds, as bound with them; *and* them
> which suffer adversity, as being yourselves
> also in the body. 4 Marriage *is* honourable
> in all, and the bed undefiled: but
> whoremongers and adulterers God will
> judge.

On the heels of his exhortation to appropriate grace from God so that they may steadfastly endure and serve Him, the author provides several practical exhortations touching on different aspects of the enduring Christian walk. First among these, he says, **Let brotherly love continue.** In many places, the New Testament exhortation is that we "love one another," that is, love our fellow brothers and sisters in Christ. (e.g., John 13:34-35, Romans 13:8, 1 Thessalonians 3:12) In these and many other similar verses, the word "love" translates the Greek verb *agapao*, so that we may often hear of *agape* or volitional love. This type of love is a volitional choice to act in another's best interest (best interest does not mean giving people what they want all of the time or allowing them to manipulate you). It does not entail emotional love and attachment, and thus Jesus could realistically say, "But I say unto you, Love your enemies, bless them that curse you, do good to them that hate you, and pray for them which despitefully use you, and persecute you." (Matthew 5:44) These are all volitional matters that we can choose to do even if we do not have an emotional attachment to the other person, i.e., even if we do not like them. In contrast, here in Hebrews 13:1, the phrase **brotherly love** translates the Greek *philadelphia*, which is a compound word from *philos* (love) and *delphos* (brethren). The Greek verb *phileo*, from which we get the noun *philos*, means "to be a friend to" or "have affection for." This type of love is more than a volitional choice to do for another and implies that there would be a developed relationship. Whereas we can *agapao* those we barely know and even those we are not fond of (e.g., our enemies), we will not *phileo* another person absent an established healthy relationship that at a minimum is a friendship.

The New Testament teaches that Christians should both *agapao* and *phileo* one another. This means we cannot be an island, but must be in one another's lives and work hard at developing deeper friendships with other believers. As an aside, when it comes to marriage, both types of love are needed, volitional love because the emotional will not always be enough, and emotional because a marriage with nothing but volition will likely lack joy, spontaneity, vibrance, and growth. To develop proper relationships with Christians, we must purposefully set aside time to have communications with them and be around them outside of church. Our talks must move beyond surface conversations about the weather, and that means we have to be able to open up a bit. May I say that I have "known" some Christians for years that I have spent time talking with outside of church about whom I know almost nothing. We need to be real with people; you will survive them figuring out that your world is not perfect (note – they may already know!). It is hard to help one another run the race when we are all pretending we already reached the finish line.

The author next exhorts them to **be not forgetful to entertain** or show hospitality to **strangers**. The context here would seem to be among fellow believers, and the reason is that **thereby some have entertained angels unawares**. The term **angels** is the Greek *angelos* and simply means messengers, with context usually determining whether it refers to angels in the technical (spirit being) sense or simply human messengers (e.g., of John the Baptizer in Matthew 11:10). The notion of showing hospitality to **angels unawares** likely alludes to the event of Genesis 18-19 where Abraham and his wife Sarah showed hospitality to three strangers that appeared to them as men, but they would learn were in fact angelic messengers from God. The text here in Hebrews, however, does not give enough detail to be dogmatic that the writer has in mind angelic spirit beings or human messengers, and perhaps that is his intent. In other words, he tells them, show hospitality to others, for God may use them to bring a message to you as He did with Abraham and Sarah. By the way, this does not mean that the other person will realize they are God's messenger at that moment, but only that God ministers into our lives through those around us. And it is those moments when we open up our homes and provide hospitality, or in some other way lend a special hand to one in need, that they in turn open up and share. God works through these experiences.

The author next exhorts them to **remember them that are in bonds, as bound with them**. In other words, empathize with the situation of those believers who are jailed (likely these were persecuted for their faith being placed in jail just like the apostles in Acts 5) and having put yourself in their sandals, **remember them**. This surely includes prayer for their release, but also seeing to their physical needs since in the ancient world, prisoners were often provided little or no sustenance by the jailors. Recall that the author commented in 10:34 that his audience previously "had compassion of me in my bonds." In the same way, they should empathize **as being yourselves also in the body** with **them which suffer adversity.** Throughout the book, the author has written against the backdrop of his audience facing persecution, but this does not mean that everyone was experiencing exactly the same **adversity.** Part of having **brotherly love** for our fellow believers is being in tune with their situation and ministering into their lives, prayerfully, but as necessary, with our material substance. The mathematics of this is simple—if someone has a genuine need and God gave you the means (i.e., money, material goods) to meet that need, then answer "yes Sir" and make it so.

Next, the author comments on **marriage**, which he writes **is honourable in all, and the bed undefiled.** The word **honourable** is the Greek *timios*, which carries the idea of being precious and valuable. (e.g., 1 Corinthians 3:12, 1 Peter 1:7) Marriage is a gift of God and tremendously precious and valuable and should be treated with great care. The area the author says we may fail in is fidelity to one another. He comments that **the** marriage **bed** is **undefiled** or pure or unsoiled, using the **bed** as an expression for the sexual union between husband and wife. Sex within marriage is pure and all other sexual expression is defilement. It is easy for believers to get all worked up about the sexual expression of those who are not believers, but we need to recognize that we have a serious problem in this area within our churches. Many Christians—both men and women and especially our teens—flaunt what God says about this issue like there are no consequences, when in fact the consequences are destructive and protracted. Paul writes: "Be not deceived; God is not mocked: for whatsoever a man soweth, that shall he also reap." (Galatians 6:7)

You can soil your marriage bed when you physically engage in sex (and by this I am not limiting this comment to intercourse so do not play lawyer) with someone other than your spouse. And make no mistake about it, when you fill your eyes with imagery from magazines, television, movies (much of what is rated "R" or "PG-13" is porn so do not kid yourself about what you watch just because the box does not say "XXX"), and the internet that is designed to excite sexual lusts for someone that is not your spouse, you soil your marriage bed and God is not winking at that. The author warns, **but whoremongers** (Greek *pornos*, a fornicator) **and adulterers God will judge**. The believer faces the possibility of temporal consequences as well as the potential of forfeiture of their inheritance at the bema. We are saved by grace, but that does not mean that there are no consequences to our actions, both temporally and in eternity. When we commit fornication or adultery, we not only breach the deepest human commitment of trust we can make with another person, but we say to God that His provision to us—in this instance of a spouse—is insufficient. We call His love and His provision as a good shepherd inadequate, and when we do this we are hopping up and down on awful thin ice before a God that the author earlier referenced as a consuming fire. Discontent is one of the most dangerous enemies to the Christian walk.

> 5 *Let your* conversation *be* without covetousness; *and be* content with such things as ye have: for he hath said, I WILL NEVER LEAVE THEE, NOR FORSAKE THEE. 6 So that we may boldly say, THE LORD *IS* MY HELPER, AND I WILL NOT FEAR WHAT MAN SHALL DO UNTO ME.

The warning about the marriage bed naturally leads to the broader issue of **covetousness**, literally the love of money. Money is not intrinsically evil, and neither is money as the reward of hard work, for God blesses us through our labors. But the love of stuff is looking to the creation for a permanent satisfaction (i.e., joy) only available from a dynamic relationship with the Creator, and so the author warns them against **covetousness**. Here is the reality of stuff—if you cannot part with it, it owns you and not the other way around. The problem with seeking from the creation what only the Creator can provide is that we can never get enough and what we do get will not last into eternity. As John wrote, "And the world passeth away, and the lust thereof: but he that doeth the will of God abideth for ever." The world and all the stuff we accumulate are part of the temporary, but our relationship with God and the service we do in His name are permanent. On this matter of never having enough, the author admonishes to **be content with such**

**things as ye have.** When our life revolves around the love of money so we can buy more stuff, our heart reflects (as with the warning above about the marriage bed) a lack of contentedness with God's provision to us for the moment. God assures us we have enough but we stand in judgment of His Word to us, and this reflects not only spiritual immaturity (i.e., lack of faith) but a rebellious spirit. This invites the negative side of discipline referenced in chapter 12.

The author continues, **for he hath said** in Deuteronomy 31:6 and Joshua 1:5, **I will never leave thee, nor forsake thee.** God provides for our daily needs. We get messed up when we convince ourselves that our wants are our needs. God knows what you need and what you cannot handle. Since God is with us and providing for us, we also do not need to fear what evil men can do to us. He quotes from Psalm 118:6: **The Lord is my helper, and I will not fear what man shall do unto me.** He does not say that evil men cannot harm us, but rather, that our life is not lived in fear of evil men. The Lord will provide not only for our material needs, but the grace we need to endure even in the midst of those who would persecute us. The point is not that there will be no persecution, but rather, that there will be no **fear,** and fearless living is liberating when the freedom is used to serve God.

> 7 Remember them which have the rule over you, who have spoken unto you the word of God: whose faith follow, considering the end of *their* conversation. 8 Jesus Christ the same yesterday, and to day, and for ever. 9 Be not carried about with divers and strange doctrines. For *it is*

a good thing that the heart be established with grace; not with meats, which have not profited them that have been occupied therein.

The author now calls upon his audience to **remember** (consider) their church leaders **who have spoken unto you the word of God.** The leaders or elders of the church are charged with teaching the Word of God, which means precisely what is stated here. Fluffy 20 to 30 minute "McSermons" or "Sermon light" where the preacher holds a Bible as a mere prop and then represents the Bible in terms of hopeful optimism, x number of steps to solving personal problems, political campaigning, social propaganda, and get rich schemes, do not satisfy this requirement. If that is what you are getting each Sunday, you are feeding on counterfeits and need to make haste and run! Moreover, elders are also tasked with modeling the Christian walk, and thus he continues, **whose faith follow, considering the end of their conversation.** The Greek term translated **follow** is the verb *mimeomai*, from which we get the English "mimic," and the meaning is to **follow** their example or imitate them. The author has in mind their prior leaders whose **faith** was lived out and thus worthy of imitation, **considering the** praiseworthy **end** or outcome of their **conversation** (lives), just like the examples of lives of faith from the Hall of Fame of Faith in chapter 11. To build on the imagery from chapter 12, these prior leaders ran the race with obedience and steadfast endurance.

This concept of imitating bears a little more attention. Throughout the Gospels and Acts we see the term "disciples," but the term never occurs in the Epistles.

Instead, we see the term "follow" or "follower" (or in newer translations, often "imitate"). This is not the place for a full discourse on this notion of discipleship, but I would suggest that discipleship is not simply being a believer, and neither is it merely learning the Bible, as important as that is. Most churches make little or no effort to disciple believers, although many churches say and honestly think they do. Many believe they are discipling because they have lots of Bible studies, but we get the picture of what it means to make a disciple from looking at how Jesus did it in the Gospels. Discipleship is an apprenticeship in the Christian faith (teaching) and practice (living), and we too often focus only on the teaching and not the development of mentoring relationships and engaging in ministry service alongside one another. In the Epistles, the word imitator or follower is used, focusing on faith lived out as the essence of discipleship. Their leaders were engaged in their lives, personal relationships were built, and so the writer of Hebrews could encourage them to imitate the faith example of these leaders whom they personally knew. If you want to disciple someone—and you should desire that—get into their lives, teach them, share wisdom, pray fervently for their spiritual well-being, and have them do ministry side-by-side with you. This will require time and commitment, but will have a tremendous impact on the lives of others.

Having mentioned their leaders who taught them the Word of God, he now exclaims that **Jesus Christ** is **the same yesterday, and to day, and for ever.** Hebrews is a book with a heavy focus on the fact that Jesus is the Son of God and thus deity. This verse cannot be saying that Jesus never changes in any way, for we know from the

Gospels that he changed when he took on human flesh and changed when he died on a Roman cross. Rather, the point is that in his divine attributes, Jesus is immutable or unchanging. When people preach false doctrine, they always seem to attack who Jesus is, and especially his deity (e.g., 1 John 4:1-3, Jude 4), which explains in part why Hebrews focuses so heavily on the fact that Jesus is no mere angel or servant, but a Son, and as such, heir and sovereign of all things. Often Paul would plant a church and it would seem that no sooner had he moved to the next town before the so-called Judaizers would move in (e.g., Galatians 1:6-9, 2:13-14), telling Christians they need to go back under the Law again, and often denying the deity of Jesus. False teaching was very real in the first century, as it is today. Thus, in light of the immutability of the Son, he warns them, **be not carried about with divers and strange doctrines**. It seems for some people who profess Christ that the more exotic the teaching and the further away it is from Scripture, the more they go for it, and attempting to correct them is usually futile. The author is especially concerned about bad **doctrines** that distort the person of Jesus Christ.

What the author was seeing as a real danger was false teachers that would push them back into Judaism or living under the Law. He addressed in detail earlier in the book that the Mosaic Covenant was replaced by a superior New Covenant, but this false teaching abounded then and does so today. He tells them that **it is a good thing that the heart be established with grace; not with meats**. He says, grow to maturity on the basis of grace-enabled living by faith, not on the basis of keeping the ceremonial aspects of the Law, such as the dietary restrictions. To be clear, there is nothing inappropriate about keeping those aspects of the Law, or even celebrating the Feasts, but you are not going to grow to maturity simply because you do those things, and so he writes, **which have not profited them** for spiritual growth or sanctification **that have been occupied therein.**

> <u>10</u> We have an altar, whereof they have no right to eat which serve the tabernacle. <u>11</u> For the bodies of those beasts, whose blood is brought into the sanctuary by the high priest for sin, are burned without the camp. <u>12</u> Wherefore Jesus also, that he might sanctify the people with his own blood, suffered without the gate. <u>13</u> Let us go forth therefore unto him without the camp, bearing his reproach. <u>14</u> For here have we no continuing city, but we seek one to come. <u>15</u> By him therefore let us offer the sacrifice of praise to God continually, that is, the fruit of *our* lips giving thanks to his name. <u>16</u> But to do good and to communicate forget not: for with such sacrifices God is well pleased. <u>17</u> Obey them that have the rule over you, and submit yourselves: for they watch for your souls, as they that must give account, that they may do it with joy, and not with grief: for that *is* unprofitable for you.

In contrast to the empty Judaism of the day, caught up in rituals like dietary restrictions and hand washings as a basis for sanctification, **we have an altar, whereof they have no right to eat which serve the tabernacle.** The **we**

are Christians, who are believer-priests under the New
Covenant, under Jesus our High Priest after the order of
Melchisedec. The **they** refers to the Levitical priests
**which serve the tabernacle** or Temple that was still
standing at that time but shortly destroyed in A.D. 70
just as Jesus predicted. We must remember that most of
the Levitical sacrifices, whether grain or blood sacrifices,
were not only sacrifices to God but also provided food
for the Levitical tribe (the priests and their families).
While they can eat those sacrifices, they cannot eat from
the **altar** that **we have**, the **altar** in the heavenly Temple.
But in contrast, the believer-priests do get to feed at the
heavenly altar. That altar has seen only one sacrifice,
Jesus, and it is that once for all time sacrifice from which
we now continually partake the grace (divine enablement)
of God.

For the next verse, it helps to first see the background
Jewish thought from Leviticus 16:27, which instructs
about the Day of Atonement or *Yom Kippur* sacrifices
performed by the High Priest:

> Leviticus 16:27 And the bullock *for* the sin
> offering, and the goat *for* the sin offering,
> whose blood was brought in to make
> atonement in the holy *place*, shall *one* carry
> forth without the camp; and they shall
> burn in the fire their skins, and their flesh,
> and their dung.

Note that the offering was taken and burned outside the
camp rather than on the altar. It is this sacrifice that is
in view when he says, **the bodies of those beasts, whose
blood is brought into the sanctuary by the high priest for**

**sin, are burned without** or outside **the camp.** The Day of Atonement sacrifice never dealt with sin permanently (Hebrews 10:4), but looked forward to Jesus' sacrifice (Hebrews 9:12). He says here that **wherefore Jesus also,** in other words, in order to fulfill this part of the Law, **that he might sanctify the people with his own blood, suffered** (i.e., was sacrificed) **without** or outside **the gate** (see, e.g., Mark 15:20-22). Jesus was not sacrificed on the Levitical altar, but outside **the gate** of the city (Jerusalem), and those that are still practicing Judaism at the Temple have no part in Jesus' sacrifice, or the true forgiveness and grace it provides. The concern throughout the book has been that his audience would return to Judaism, in other words, that they would go back through the gate into the city to worship with animal sacrifices. So he says, **let us go forth therefore unto** Jesus outside **the camp, bearing his reproach.** Here, **the camp** symbolizes empty Judaism, inferior sacrifices, the Temple that will shortly be destroyed, and the inferior priesthood, which continues outwardly even though the old covenant was already set aside. "Don't go to the camp of Pharisaic Judaism," he says, "but outside the camp to Jesus. The camp rejected Jesus. Bear his reproach by identifying with his rejection and not those that rejected him."

To exit the gate to get to Jesus is to exit the earthly city altogether. So he continues the logic of the imagery, **for we** Christians **have no continuing city, but we seek one to come.** His point is simply that Jerusalem and the empty Judaism centralized there is not **continuing** or permanent, but temporary, shortly to be removed by the Roman troops (see Matthew 24:1-2). Of course, we know it would be rebuilt, but the Temple and the Levitical system as it then was is gone to this day. Believers are not citizens in the earthly Jerusalem, but the heavenly Jerusalem. We may sum up this picture of leaving through the gate, going outside the city to Jesus, and not identifying with the earthly Jerusalem but the heavenly city, as again teaching commitment (obedience) and endurance in the face of adversity and persecution.

Since we are believer-priests, this naturally raises the question of what sacrifices we offer at the altar in the heavenly tabernacle, and two are taught here. The idea is not that further sacrifice needs to be made for sin, for Jesus dealt with that issue permanently through his sacrifice of himself. Notice first that we are **therefore** (because we have the altar) to **offer the sacrifice**, and notice that it is **by him**, that is, **by** Jesus. He is the High Priest through whom we serve. And as we continue reading, the first sacrifice is **praise to God continually.** While we should obviously gather corporately on the Lords' Day to praise God, the author is not talking about only a "Sunday thing," but rather, says this sacrifice should be made **continually.** Moreover, what he has in mind is not just **praise** in general, but **the fruit of our lips giving thanks to his name.** The Old Testament background for this **sacrifice of praise** would seem to be the concept of a thank offering (e.g., Leviticus 7:11-15). Often a worshiper would pray to God for deliverance in some area and vow to make a thanksgiving offering. When God answered the prayer, the worshiper made the thanksgiving offering and fulfilled his vow by giving a testimony of praise to God's goodness in his life. We see an excellent example of this in Psalm 66:

Psalm 66:13 I will go into thy house with burnt offerings: I will pay thee my vows, 14 Which my lips have uttered, and my mouth hath spoken, when I was in trouble. 15 I will offer unto thee burnt sacrifices of fatlings, with the incense of rams; I will offer bullocks with goats. Selah. 16 Come *and* hear, all ye that fear God, and I will declare what he hath done for my soul. 17 I cried unto him with my mouth, and he was extolled with my tongue. 18 If I regard iniquity in my heart, the Lord will not hear *me*: 19 *But* verily God hath heard *me*; he hath attended to the voice of my prayer. 20 Blessed *be* God, which hath not turned away my prayer, nor his mercy from me.

Also notice that the **thanks** is to be given **to** God's **name.** It is not the word "God" or even "Yahweh" that is in issue, but God's person, reputation and works. Chief among those works, of course, is that "God so loved the world, that he gave his only begotten Son, that whosoever believeth in him should not perish, but have everlasting life." (John 3:16) But in our lives, the more we come to know God's person, the more we will see His outworking in and around us, for which He deserves a continual sacrifice of praise. This issue of giving thanks gets preached around our national holiday of Thanksgiving (as it should) but often gets little attention the rest of the year. I suggest we need to heed this issue with all seriousness. One of the very first steps a believer takes away from God is a lack of gratitude in his heart, and when we stop giving thanks it usually reveals a heart of discontent, which in turn leads to our seeking from the creation what only the Creator can provide. Consider these words from Paul:

> Romans 1:20 For the invisible things of him from the creation of the world are clearly seen, being understood by the things that are made, *even* his eternal power and Godhead; so that they are without excuse: 21 Because that, when they knew God, they glorified *him* not as God, **neither were thankful**; but became vain in their imaginations, and their foolish heart was darkened.

So as believer-priests we have no sin offerings to make at the heavenly altar, but instead we **continually** offer **praise to God** with our words by **giving thanks to** God's person (attributes or perfections), reputation and works. We cannot properly praise who God is if we do not know, and what we know of God's deeds and person is primarily revealed to us in the Bible. We must eschew the notion that portions of the Bible, especially the doctrinally "heavy" portions like Hebrews, lack relevance. If we are tasked with praising God **continually**, then we must engage the Word and know Him as the creator, sustainer, omniscient, and holy God. And further, we must be attuned to His working in and around us, not only in our lives but our brothers and sisters in Christ. We are called upon to praise God both privately, as in our prayer, as well as publicly to our brothers and sisters in Christ, both to glorify God and bring encouragement to them about God's grace.

The second sacrifice is **to do good and to communicate...for with such sacrifices God is well pleased.** The phrase **to do good** means simply to do good or kind deeds for the benefit of other people. We may think of Dorcas, a disciple we meet in Acts 9 who was described as follows: "this woman was full of good works and almsdeeds which she did." What a testimony her good works were. Jesus said in the Sermon on the Mount, "Let your light so shine before men, that they may see your good works, and glorify your Father which is in heaven." (Matthew 5:16) He even said, "do good to them that hate you." (Matthew 5:44) Paul told the Galatians, "As we have therefore opportunity, let us do good unto all men, especially unto them who are of the household of faith." (Galatians 6:10) And he told the Ephesians, "For we are his workmanship, created in Christ Jesus unto good works, which God hath before ordained that we should walk in them." (Ephesians 2:10) As believers, we have a fundamental purpose of worshiping God with our lives by our words (praise) and our works (good deeds). Thus, Paul would tell the Romans, "by the mercies of God...present your bodies a living sacrifice, holy, acceptable unto God, which is your reasonable service" or worship. (Romans 12:1) There does not need to be another sin offering (a sacrifice that sheds blood and dies), but we should offer our bodies (the emphasis is what we think, say and do) as a sacrifice. To do this, we must have a heart for other people, compassion for their suffering and concern for their spiritual well-being and growth. What starts in our hearts must come out in actual deeds, not like the negative example in James 2:15-16: "If a brother or sister be naked, and destitute of daily food, and one of you say unto them, Depart in peace, and be ye warmed and filled; notwithstanding ye give them not those things which are needful to the body; what doth it profit?"

As part of doing good, he says **to communicate**. The word **communicate** is the Greek term *koinonia*, which means partnership or fellowship or sharing, and in the right context means partnering through our giving of money, as in Philippians 1:5. That would seem to be the point here, that is, both to do good deeds and to share our material blessings with those in need. This was amply demonstrated in the life of the churches in Macedonia that provided for the saints in Jerusalem, "praying us with much intreaty that we could receive the gift, and take upon us the fellowship [*koinonia*] of the ministering to the saints." (2 Corinthians 8:1-5) In most places in the world there are believers whose lives could be radically improved, from a material perspective, if we only shared the cost of one meal dining out, people who do not earn in a day what we spend on our morning coffee. More than being willing to give, we need like the churches in Macedonia, out of "the abundance of...joy" to look for opportunities to share with others. Someone may say, "I do not have enough to share." Look at 2 Corinthians 8:2: "How that in a great trial of affliction the abundance of their great joy and their deep poverty abounded unto the riches of their liberality."

Finally, returning to the issue of their leaders or teachers, but now focusing on their current leaders and not the prior leaders they were encouraged to imitate, he says, **obey them that** presently **have the rule over you**. Obey means obey. Much could be said about proper leadership by elders (or pastors), who are to be shepherds who lead out in front with the sheep following behind them, and not cattle drivers wielding their authority like mad arrogant fools. But the reality is that many people say with their lips they want to follow God's will, but when God's man tries to lead them, they rebel, cause division, or get angry and leave the church with some pathetic effort to sound spiritual about it ("I just wasn't being fed there"). He says, **submit yourselves**, and may I say this does not require that you agree with every word they speak, but that you recognize that God is working through His appointed leadership. The reason given is that these leaders **watch for your souls** or lives, meaning your spiritual well-being. Further, they are witnesses **that must give account**. Of course, according to James 3:1, at the bema judgment they will give account for discharging their duties to you as teachers of the Word of God, but here what is in view is their giving the eyewitness account of your obedience to the Word. Those who teach and preach get the greatest joy from seeing those under their ministries pursue the Lord with vigor and humility, and they **may do it**, that is, give the account for those folks, **with joy, and not with grief**. There is tremendous grief to God's appointed leaders who pour their lives in to the lives of others only to see them not submit to the Word of God, and they will take no joy in testifying or giving account for the life of the rebellious Christian that was under their ministry. Rebelliousness will be **unprofitable for you** when you stand to give account to Christ (e.g., 2 Corinthians 5:10).

> 18 Pray for us: for we trust we have a good conscience, in all things willing to live honestly. 19 But I beseech *you* the rather

to do this, that I may be restored to you the sooner. 20 Now the God of peace, that brought again from the dead our Lord Jesus, that great shepherd of the sheep, through the blood of the everlasting covenant, 21 Make you perfect in every good work to do his will, working in you that which is wellpleasing in his sight, through Jesus Christ; to whom *be* glory for ever and ever. Amen.

Now, in the closing words of the book, the author asks his audience to **pray for us**. We do not know for sure who authored the book of Hebrews, nor who he was with, i.e., the **us**. The author many times referenced the notion of the conscience, teaching that the Levitical sacrifices could not clean the conscience, but the blood of Jesus could. (Hebrews 9:9, 14, 10:2, 22) The author's **conscience** was cleansed by Jesus, and he confesses his heart to **live honestly... in all things**. On this basis, as a fellow child of God, he seeks prayer, and especially prayer **that I may be restored to you the sooner**. This means he was not only known by his audience, but had previously been present with them, and now hoped to return to them soon.

Having requested prayer, he now prays for them: **Now the God of peace, that brought again from the dead our Lord Jesus, that great shepherd of the sheep**. The basis for his prayer is that the God whose power raised Jesus can meet their needs also on the basis of Jesus' **blood**, which is **the blood of the everlasting covenant**. Recall that the old covenant or Mosaic Covenant was temporary, and indeed replaced by the New Covenant, inaugurated by Jesus' **blood** and a permanent or **everlasting covenant**. His prayer is that God would **make** them **perfect in every good work to do** God's **will**. In other words, he prays that God would **perfect** or complete—essentially that He would equip—them with everything they need to do His **will**. Further, he prays that God would work **in us** (that is, both the author and those with him as well as his audience) that which **is pleasing in His sight**. Putting this together, he prays for God to equip them **to do his will** and that God would work out His will through them, and all of this **through Jesus Christ,** the one whose sacrifice made it all possible. Finally, his prayer that they would do the will of God is so that their good works that God does through them would ultimately bring to God **glory for ever and ever**. He ends the prayer with the traditional **amen,** meaning let it be true.

> <u>22</u> And I beseech you, brethren, suffer the word of exhortation: for I have written a letter unto you in few words. <u>23</u> Know ye that *our* brother Timothy is set at liberty; with whom, if he come shortly, I will see you. <u>24</u> Salute all them that have the rule over you, and all the saints. They of Italy salute you. <u>25</u> Grace *be* with you all. Amen.

He now urges them, as his fellow Christian **brethren,** to **suffer** or receive his **word** or message **of exhortation**. Here, his is referring to the entire epistle of Hebrews as **the word of exhortation**. He also says that he wrote the letter **unto you in few words**. The point seems to be that he could say a great deal more about the argument of the book, but chose instead to present what he wrote and stop. He gives them the good news that **our brother Timothy is set at liberty** from prison. His hope is that if Timothy can **come** to him **shortly or quickly**, he will be able to bring Timothy when he comes to **see** them in person. In the meantime, he asks them to **salute** or greet their leaders (presumable elders) **and all the saints**, meaning their congregations as a whole. The author then says that **they of Italy salute** or greet **you**, which suggests that he writes from Italy and most probably Rome, although it is possible that he is elsewhere and accompanied by some Italians. In any event, he closes the letter that points us so much to the grace of God with the words, **Grace be with you all. Amen.**

## Closing

The book of Hebrews opened by telling us that God's ultimate revelation was in His Son Jesus Christ, who reflects God's glory and person and is the creator/sustainer of the universe, and who presently is seated at the right hand of God in heaven. When he brings the book to a close, he calls on those who identify with Christ by faith to treat fellow believers within their family, their church, as well as strangers, with love, and in the context of church leadership, with submission. Our treatment of others, and our responses to them, should reflect a firm conviction in our thinking of who the Son is with whom we profess to identify ourselves with. We call him Lord, and rightly so, and our day-to-day lives in even the smallest details should reflect the reality of who Jesus is.

## Application Points

- **MAIN PRINCIPLE:** Our relationship with one another and with our church leadership should reflect brotherly love and an appreciation for God's sufficient provision for us at the moment so that we can run the race with endurance.

## Discussion Questions

1. What is the difference between agape love and phileo love?

2. How can we entertain strangers and how might that bring us a message from God?

3. Is there a Biblical basis for prison ministry?

4. When we commit infidelity or covetousness, what message does our conduct speak to God about His provision for us as His child?

5. Is it wrong to imitate other people?

6. In the Old Testament, the sacrifices were eaten by the priests and sometimes the worshipers. In what way can we continue to partake of Jesus' sacrifice?

7. What does the prayer in verse 21 suggest we should be praying for in regard to other Christians around us?

# Bibliography

I have found the following particularly helpful in studying the book of Hebrews:

F.F. Bruce, *The Epistle to the Hebrews Revised* (Grand Rapids: William B. Eerdmans Publishing Company 1990).

Arnold Fruchtenbaum, *The Messianic Jewish Epistles: Hebrews – James – I & II Peter – Jude* (Tustin: Ariel Ministries 2005).

G. Harry Leafe, Exposition of Hebrews (mp3 audio series available at www.scriptel.org).

J. Dwight Pentecost, *Faith That Endures* (Grand Rapids: Discovery House Publishers 2000).

Jeremy Vance, *Companions With Christ* (Grace Theology Press 2014).

# About the Author

HUTSON SMELLEY is an attorney and Bible teacher residing in Houston, Texas with his wife and six children. He holds advanced degrees in mathematics, law and Biblical studies. He can be contacted at proclaimtheword@mac.com.

www.proclaimtheword.me